Prospects of Power

Prospects of Power

Tragedy, Satire, the Essay, and the Theory of Genre

JOHN SNYDER

THE UNIVERSITY PRESS OF KENTUCKY

Publication of this book has been assisted by
a grant from the University of Houston–Clear Lake.

Scholarly publisher for the Commonwealth,
serving Bellarmine College, Berea College, Centre
College of Kentucky, Eastern Kentucky University,
The Filson Club, Georgetown College, Kentucky
Historical Society, Kentucky State University,
Morehead State University, Murray State University,
Northern Kentucky University, Transylvania University,
University of Kentucky, University of Louisville,
and Western Kentucky University.

Editorial and Sales Offices: Lexington, Kentucky 40506-0336

Library of Congress Cataloging-in-Publication Data

Snyder, John, 1942-
    Prospects of power : tragedy, satire, the essay, and the theory of
genre / John Snyder.
        p.   cm.
    Includes bibliographical references and index.
    ISBN 0-8131-1724-0 (acid-free)
    1. Literary form.   2. Criticism.   3. Tragedy.   4. Satire.
5. Essay.   I. Title.
    PN45.5.S6   1990
    801'.95—dc20   90-38952

This book is printed on acid-free paper meeting
the requirements of the American National Standard
for Permanence of Paper for Printed Library Materials. ⊗

In memory of my father
and with special thanks
to Elsa and Tom

Contents

Preface

Genres are my longest-term theoretical and critical interest. My teaching and previous publications have consistently reflected the unity-diversity appeal of all genres—large and small, traditional and popular, literary and nonliterary. The ultimate attraction, though, I cannot explain except by noting in the fact of genre the paradoxical bonding of the completely obvious with the completely mysterious. Like history in this teasing assurance of answers, which then disclose unsuspected prospects of perplexity, genre itself beckons as the clear inscription of power on what remains an ineffable body of intertext: clarity *and* mystery *in* the texts *as* they operate—that is, as a *kind* of history.

Indeed, the compounding of the self-evident and the opaque in genre I have found to be fascinating mainly to historians alert to the powers of discourse, from Marx to Foucault and Serres, rather than to literary historians, who for the most part (Bakhtin and Benjamin are two notable exceptions) tend to assume that literature contains mysteries and history, the clarifying referents. Genre, however, as the intersection of history and texts, while organizing texts makes history less obviously factual, or separable from words; and that tendency, of course, lends a new potency to textuality.

For the development of the genre theory presented in this study, I am much obliged to essayistic discussions over many years with a historian, Bruce Palmer. His absorption in the meaning-generating processes that activate Southern history makers and historians alike has pushed me to more and more thoroughgoing formulations of genre as the historical construction of texts by the texts themselves. Tragedy is not what has been called "tragedy." Tragedy *is* what tragedies *have done* toward the political ends of victory, loss, and stalemate. Satire is what satires *intend to do* but never succeed in doing except by becoming other, more effectual genres. Essays are what they say they are doing in saying "essaying." If genre is the deployment of symbolic power, the individual genres are historical degrees of inscription cut into the body of history itself.

In the curious fact of genre, then, the literary theorist can discover how history can be both entirely verbal and entirely actual, both symbolic and nonrepresentational, both literary and historical. The historian can discover in texts that have organized themselves generically (and not only the literary) more than mere monuments of power. The historian can tap onto the genres as the differentiating textual operations of power, symbolic configurations that are not merely figurative but figural, not only ideological but ideology-making—prospects not *on* but *of* power. Language through genre becomes history, and history, discourse.

I am indebted to my literature and film colleagues as well as to historians and a historian friend. This study would not have materialized had I not been allowed by the Literature and Humanities programs at the University of Houston–Clear Lake to rove freely across the disciplines and to organize virtually all my courses with an aim toward solving the problem of textuality apprehended generically. I owe special thanks to Ed Hugetz, a filmmaker whose breadth of teaching interests and aesthetic obsessions have affected my thinking in many ways hard to specify. And Pam Sisk, my original manuscript typist and retypist, was wonderful over a very long haul. Various research committees at UH-CL deserve my thanks for occasional released-time support, which allowed me to write the satire and essay portions of *Prospects of Power.* Finally, for her editorial acuity and patience Nancy Atkinson has won my ungrudging admiration.

CHAPTER ONE

Contemporary Genre Theory

Genre, or the articulation of "kind" in aesthetic production and consumption, is both too general and not general enough. It is as close to a common assumption as anything in literary theory and history. Yet the more genre attains in specificity when applied, the more it tends to evaporate as an abstraction. Still, certain features of genre can sustain the tightest theoretical focus as well as accommodate the widest angles of application and interpretation. First, every work deviates from any particular set of characteristics that may be attributed to its kind. And over time every work combined with all others of more or less the same kind constitutes the history of the genre: the genre *is* its history of individual instances. This history, of course, signifies changes, even transformations in the genre: *Hamlet* both is and is not a tragedy in the same sense as the *Oresteia*, and *Othello* both is and is not a tragedy in the same sense as Imamu Amiri Baraka's *Dutchman*. A historically transformed genre necessarily includes all its moments. That is how it changes.

Hence, the question confronting theory cannot be "What is genre?" Nietzsche's cryptic definition of the dialectic applies perfectly to genre, which cannot be defined because as a historical phenomenon it possesses no nature: "Only that which has no history is definable" (*Genealogy* 80). All theories that claim genre "is" this or that miss the inherent historicity of genre. Aristotle, Corneille, Johnson, Frye, Genette, Derrida—all miss this mark, though in different ways and from various intents.

For the same reason, their historicity, any system of genres is an arbitrary imposition. Such classification schemes must remain alien from their materials. Yet so must all putative sciences, which cannot be disqualified simply because they are arbitrary. However, our understanding of the interrelation of the genres must adhere exceptionally closely to their diachronic operations as these compare and contrast with one another, and

neither start from nor rest content with any detectable synchronic order-
ing. There can be no grammar of genres.

The real problem of genre as it relates to system, then, requires
solution by means of a description of the *range* of genres with respect to
their individual histories. Genre study is converted into a kind of dialectical literary history, which in turn gains in theoretical sophistication from
genre study. Power, the *dynamis* of history, is the only way historical
pheomena relate to one another. History itself resists both geometrical
rule and classification, as is clear from the failures of Vico or Toynbee or
Spengler. So, too, do the genres evade systematic categorization. Instead,
they invite dialectical attentiveness, which may map though it cannot
secure.

But just how can genre be conceived as power? First of all, genre as a
historical phenomenon is operational rather than essential. Genre is not a
theoretical construct but the actual construction of texts. For example,
symbolic power in literature can operate straightforwardly, in political
configurations of victory, loss, and deadlock, as in tragedy. Power can
recoil upon itself, in contradiction, as in satire. Or symbolic power can
deploy itself freely, opening up a prospect of self-liberation, as in the essay.

Power can also be characterized as stable or unstable to one degree or
another. Tragedy, for example, maintains a high degree of stability, or
identifiability, however great its transformations. Other genres, such as
satire or the lyric, perpetually dissolve into modes qualifying the stabler
genres. When genres are mixed, discursive power acts to subordinate one
to the other (or others), so that formally the earlier genre attenuates to a
mode. The novel can absorb tragedy or comedy, for example, and in doing
so it reduces them to the qualifiers "tragic" or "comic." Formal satire, a
major distinct genre at least through the eighteenth century, appears less
and less frequently as itself, more and more as a flavoring. Because the
novel is the overridingly dominant contemporary genre, even those with
potentially the most to gain from the effects of Menippean satire—femi-
nists and racial and ethnic minorities for example—rest content with
narratives that stress novelistic development of progressive characters
while subduing the target-intent rhetoric of satire: Doris Lessing, Marge
Piercy, Ishmael Reed, Philip Roth.

Furthermore, there can be different formal ends wrought by different
configurations of power. Thus genres that are mimetic, such as tragedy and
comedy, achieve different ends from genres that in their operations are
rhetorical (in the classical sense of audience-directed) or textual (rhetorically mimetic, or self-directed): Aeschylus's *Persians* and Aristophanes'
Birds aim at a kind of effect that is quite distinct from the kind of formal
effect achieved by Juvenal's *Satires* or Montaigne's *Essais*.

Equally important, genres conceived, if not defined, as configurations of power eliminate entirely the aspiration to form a system of genres. All systems imply closure. Power is interminable, though it can increase and decrease. Yet power can accommodate—it indeed requires—the conception of range, which traces shifting boundaries. What are the boundaries of such genres as tragedy, satire, and the essay? And what curve tracks the extension of power from the relatively stablest genre to the least definite genre? These twin questions, it seems to me, set the correct theoretical beginning for a diachronic understanding of intrinsically historical genre. For they initiate an orderly method of genre study as a kind of dialectical literary and cultural history without imposing a system.

Two more provisions are needed properly to launch a comprehensive investigation of genre itself combined with a close inquiry into the operations of certain exemplary kinds. First, genres relate to different "substances"; they have distinct "material causes." Second, since they are historical, thus nonnatural, genres must be correlated, if very loosely in most cases, with differences in media: literary, visual, musical, and mixed (opera and film, for example). Generic difference, however, is not *constituted* by difference in medium. To review briefly: the intrinsic historicity of genre is combined with the variety of formal effects in the distinct genres to produce the theory of genres as configurations of power. But it then becomes necessary to add the material cause of genres. This material cause allows for, though it does not constitute, differences among the media.

In the literary genres the material cause is language—not in itself but already shaped dynamically as discourse serving formal ends. Thus discourse is to be taken as the mediatory power acting between language as such and the formal effects of individual generic operations in literature. Within discourse as power I can distinguish three key formations (not exactly the same, it will be seen, as Foucault's comparable "discursive formations"): mimetic (tragedy is the purest example), rhetorical (satire), and textual (the essay). These three both establish the range of all literary genres taken together and suggest how properly to correlate them with differences in media.

Discursive formations as such attach exclusively to language compositions. Only by analogy can they be applied to the visual, musical, and mixed-media arts. The theorist must therefore take care to hear in Wagnerian *sprechtstimme* what may be termed the "tragic" in mode, but never the recitations-minus-music (except in the sense of the Greek *mousike*) of the mimetic genre par excellence, tragedy. Similarly, Daumier's prints can be seen as rhetorically satiric if not as satires, and a film by Godard may be essayistic but not an essay. Analogies connect separate formal worlds that

obey their own sets of laws. But media are independent even of these
formal differentia. The reason is that differences in media are always
derived from technological innovations. However, generic power differentials operate together with formal differentia, which are integral with
different material causes. And these distinct substances, such as language,
visual imagery, and harmony or counterpoint, are not technologically
based, though literature, painting, and music are, as media.

While technology inevitably results in the creation of new genres and
the demise of old genres, media differences neither cause nor constitute
these consequences. New chemical compositions, for example, permitted
but did not constitute or determine the transition from early Renaissance
mural painting, one genre, toward the dominant late Renaissance framed
oil painting, another genre. Nor can the novel as a genre be said to have
been caused or constituted by techniques of mass printing. To lay such a
claim is as mistaken as to concentrate on steam power for an account of the
Industrial Revolution. More productive is tracing the development of a
middle-class readership mainly composed of informally educated women,
for this development framed the truly generic dimension of the final formal
shift from romance to novel in the eighteenth century.

With all these preliminaries in mind, I should like to prospect the
territory ranged over by my theory of literary genre and map it into
discursive configurations of power: a kind of tectonic plate theory insofar as
literary genres are constantly shifting in response to the conditions and
forces of discourse. I see such an approach completely situated in history.
It thus occupies another theoretical world than, say, Northrop Frye's, the
axes of which are immanent and transcendent, or the structuralist Gérard
Genette's, whose analytic grid is composed of linguistic and "architextuel"
axes. And I hope my study begins to reconcile the deconstructionist
critique of genre as a deep structure with the post-Althusser Marxist
emphasis—which is deepening thanks to Fredric Jameson and John Frow
among others—on genre as the crucial juncture between history and
aesthetic production and consumption.

In the remainder of this chapter and in the final chapter, I shall show how
this reconciliation can take place by sifting through those genre theories that
have come to the fore since Frye's *Anatomy of Criticism*. In the middle
sections of the book, I shall try to specify, by means of three dialectical literary
histories, exactly how my own theory of literary genres as discursive configurations of power can mediate between the particular powers exerted in and of
history by the selected genres: tragedy, satire, and the essay.

Genre has set contemporary theorists since Frye off in divergent directions. At one limit of the range are the poststructuralist and hermeneutic

interests in genre, most adventurously pursued by Derrida[1] and Hirsch,[2] respectively, and, at the other limit, the traditional literary history of Alastair Fowler (*Kinds of Literature*) and the empirical literary sociology of Natascha Würzbach. Mediating between these extremes is Fredric Jameson's appropriation (in *Political Unconscious*) of genre as a key element in his proposed postdeconstructionist restructuration of the Marxist aesthetic model along lines originally drawn by Lukács and Althusser.

Fowler, applying Wittgenstein, defines genre as family resemblance rather than class inclusion and exclusion. Moreover, he stresses diachronic transformation as the most profitable application of genre. In place of new definition, Würzbach offers empirical study of genre within a communication model. Thus genre study amounts to an orderly method of totally describing regulative conventions and devices: "Genre conventions can be looked upon as rules for the communicative interaction associated with composition, propagation, and reception which is rooted in the sociocultural context" (65).

For Hirsch's continuing struggle to anchor "meaning" and "significance" through epistemology and linguistics, genre remains "intrinsic."[3] "Intrinsic genre" is the means whereby a given work can be read—both registered and made understandable—its meanings realized by being put to their generically marked *use*: Hirsch's genre "generates" meanings in the sense of establishing, regulating, and qualifying the various kinds of discourse.

Derrida leads the deconstructing and disseminating genre theorists, all of whom respond to the successive puns on "genre/gender" that are accessible within French and English as well as to most Latin-absorbing linguistic practices. Thus they fasten upon the definition of genre as original matrix and emphasize the generative power of literature, or its vital "generativity," rather than its automatically generating functionality. Accordingly, their critical applications feature the symptomatics, or even obstetrics, of the coming-into-being of new forms, both within and between texts.[4] With deconstructionists, then, the focus of genre analysis shifts from kind to the most general radiation, or dispersal, of kinds of signification—which turn out to be endlessly intertextual (Frank).

Derrida's own sense of genre is that it *is* the unfolding process of textual openness and closure. Thus genre is an odd categorical imperative that dictates against "mixture" and, by doing so, points up the lapses of genre's putative purity. Though like dialectic in its generativity, Derrida's "law of genre" is more like irony in its infinite escapes from itself, and from history: "There is always a genre and genres, yet such participation never amounts to belonging. . . . The clause or floodgate of genre declasses what it allows to be classed" (Derrida 212-13).

A faithful Nietzschean, Derrida gaily propounds the subversiveness of such a law, which legislates against impurity yet constantly decenters itself by the miscegenation it makes inevitable in the very act of legislation. Instead of a "conventional fiction" (*Beyond Good and Evil*) requiring demythification, genre is its own unfolding, both destructive and creative. This law of genre, then, is not really *a* rule, or even a principle of rule as it is for Hirsch, but the very process of a language-constituted form as it discloses itself and, in so doing, regenerates itself as an evanescent phenomenon. Genre, like Nietzschean discourse, inverts, subverts, re-creates ("plays"). This re-creation is a sexual matter of engendering and detumescence: "At the very moment that a genre or a literature is broached, at that very moment degenerescence has begun, the end begins" (Derrida 213).

Paradoxically, as within Nietzsche's own "genealogy," within Derrida's diachronic genre lurks a shadow of synchronicity. Or, to apply Foucault as an overlay to Derrida, genre is the act of clearing and claiming its own "space," where discursive signifiers can slide home, scoring their points within the game configuration of power-knowledge. Yet a game, which may change itself, even degrade itself in insisting on being played strictly by the rules, remains a structure; indeed a game is sheer structure, equatable with the starkest synchronicity.

Derrida's genre certainly sidesteps the specter of sterility in Hirsch's apodictic "intrinsic genre," whereby all communication is based on self-contained types. It escapes by focusing on the freedom of genre's self-disclosure, which builds into a given work the opportunity to subvert its own significations. Thus literary history becomes a nonprogressive *gaia scienza*: "Making genre its mark, a text demarcates itself" (Derrida 212). But such Nietzschean escape remains a fertile ploy, even a practical one; for Derrida's genre would be a starting point, or "constellation" of points to borrow Walter Benjamin's concept, a pliant yet substantive discursive place of passage (Derrida's "womb-vagina" metaphor pervades "The Law of Genre") that indicates "where" a work will take place without enclosing it. Genre, first deconstructive, becomes disseminative: it becomes the not-quite-wholly predictive yet always promissory and fully generative possibility of meaning for a literary work.

If there is structure, or the shadow of synchronicity, in Derrida's deconstructive genre, it is the kind of structure that allows for *both* immanence of meaning *and* diachronic transformation. However, Derrida's trick remains a trick: a given work can both obey and disobey his law of genre, thus both it itself and genre subsume all meaning. The work and genre require a hookup with history, the last of a text's immanent references this side of any transcendent possibilities.

Only the Marxist appropriation of genre provides such a hookup. The sociological empiricism of Würzbach issues in total classification minus meaning, while Fowler's literary history may establish the limits of meaning but fails to generate any meanings beyond the obvious. Poststructuralist genre generates meanings but shies away from complete congress with historical forces; parthenogenetic literature is certainly real *within* the limits of textuality and intertextuality, but literature is also real, in some way, *for* history, perhaps even *as* history.

To employ genre as an especially valuable dialectical technique closely coordinating textual form with history, both literary and historical, is Fredric Jameson's answer to both the ideological revisionism of Althusser and the literary anarchism augured by such radical poststructuralists as Deleuze and Guattari. Jameson takes his stand midway between Lukács, whose animus against mechanistic sociological determinism he shares, and Althusser, with whom he shares the conviction that history does not "express" itself (*Political Unconscious* 23-26) through events or cultural manifestations which then require explanation as effects of ultimately economic causes. Above all, Jameson wishes to avoid the simplistic centeredness of "expressive causality" (27), which reduces, via crude mediations, all levels of the superstructure to "homologies" (43-46) mutually reflective of the base. Consequently, literary works, like historical events and movements, need to be seen as continuous with or contradictory to or both—yet never merely reflective of—their social causes. Literary works are constitutive elements homogeneous with their history-saturated structure and not signs of another, base structure.

Genre, then, to Jameson, is the bridge necessitated by Althusser's critique of ideology: "The strategic value of generic concepts for Marxism clearly lies in the mediatory function of the notion of a genre, which allows the coordination of immanent formal analysis of the individual text with the twin diachronic perspective of the history of forms and the evolution of social life" (Jameson 105).

At this point it bears recalling certain poststructuralists' admonition about genre, whether it be construed as a vital generator of meanings and their negations (Derrida), an epistemological-linguistic control of meaning (Hirsch), a historical condition of meaning (Fowler), or a mediation between formal textual meaning and history (Jameson): genre may be a nonconcept altogether, a figment convenient to those who mistakenly essentialize texts by reiterating such questions as "What is genre?" or "What is the novel?" or "What is comic in this drama?" or "Is the romance a genre or a mode?" or "How does the subgenre anatomy affect the interpretation of *Moby-Dick*?" or even "Does Emily Brontë meet the threatening implications of the capitalist transformation of the countryside by making Heathcliff a composite of romantic and realist traits whose function is to mediate between the rural gentry's past and its future?"

Manfred Frank locates the essentializers' mistake about genre in their presupposition "that the systematic, self-contained quality ('clôture'—closure) of the text represents something approaching a transcendental signified ('signifié') or an expression-founding, originary sense which, as the independent organizational basis of the entire construct, serves like a magnet to hold together the field of all other meaning in a coherent order" (74). Then there is the tempting possibility of dismissing all current definitions of genre, from Fowler's to Derrida's, by applying a special sense of genre derived from certain Romantics' "conceit of one Genre." This conceit Michel Beaujour describes as opposition to the "taxonomic distribution of discourses and texts into a hierarchical genre system"; for "genre, as opposed to genres, intimates what it does not denote: a line must—but cannot—be drawn somewhere between *everything*, and *something* that is unnamable" (15).

Whether figment or no, error or merely pragmatic practice, some kind of essentializing is something I see no way to avoid in the following work on genre through investigations of tragedy, satire, and the essay. For I need versions of presence—such as heroic integrity in tragedy, target-bound critique in satire, and prolongation in the essay—if only to articulate their equally present contradictories. Nor do I intend to ignore the adhesiveness of history, although derivations are not a central concern of mine. I do wish to proceed, however, within narrower bounds than infinite intertextuality, and within a lower sphere than the absolute Genre of post-Romantic poetics.

Yet I share the deconstructionist bias against the conviction that genre is centered by either authorial intention or a "transcendental signified": "The history of widely differing semantic realizations, even the everyday experience of the nonidentity of the two readings of one and the same text, attest to the dubiousness of this supposition which considers reading and understanding to be performances of a fixed, self-identical score. This score—the grammar of a text—would be something like a truism removed from the differentiating play of functions; like a verity which fixes once and for all, from without or from above, the sense of the 'marks' and determines them as its 'expression' or 'realization'" (Frank 74).

In the place of these suspiciously soft centers for genres, I should like to emulate Jameson and do, or attempt, the right thing given the unavoidable historicity of genre itself, by inserting or constructing configurations of power—political in tragedy, rational in satire, and textual in the essay—into both individual works' "differentiating play of functions" and overall patterns of generic transformation. However, for a concept of history specifically applicable to genre as either practice or extrapolation, I shall adopt Benjamin's deductively dialectical notion of *Ursprung*: "Origin [*Ursprung*], although an entirely historical category, has, nevertheless, nothing to do with genesis [*Entstehung*]. The term origin is not intended to describe the process by which the existent [a genre] came into being, but rather to describe that which emerges from the process of becoming and disappearance. . . . There takes place in every original phenomenon a determination of the form in which an idea will constantly confront the historical world, until it is revealed fulfilled, in the totality of its history" (45-46). Put in a less Hegelian, more Marxist way, this turn from the synchronic approach—as it is characterized, for example, by Frye's account of the myth of romance—to indeterminist and formalist dialectic will allow me to conduct genre study as a matter of laying a foundation for a nonteleological explanation of what tragedies, satires, and essays have become, as well as what they cannot become, from Aeschylus to Büchner, Juvenal to Hašek, Cicero to Nietzsche. Such a strategy, I hope, will not produce merely empirical nonmeanings, but, instead, a literary-historical map marking certain crossroads in the evolution of Western culture, a map to be added to those already devised by Lukács, Benjamin, Adorno, Jameson, Habermas, and Serres.

Besides, genres have themselves been plied consciously and unconsciously as guides to both execution and exploration and have sometimes enjoyed privileged sway as unconscious and conscious manipulators of potentially real signifiers. Genres have been practiced, have as it were practiced themselves, and they will continue to be hypothesized of all sorts of texts in all sorts of ways. More important, perhaps, in their very lingering as purely formal, often futile directives, genres always fall into desuetude, thus proving their temporality: it is a truism that tragedy, perhaps even the ability to understand tragedies, is no longer, and it is obvious that satire and the essay have been almost terminally trivialized. Therefore, I feel fairly secure in offering at least one theoretical presupposition: that hard historical residues, or "sedimentations" (Jameson)— political in tragedy, rational in satire, and textual (liberationist) in the essay—make up the skeleton of that discursive ghost called "genre." It needs to be reasserted at this point that authorial intentionality is not entailed by this historical sense. One need not, should not out of respect for the distinction between literature and life, refer to intention as determining the working of genres any more than as determining the drifts and crises of history itself. If intentionality is important in genres, it is, as in history, only as one of a complex of larger factors such as nature, will, violence, order—each of which requires further explanation in still larger terms such as interest, or power, in all its modes.

Beyond the absorption of intentionality by these stronger categories, there is another, even more expedient reason for dismissing it as an interpretive vector. Recognition of intentionality in literature tends to blind readers to the moral-formal distinction between the compound of signifier and signified, on the one hand, and experience, on the other. Characters in tragedies, attitudes in satires, and voices in essays are *presentations as* characters, attitudes, and voices. We must therefore read them as composites of arbitrary signs. If we were to regard tragic heroes, satiric denouncers and butts, or essayists as real people or even symbolic surrogates, we would be violating a taboo prescribed by the illusionistic nonnature of literary acting:

> Fictional characters exist only in literature. . . . Everything moral is bound to life in its extreme sense, that is to say where it fulfills itself in death, the abode of danger as such. And from the point of view of any kind of artistic practice this life, which concerns us morally, that is in our unique individuality, appears as something negative, or at least should appear so. For art cannot, for its part, allow itself, in its works, to be appointed a councillor of the conscience and it cannot permit what is represented, rather than the actual representation, to be the object of attention. The truth content of this totality, which is never encountered in the abstracted lesson, least of all the moral lesson, but only in the critical elaboration of the work itself, includes moral warnings only in the most indirect form. [Benjamin 105]

Indeed, the concept of genre itself means, if anything, simply "presentation as . . . ." Thus a tragedy or satire or essay is there to be considered for what is being presented, not for "its" intention or the speaker's or the author's, which are erroneously presumed to be re-presented by the work. In short, genre in this sense amounts to the self-advertisement of a work, or grouping of works, to be deliberated upon for what it appears to be, as presentation, and not for the intentions purportedly behind it. Genre, like Benjamin's characters, is only literary, a performance of the apparent: life is neither tragic nor satiric nor essayistic; tragedies, satires, and essays are.

I mount this curiously moral defense of literature against life's incursions as a corollary to an approach that has been announced as part Marxist and part deconstructionist because of a certain humanist retort to the reputed destructivism of poststructural thought of all stripes, Foucault to Derrida. This retort finds fullest articulation in Charles Altieri's *Act and Quality*. Altieri, discontent with life as life, art as product, wants life to be *in* art, a desire I would judge to be hardly different from the rather mandarin desires of the old New Critics and I.A. Richards: "Texts afford

knowledge not because they describe particulars but because they embody ways of experiencing facts" (Altieri 12). "Embody," "ways of experiencing," and "facts" have never been possible predications of literature: as
the shadow Hamlet "himself" knew, literary gestures are mere shadow
acts—play, apparition, and dumb show—not living acts with consequences, but signs spawning interpretations and misinterpretations. Literature derives its forcefulness not from experience, and not directly from
knowledge, but from symbolic incursions into history, serving interests
and betraying them, from the local to the universal, the humble to the
proud.

Some of my departures from previous theoretical or critical tracks may
be ascribed to my comparative, nonpolarizing procedures. I have selected
three genres representing three very different categorizing principles—
classical, represented by tragedy; attitudinal, by satire; and formal, by the
essay. These principles and genres I analyze through the dissection and
reassembly of examples of each; the three genres are then differentiated
with the object of constructing, or reconstructing, a theory of genre.
Tragedy is my first consideration because, while definitely the solidest and
least questionable genre, or the quintessentially classical genre, it as often
wanders away from "the tragic" as it keeps on track—rather, they do, the
individual tragedies I have chosen. Tactically, then, I shall follow the ways
the action appears in the course of a given tragedy's plot to take syntag-
matic shape as a version of the hypothetical tragic, then diverges to assume
more or less contradictory shapes. Indeed, the very problem I find en-
grossing in the next two chapters is why all the tragedies I know are never
tragic, whether those of Aeschylus, Euripides, Beroul, or Kleist—and
whatever the specific definition of tragic action or signification one adopts.

Chapters 4 and 5, on satire, propose the most shape-shifting of all
genres as a "semigenre." Partly because the Romans, who made satire,
verse or prose or mixed, a full-fledged albeit muddled (*satura*) genre,
never figured out how to be classical, and partly because it is an almost
exclusively expressive rather than constative genre, satire proffers no
essence at all, no in-itself. Indeed, as Koenraad Kuiper seductively argues
in "The Nature of Satire," satire may be said to lack nature because it is
"perceptual": "neither a matter of form nor of function but a matter of the
way both these are perceived in particular contexts by particular people"
(459). Yet at the same time as it blocks critical attempts to essentialize,
satire compensates for its inner vacuum by sliding, up until the nineteenth
century, into tragedy—and, since the era of Romanticism, into the novel.
Thus the problem of satire is how something as vaguely attitudinal yet
pervasive as the satiric ever comes to be satire, generically speaking, and
how, typically, it lap-dissolves into tragedy or novel. Juvenal's *Satires*,

Petronius's *Satyricon,* then Cervantes' *Don Quixote* and, subsequently, quixotic narratives in either prose or poetry, from Samuel Butler's *Hudibras* to Hašek's *Švejk,* furnish the semigeneric traps most suitable to this inherent instability of satire.

I shall finish the sequence on the three selected genres by exploring, in chapter 6, what is both more than a literary kind and less than a traditional genre. For too long the essay has been relegated to the generic closet, to hang with other formal, only vaguely literary genres such as the Platonic dialogue, the Ciceronian dialogue, the Renaissance discourse or commentary, the Enlightenment treatise, and the nineteenth-century philosophical or scientific essay. Some literary historians marginalize it further, by labeling it the bellettristic "personal essay," practiced by such as Hazlitt, Lamb, Chesterton, or Mencken, as well as by Montaigne, Emerson, and Nietzsche. Formalist purists, on the other hand, often reserve "essayist" for a handful of greats, Montaigne to Matthew Arnold.

The essay, however, possesses, or lures one into thinking it possesses, an ontology and epistemology all its own. Even an ethics and a politics. But the defining trait of the essay taken as a genre is its traitlessness. Musil characterizes it rather aptly, if tantalizingly, when his protagonist, Ulrich—the premodern postmodernist "man without qualities" of the unfinished novel's title—appropriates the term "Essayism," following Emerson and Nietzsche, to name his antipresence philosophy. This amounts to a deliberately tentative "absentism" that occasionally verges on the inevitable Germanic—at least Hegelian, Husserlian, Heideggerian, and Heisenbergian—rediscovery and recovery of presence through a notion of potentiality. Yet from Cicero to Montaigne and Rousseau, from Emerson to Nietzsche, the essay has traced out its eccentrically positive yet diffident ideology of critical absence. This program represented by the essay has something to do with freedom from generic limits, with an unboundedness sufficient to justify treating the essay as a nongeneric genre—or "nongenre."

I shall, then, attend primarily both to the problematic intersection among interpretive directions in individual examples of each selected genre and to the theoretical problem of genre itself; scrutiny of the conceptions implicit in each particular genre will provide a hermeneutic mediation between these two levels. In the interests of method, I shall construe the sense of closure implied by genre in the Kantian way, namely, as "boundary," constrictive when regarded, as it must be, from within, yet expansive, indicating the horizon always already beyond, when regarded from our situation as readers looking across the text: "Bounds . . . always presuppose a space existing outside a certain definite place and inclosing it; limits do not require this, but are mere negations which affect a quantity so far as it is not absolutely complete. . . . A boundary is itself something positive, which belongs to what lies within as well as to the space that lies without the given complex" (Kant 93, 101). Thus tragedy will be understood as much by what it cannot or may not be as by what it can or may be; satire will be seen as sticking to its target all right, as satire, but equally as never aiming at it in the first place. And the nongeneric extremism of the essay will be seen, perhaps, as an obsessive effort, conserving and preserving much more than it seems to risk.

Actually these are not critical-theoretical paradoxes of being, but standard ways of writing. For all the genres work, however problematically, with a kind of propaedeutic willfulness that is self-consciously arbitrary, thus inevitably self-canceling. Aeschylus, Sophocles, and Euripides worked up, or executed, their tragedies as skill displays, commensurate for the Athenians with the athletes' displays—demonstrations, both, of many kinds of prowess. Likewise, to be a satirist has always been much more an act of public impersonation than a status of *being* an author; noms de plume—more satirists are "Anonymous" than tragedians or essayists—are not simply safety devices. And to write an essay, with its predilection for untrammeled gestural imperatives and exhortations, requires nothing short of ultimate gall. That is, all these genres—genre itself, I think—are illusionistic, like the slippery signifiers composing them. Their temporality, their historicity, further exposes their vulnerability as writing. As Augustine in his *Confessions* of a rhetorician admitted, words merely pretend to the absolute; they are acts of will as pathetic as they are supreme. Derrida's figures catch this illusionism of genre with particular delicacy: genre is a "floodgate" (*écluse*) and "the blinking of an eye," but also the intrinsically rhetorical "clause":

> The clause or floodgate of genre declasses what it allows to be classes. It tolls the knell of genealogy or of genericity, which it however also brings forth to the light of day. Putting to death the very thing that it engenders, it cuts a strange figure; a formless form, it remains nearly invisible, it neither sees the day nor brings itself to light. Without it, neither genre nor literature come to light, but as soon as there is this blinking of an eye, this clause or this floodgate of genre, at the very moment that a genre or a literature is broached, at that very moment, degenerescence has begun, the end begins. [Derrida 213]

Genre, which strikes us at first as the entry to permanent meaning, as the sharpest focus of a work's beams, is itself directed by the work, just as it irradiates the work. Neither is less illusory than the other, neither is more so. Yet, for the sake of thinking about genre, Aristotle's rule still sounds sensible: "Always, the inclusive factor is prior to individual factors" (*Aristotle's* Physics 29). Again, Derrida clearly expresses the inscrutable priorism of genre in itself, as "the law of the text," with the requisite balance of transparency and opacity: "Such is the law of this textual event, of this text that also speaks the law, its own and that of the other as reader of this text which, speaking the law, also imposes itself as a law text, as the text of the law. What is, then, the law of the genre of this singular text? It is law, it is the figure of the law which will also be the invisible center, the themeless theme" (221). Still, literary texts have content as well as rule: "The remarks that have just been made . . . should suffice to exclude any notion linking all these complications to pure form or one suggesting that they could be formalized outside the content. The question of the literary genre is not a formal one" (Derrida 221). Derrida is the first to emphasize this distinction between genre in the figure of ineffable law and Kant's truly "formless form" of *Freiheit* in the categorical ether.

The content of genre, the material cause imbedded within the formal, is the singular text: the tragedy *Philoctetes,* the satire *Don Quixote,* the essay "On some verses of Virgil." How, then, can one move around according to the law and at the same time freely, tracking the textual traces where they lead? What, that is, can I ultimately propose as a theory of genre that might withstand the criticisms aimed at other theories of genre, indeed at the concept of genre itself? And what can I propose that would offset my own diffidence about genre, which is certainly illusionistic?

Genre, then, I shall define the way Michel Serres defines the "encyclopedia" of sciences (his "elements") and their relationships (his "operations"), which he uncovers while attempting to explicate some texts of Michelet: "When I say 'a set of elements plus operations upon these elements' I am not defining a structure . . . I am defining structure itself; for the definition of structure is indeed a set of elements provided with operations" (*Hermes* 37). Serres's definition of "structure itself" is "set of methods": "I can no longer entertain the idea that I have explicated a text. . . . The object of explanation explains in turn the set of methods that were to explicate it" (37). As a historian, Serres concludes, then, much as Althusser concludes as an ideologist: "It is not necessary to introduce methods to read this text: the method is *in* the text. The text is its own criticism, its own explication, its own application" (38, emphasis Serres's).

Following Serres in this justification of reflexive textualism, I shall define genre as method itself. He gives content to this method in "The Algebra of Literature: The Wolf's Game"[5] and thereby avoids the solipsism of the view that method equals procedure: genre is to be understood as the deployment of power in differential curves. Thus tragedy is its own application and criticism and explication of power deployed politically, as an earnest game allowing victory, defeat, and stalemate. Satire is, similarly, its own characteristic deployment of power, the power of rational superiority gesticulating at declining, corrupted others. And the essay allows the personal voice to deploy itself, textually, as sole structure, with the aims of self-control and self-abandonment.

Expressed as hypothesis rather than as "method itself," genre will be understood as the differential configuration of discursive power—as the figural deployment of power in literature. Specific genres channel this power by following different historical topographies and realizing different potentials of language itself. My three foci, tragedy, satire, and the essay, are to be taken as tests of the critical and literary-historical value of this theory and of the theory's possible limits.

Tragedy I analyze as an aesthetic configuration of *political* power, given the conditions of its origination during classical Athenian history. Following Aristotle but expanding his notion of "action" with contemporary definitions of "power knowledge" (in *Hermes* by Serres, in *Power/Knowledge* by Foucault), tragedy may also be seen as the genre that realizes the potential of language to imitate action—but not to *re*-present historical actions. Consequently, a tragedy is immediately recognizable, even by illiterates, as a game, as a teleology of objective action culminating in one of three distinct outcomes: victory, loss, or stalemate. Developments in tragedy after the Greeks show these same three outcomes transposed to new genres in the tragic mode.

Satire is the second test case for my hypothesis. I begin with Roman *satura*, again for generic origination, then trace developments up to the twentieth century in a subspecies of *satura* called "Menippean satire." All satire I have found to be a good litmus for genre as power in that, unlike tragedy, it is an unstable genre, what I term "semigenre." The set of operations in both Augustan verse *satura* and Menippean *satura* shows, in midwork, a marked shift into modes of other genres, particularly tragedy and the novel, when satiric deployments of power prove unable to resolve dilemmas caused by the genre's concern with matters as they are *rationally* conceived and perceived. Moreover, satiric configurations of rational power are rendered even less stable by their typical composition, which is rhetorical and gestural, unlike political tragedy, which is anchored in imitative action.

This line of thought, as well as the method, I wish to develop to its terminus with a study of the essay, a kind I define as a distinctive set of operations in nonfictional discourse that can be traced back to Cicero's nondialectical way with the Platonic dialogue and that develops into the fullfledged *essai*, or "essaye," with Montaigne and Bacon until it becomes a mode of experimental philosophy in Rousseau, Emerson, and Nietzsche.

The essay, though it is usually merged because of its indeterminate subject matter into the amorphous category of prose discourse, is neither formally stable and definite in its outcomes like action-based tragedy nor unstable (degenerescence, "de-genre-essence") and ambiguous like rhetoric-based satire. Instead, the essay's set of operations requires definition according to contemporary notions of textualism. That is, precursively in Cicero and then definitely in Montaigne, the essayistic voice talks itself out of finality: Montaigne's "I do not portray being: I portray passing" (*Essays* 3.2 B, p. 611). Thus the essay provides an excellent component for my testing frame because it takes for its generic identity a *rhetorically active*, noncentered identity I call "nongenre." Positively stated, the essay as a genre frees the self from genre, by making writing a reciprocal process of self-discovery and self-abandonment. Yet, paradoxically, this subversive set of operations eventuates, by the late nineteenth century, in a potent transformation of philosophy-philology-confession into critique of ideology. Linguistically, the essay, unlike action-tragedy or rhetoric-satire, converts rhetoric into constative action through textualism.

I believe such a study will produce a fresh concept of the literary kinds, one that will take advantage of their status as moments of genre conceived as the figural deployment of power. Political (action), rational (rhetoric), and textual (rhetoric *as* action) would be only three such distributions—tragedy, satire, and the essay, respectively. The sonnet from the *dolce stil nuovo* and Petrarch to at least Wordsworth, might, for example, be fruitfully pursued for its power capacity: the intellection of love for a variety of ends, from diplomacy in its broad cultural significations of arbitration and mediation to secular figurations of the tragedy of time. Moreover, genre as power can apply in immediate ways to the welter of current literary configurations, most of them radically unstable, that self-consciously call into question the relationship between communication and social change. For example, what ideological implications does the feminist theoretical and critical essay, especially the academic variety,[6] possess when considered as a subgenre of the genre practiced since Cicero and Montaigne? Or what signs of renewal can be discerned in the contemporary trend of the hypermixed genres produced by many postcolonial cultures, for example, in the tragedy-satire-documentary-musical-dance in South African theater of protest (*Asinamali!* and *Sarafina!* by Mbongeni Ngema and the Committed Artists, 1984-87) or in El Teatro Campesino (1986)? Genre conceived as power can trace the new as well as reorganize the traditional. For it can coordinate without collapsing changing forms and varying historical content.

Finally, I should like to see genre thus reworked realize its potential as what Fredric Jameson has called an "ideal tool" for the dialectical study of culture. As deployment of power in the different kinds in ways responsive to and co-constituting historical change, genre can mediate—*more* than mediate, as I hope to explain later—between history and cultural artifact, avoiding both empty abstractions and trivial empiricism.

Before tracing tragedy, satire, and the essay as sets of operations disclosing their own dialectical traces in particular works, thus accounting for the intrinsic historicity of genre, I should establish some sort of lexicon, in descriptive rather than glossary form. These terms will not assume their full definitions, of course, until activated by the operations they indicate. Still, indicants in poetics always seem to need their indicators. I hope a brief discussion of the key implications of my terminology will steady the reader's focus on the different prospect afforded by each kind's deployment of symbolic power. Yet at the same time I want to keep the peripheries clear, so that a sense of genre as power will develop naturally rather than impose itself schematically. Genre theory has for too long been afflicted with schematisms of all kinds, from the classificatory to the definitional and structural.

First, *power* in my title *Prospects of Power* I take to be both symbolic and dynamic in that genre operations are nonrepresentational, self-referential, more or less violent *interventions* between history and literature. These operations are, then, themselves historical actions. Genre intervenes, rather than mediates in the usual sense, between literary languages, on the one hand—whether they be *political/mimetic, rational/ rhetorical,* or *textual*—and events, deeds, and institutions, on the other. Tragedy, for example, intervenes between history as action and its activation in emotion: it *is* history as political force experienced through mimetic presentations (not *re*presentations) of victory, loss, and stalemate. Satire intervenes between rhetorical gestures and rational frames of evaluation, whether moral, social, religious, or ideological. Unlike the symbolic-dynamic mimesis of tragedy, the symbolic-dynamic rhetorizing of satire rebounds against itself, aspiring to correct or condemn *really* yet stalling at the level of evaluation without penetrating to the political realm of felt power differentials. From satire we acquire sharper or duller discernment; through tragedy we experience definitive celebration, mourning, or suspension. The essay, which is neither mimetic like tragedy nor rhetorical like satire, can be said to intervene between the writing or reading self and the words constituting that self through the liberating play of textuality. First the essay frees itself from history by means of the self-reproductive Word, then it frees itself from the essayist's self, and finally from genre altogether. The essay is the literary kind that intervenes as it were sexually, with the on-again, off-again violence Montaigne is so ironic about in "On some verses of Virgil": the self re-creating itself by means of the eroticism of the Word, the autosuggestive fertility of language, rhetoric as constative act rather than gesticulation. The prospects of power offered by all these genres are, therefore, at one and the same time symbolic, or literary (prospects), and dynamic, or historical (power in the mode of intervention).

If "intervention" appears insufficient in defining the kind of power I see operating in genre, all I can say here is that after my treatment of the three selected genres I should be able to argue, in a final chapter, that the post-Althusser Marxist notion of mediation among levels of culture all relating in some way to a dominant needs to be revised according to my understanding of how genre acts historically as the kind of violence I term "intervention." For power in generic configurations is a mode of both cultural and historical violence: undiluted, or political-mimetic, in tragedy; self-defeating, or rational-evaluative, in satire; and inwardly political-sexual, or textual, in the essay. These may seem odd formulations now, but I hope to make them real in the chapters devoted to the particular genres I have selected.

At the end of this first chapter, I shall rest content with some initial definitions of the terms I have just applied in attempting to define "power" in genre. By "political" as it applies to tragic configurations, I mean to indicate the power differential as such, politics as Machiavellian form, with no specific ideological content implied, just the edges of power in history. This differential is realized in a tragic action as one of three possible outcomes: winning, losing, or stalemating. It does not matter which of the three comes to pass, merely that some outcome be realized—and there are *only* the three possibilities. Politics in tragedy is no empty form, however lacking it may be in specific factional, moral, social, or religious significance. For in history *as* political form, the shifting configurations of friend and enemy, good and evil, us and them, godly and impious signify nothing; only the result, whether victory, loss, or stalemate, counts. Tragedy as an action in mimesis of historical action is, then, a game, but one that in the symbolic-dynamic sense of power is as perfectly serious as history, since the aesthetic ends of tragedy are the emotional experiences of celebration, mourning, and suspension.

Moreover, if tragedy is mimetic action and its outcomes are the same in form as historical results, the power deployed by tragic genre is pure, in that it is not an effect of a *re*presented action but a real, that is a game, presentation in itself. Power is directly rendered—this is the sense of Aristotle's "imitation" as I take it—by tragic actions; it is not evaluated, as in satire, and it is not mentalized, as in the essay. And as emotion, tragic power remains historical, free of rationalization (satire) yet equally sealed off from the freedom of textual play (the essay).

By "rational" as it applies to satiric configurations, in distinction from tragic, I mean the diversion of power away from imitated action and toward evaluation in terms of morality, taste, religious faith, political faction, and ideology. These two latter senses of "political" refer to content, unlike the formal "political" of tragedy. While tragedy's mimesis is conveyed in part by real-time imitated action and in part by the actor's speeches, satire, even when it renders indirectly imitative action as it does in its Menippean variety, depends entirely on the ability of the rhetoric, particularly irony, to secure the direction of critique. The combination of evaluation and reliance on rhetoric for aim makes satire a thoroughly rational enterprise; its effects are entrapped within the brain, manipulating for advantage always but never breaking out even at its most raging into the political realm of definitive outcome. Yet satire aspires to make the breakthrough because only through political force can there be outcome. And what else could inspire satiric critique besides the will to win? All it can win, though, is its point. For unfortunately reason requires another base besides itself to produce victory, loss, or stalemate. Indeed, the occasion of satire is typically despair with its own identity as rational critique, which, while never winning, yet never loses—or it would not satirize at all—and never stalemates—or it would not find expression as critique in the first place. Or, put another way, in winning its points in the sense that slander permanently stains its target, satire removes itself completely from the world of the power differential: automatic winning is no victory at all.

Despairing of its rational despair, satire turns itself toward other genres, for example tragedy, in the hope of achieving a definitive outcome even if it consists in loss or stalemate: witness Juvenal's turn to Greek tragedy, specifically the Sophoclean and Euripidean varieties. Otherwise, if it does not abandon its identity, satire must content itself with a merely gestural reality, that of rhetoric guided by reason in its attempts to evaluate. These attempts produce values aplenty but never results, which are available solely through history and the historical game of tragedy.

By "textual" as it applies to the essay genre, I mean rhetoric *as* action, rhetoric become constative instead of expressive. The essay, unlike tragedy or narrative satire, lacks all mimetic function. And although the essay may include critique, as it obviously does in Montaigne, Emerson, and Nietzsche, its directionality, or rhetorical aim, is not determined by the evaluative categories of good and bad, friend and enemy, this side and that side, which are typical of satire. Instead, the essay is generically controlled by desire alone, the desire of the reflexive self for liberation through the play of words—what I term "textualism." Essayistic rhetoric fuses the gap between tragedy's action-based rhetoric—Aristotle's "diction" combined with his *dianoia* "thought," both subordinate to plot—and satire's gestural rhetoric. By substituting the Word for all pretense to the form of the historical world, which is the power differential, the essayist also eliminates the need to harness rhetoric to evaluative reason. The result is a freedom eluding satire except when it is transformed into fantasy. The essayist is free to cultivate the politics of the self by opening up to the prospect of language as a virtually corporeal extension of the self into the reader— *and* back into history. There, refusing even to acknowledge the game of power as relevant, constative rhetoric always wins. Yet this kind of victory, unlike the empty victory of rational satire, brings the benefit of freedom not only from history but from rationality as well. And while remaining prose, the essay assumes the Platonic privileges of Romantic poetry.

Perhaps a disclaimer is in order before I turn to the operational literary history of particular genres. In choosing tragedy, satire, and the essay, I not only wish to compare genres the differences between which can establish my argument that for *all* genres, genre is the figural deployment of power: political-mimetic tragedy, rational-evaluative satire, textual essay. More important, in selecting these three I stake out the limits of the concept of genre: from the core, where the purest instance is completely stable, the genre of tragedy; through a midpoint where a bona fide genre shows itself unstable, the semigenre of satire; to the extreme where expression finds liberation from the concept of genre altogether, the nongenre of the essay. I do *not* mean to suggest that a systematic spectrum of genres can be established, with ordered gradations and set positions for particular kinds. The sonnet, for example, cannot be thought of as being situated "halfway" between the gestural rhetoric of satire and the free rhetoric of constative essayism. Such an explanation would be confusing, to say the least, although it would properly show up the absurdity of equating genre with any kind of classification scheme.

What I hope to accomplish is to describe the *range* of genre, not to elaborate its taxonomy. Simply, since I believe genre *is* power, I wish to show what genre at its maximum efficacy, the genre of tragedy, can *do*; what a perfectly unstable genre, satire—which must become other genres to resolve the problems it poses and attempts to solve through rational critique—*cannot* do; and what a kind that generates itself, the essay, can *avoid* doing, namely, paying obeisance to absolute generic directives, such as the requirement of political outcome in tragedy, and running up against generic deadlock, such as the permanent irresolution of rational evaluation in satire.

Instead of a system of genres, I propose a systematic approach to genre as a dialectical phenomenon in cultural history, indeed a dialectic all by itself. Every other kind besides the three I describe has to be understood as more or less like and unlike *all three* taken together, for they articulate the range of power. That is, all genres must be understood for the ways they deploy figural power. In establishing a range rather than a system, the three selected genres imply a whole new set of questions. We should not wonder "where" the sonnet is "situated" in the "spectrum" of genres. Instead, might not the sonnet deploy power in its *own* way; might it not be both like and unlike tragedy, satire and the essay in the way it *operates*? Or might not comedy even be a *kind* of tragedy? For if tragedy is the political deployment of figural power toward the outcomes of either victory, loss, or stalemate, comedy might well be apprehended as the directly mimetic genre limited to only one of these three, victory. Or the novel of social realism, which is already contained, albeit contradictorily, in Menippean satire from Petronius to Cervantes and Twain, might represent the historical development of a basically aristocratic form into a form more consistent with bourgeois ideologies of hope and progress. Byron's nostalgia for Menippean satire may be cited to illustrate this development, for it was a fondness not shared by most Romantics in England, who committed themselves to the historical novel. And the Victorian Thackeray, who from *Pendennis* through *Vanity Fair* was basically a satirist, gradually transformed himself, in *Henry Esmond*, into a realist novelist. The crucial point I wish to make in describing the *range* of genre is a matter of dialectical poetics, or formalist dialectics: figural deployments of power are the constituent elements of genre.

Still another introductory statement is necessary here, about the relation in this book between specific analyses of works in a literary-historical format and the theory I am urging. In the succeeding chapters analyses of specific tragedies, satires, and essays as configurations of power, as prospects of power, keep my project within the boundaries of the literary genres as they are or have become in history. These analyses may look like traditional critical explications, but they do not translate, or interpret, generic power by applying another *type* of discourse, say, exegetical, structural, philosophical, linguistic, historical, or sociological. My analyses are instead exercises in the *poetics*—in the sense made familiar by such writers as Todorov and Culler, among many others—of genre. Again, I simply wish to show how both genre and specific genres *operate*, as modes of historical signification.

My models for such a method of discussing literary works as operations would be Serres's and Foucault's ways with their materials. I take perfectly seriously Serres's rule, "The text is its own criticism, its own explication, its own application" (*Hermes* 38). Following this rule, however, does *not* mean, for either Serres or myself, that bald quotation is logically the only way to proceed with texts. Their operations, after all, must be uncovered, just as ideologies, while applying, explicating, and even criticizing themselves, still need the X-ray vision of theorists necessarily working from the inside of these same ideologies. To show tragedy as deployment of power requires penetrating that power configuration; individual tragedies must be penetrated to disclose *where* they are *going* as operations, not *what* the channels of power "mean." My mode of analysis thus becomes as violent as the generic interventions I respond to.

Serres and Foucault, both theorists who call themselves historians rather than poeticians, can indeed serve me as guides toward the ideal of transparency, if not its accomplishment. Actually to achieve such transparency would preclude both theory and criticism; by analogy, it would also be as if Aeschylus's *Persians* did *not* have to be created since the Athenians and Spartans *had* won at Salamis and Plataea. Were the genre theorist to get to the point where the texts discussed actually appear *as they operate*—transparency, in short—it would be tantamount to theoretical silence (not a bad idea, many would say).

My own situation as a theorist dealing with purely literary materials is further complicated by the peculiar status of my matter, it is true. For when verbal art operating as generic power is the subject instead of Serres's philosophical-aesthetic texts or Foucault's documents, I necessarily fall even shorter of the ideal of transparency than they do. They can be literary about the genesis of institutions or ideologies. However, I am often forced to talk, unliterarily, about tragedies and satires as I try to show them operating. I must also pull back occasionally to insert summaries on the tragedies and satires traced in their operations, as I do in chapters 3 and 5. With the essay, theoretical transparency is more possible; thus I treat the operations of the essay genre in one unified chapter, with no separation required between "on" and "of." What else is the theory of the essay but an essay on the genre? For the only available form to theorize about anything at all in the field of literary subjects is going to be some version of the essay. The ambiguity between "on" and "of" was thus a standard ambiguity from the sixteenth through the eighteenth century: for example, Montaigne in Florio's translation ("Of repentance," now routinely modernized into "On repentance"), or, in essayistic philosophy, Hume's *Treatise of Human Nature*, meaning our "on."

In other words, the analyses of particular tragedies, satires, and essays will be tracings of genre operating as power, not interpretations of something called "literature" correlating these works with historical events, deeds, and institutions. For example, an analysis of *Philoctetes* will unfold the history of tragic genre configuring itself as Sophoclean stalemate, which unfolding is itself a political action. Similarly, the section on *Don Quixote* will disclose the shifting from satiric critique to the securities offered by other genres such as fantasy and the romance; and it is precisely this instability that accounts for the rational-rhetorical gesture describing the nonmimetic, non-outcome prospect of satiric genre—and, in turn, the gesture accounts for the instability. My attempt to follow Montaigne's "mental metonymy" will be both on and of essayistic nongenre as it operates by freeing the self from both history and self by means of libertine acts of reflexive textualism.

Clearly, an exclusively theoretical statement of the modus operandi of my theory of genre in *Prospects of Power* will be possible only once my selected genres have worked themselves, as particular works and as literary-historical kinds, as acts of power. For tragedy, satire, and the essay *are* history. To elaborate such an extreme pronouncement, however, I must wait until chapter 7.

CHAPTER TWO

Tragedies

I begin this sequence of chapters on the operational literary history of three specific kinds with a study of tragedy because it possesses uncontested credentials as a genre, with a definite if still obscure origin, a clear set of developments, a demise (or many demises), and a discernible effect on certain other genres. Satire, by contrast, is both in itself, formally, more diffuse and more intricately compounded with other genres from the start. The essay, which provides the terminus of my range of genre, is, of course, extremely different from both tragedy and satire, not only formally but in its peculiarly discontinuous history; and this extreme difference makes it unsuitable for a beginning.

Greek tragedy as we know it falls into a weirdly neat division caused by the historical accident that gives us, aside from a few fragmentary exceptions, only Aeschylus, Sophocles, and Euripides—and, with overlaps, in that chronological order. If, however, we necessarily depend on Homer for our understanding of epic, there should be nothing strange about accepting this triangulation of fifth-century Athenian tragedy, even if it is impossible empirically to extend our conclusions to Megarian and Corinthian tragedy, or to later Athenian tragedy for that matter.

Still another tripartite division immediately suggests itself concerning the overall form of Greek tragedy. The telos of Aeschylean drama is not tragic, for the outcomes of his tragedies all either celebrate Athenian victory outright or indicate it down the mythical-historical road. Sophocles' objective is not victory, but instead permanent suspension between winning and losing, or stalemate. The Euripidean telos is either devastation of the "winner" *(Medea, Heracles,* the *Bacchae)* or, less typically, inexplicable and even perverse deliverance from disaster *(Iphigeneia at Tauris).* Athenian tragedy is, then, formally definable in terms of three possible outcomes: victory, loss, stalemate. These formal differentia transparently indicate, they in fact signify, the historical power differential. For whatever the content of historical action, whether it be good versus evil or simply "us versus them," the sole form of history itself—what makes events, deeds, and institutions happen, or *politics* as the practice of power—is winning, losing, or stalemating.

Obviously, tragedy must be described in terms of the operations of political power. Immediately we can see no other genre so starkly dependent on the interplay of forces: stronger, weaker, as strong as weak. Reason, which has everything to do with a genre such as satire, for instance, with its critical sorting-out of the relatively good and bad, tasteful and tasteless, pious and blasphemous—has nothing to do with power *as* power, which registers only outcome with complete disregard for values. Furthermore, as a genre of direct mimesis, tragedy seems less dependent on words and more dependent on action—even to the point of real-time, or nearly real-time, presentation instead of representation—than the kinds of genre, like the lyric or the essay, that acquire their character from the nature and effects of language as such. No wonder, then, that tragedy is so slippery for poetics, beginning with Aristotle's formalism, and so inviting of other kinds of explanation than the literary, from the tracing of religious or historical origins to moral-social thematics and myth study.

Power in a political configuration, however, as a discursive frame sufficiently general yet specifically applicable to Athenian tragedy, will properly initiate my own tripartite treatment of the range of genre. For the world of power in a kind such as satire, which is often about things political, is remarkably lacking in efficacy; satire's rational critique of political values means satire is incapable of presenting the straight power differential that determines tragic plots. But now tragedy, easily contrastable with other generic operations, needs a surer outline in itself.

Defining a particular genre is as problematic as adequately articulating the concept of genre and deciding upon a proper theory and method. Aristotle claimed tragedy offers us men as better, and comedy as worse, than they are. That is a nice dictum. But one could just as well turn it around: even in Old Comedy men appear better than they really are—innocent rather than guilt-ridden, lively and sometimes lyrical instead of reduced. We need not worry about our better's having diverged all that far from the Greeks': the *Frogs* (405 B.C.) reassures us that we can, after all, be presumed into basic agreement with certain criteria of Old Comedy as they are applied at least to Euripides and Aeschylus, from whom contemporaneous Athenians were as distanced as we are today.[1]

Or we could leap to our present and be Saussurian, identifying tragedy in terms of what it is not, both its internal and its intertextual *differances*. However, the fullest, most mature work of Aeschylus, the virtual founder of tragedy, that has come down to us shows, imperturbably, important traces of several other genres, some of which were already available *as* genres to fifth-century Athens: not only comedy and a kind of satire, but also the lyric, in the choral odes framing the mimetic episodes, and the epic, in the gods/men antithesis and synthesis. Aristotle himself, we should not forget, admitted generic mixture, particularly that of epic and tragedy.

For greater clarity we could fall back on literary convention, sustained presumably by some degree of consensus throughout Western history. Convention and consensus operate formatively at the level of aesthetic traditions, yet experientially as well, at the level of audience and reader response: that is, they should explain something about the effectuality of a genre such as tragedy. Yet even such a reader-oriented critical concept as expectation, which aims at combining epistemological, aesthetic, and social determinants, has to straddle too many contradictions to cohere: one expects the worst from matricide, yet the "innocent murder" in Aeschylus's *Libation Bearers* is the conceptual foundation of a progressive civilization. If we conclude, then, that tragedy is the genre appropriate to these fearful paradoxes that surprise us, moving us away from our settled expectations of how things either do or should turn out, we can just as easily move on further, to conclude that a kind of wildly improbable comedy—especially if it is Christian in its ontology, perhaps Shake-spearean tragicomedy—would be even more appropriate. Indeed, one of Euripides' works that critics never have secured in any genre, *Iphigeneia at Tauris*, gives us an alternative from an era immediately following that of Aeschylus. Or plain satire, directed against both man and the gods for their perversity, might have served Aeschylus's paradox with still cleaner gener-icity—the way, for instance, popular American satire of perversity serves contemporary paradoxes of dissidence and racial experience far more efficiently than most current attempts at tragedy, whether mainstream or countercultural.

Then there is the kind of explanation that makes tragedy deeply performative of still-obscure Dionysian rituals. Tragedy certainly does relate, genetically, to certain predecessor rituals. Yet Aeschylean tragedy, which one must start with, is obviously not itself a ritual, nor were the political-social circumstances of tragedy competitions the kind stipulating ritual functionality.

Politics fairly subsumed religion in Athenian public life during the fifth century, at least by the time the sponsor, or *choregos*, of the tragedy writer appeared—notably Themistocles, who backed Phrynichus (Pick-ard-Cambridge 64), then Pericles, who backed Aeschylus. Indeed, from the time of Peisistratus, a half century before Aeschylus, not only was cult itself being co-opted by politics or preemptively consolidated with it, but specifically Dionysian and Eleusinian cults were also being fostered by Peisistratus, precisely to extend the antiaristocratic and "nationalist" polit-

ical base of his *tyrannis* (Andrewes 113-14). He is even credited with
presiding over the formal birth of Athenian tragedy: "The festivals of
Dionysus also received his attention, and he introduced the competition of
tragic choruses from which the art of the great fifth-century tragedians
grew. Dionysus was a god whose appeal was universal, not the special
preserve of a noble family" (Andrewes 113-14). Moreover, from Peisistratus's emphasis on the Panathenaic festival—perhaps to offset the political influence of Delphi, which was biased toward the Peloponnesus—we
can form a sense of how Athenian identity came to be reinforced more by
secularized, that is desacralized, communal activities such as athletic
contests and choral lyric-tragedy competitions than by anything properly
ritualistic: "all attempts to ascribe a Dionysiac content to the earliest
tragedies, or even to turn Dionysus himself into the earliest actor, are
unfounded" (Lesky 57). The secularization of medieval English drama
during the interval between *Quem quaeritis* and *Corpus Christi* "plays,"
on the one hand, and *The Four "P's,"* on the other, may be a comparable
phenomenon in the history of theater. In the history of public competitions, Rome's and, later, the twentieth century's pseudoritualist way with
the Olympics probably goes far beyond the degree of secularism meant
here, but the basic analogy illuminates more than it may shock.

An opposite tendency, religion's pressuring of politics, may seem to
have been operating in Athens between the early 500s and the eras of
Themistocles and Cimon, Pericles and Cleon, and later popular leaders.
Instances impinging on tragedy abound, but all suggest meanings of
scandal and clandestine political maneuverings rather than genuine sacri-
lege or violation of religious taboo. First, Aeschylus was reputedly tried
for violating the Eleusinian mysteries, though in the end he was exonerated (Lesky 57). Then Sophocles' deme, or more generally his ancestral
(genos) and spiritual home base, Colonus, served as a religiopolitical
rallying site (perhaps like the Nuremburg Festival of the 1930s) for the
reactionary Four Hundred before their putsch against a beleaguered
Athenian democracy toward the end of the Peloponnesian Wars
(Thucydides 576-77). Evidently the Four Hundred at some point went so
far as to offer Sophocles a position in their oligarchy in return for his
support, which he subsequently withdrew (Ehrenberg 318-19). And of
moment, perhaps, to Euripides, the notorious *hermokopidai* provided
Alcibiades' enemies, including the priests at Eleusis, a pretext for summon-
ing the leader of the Syracusan expedition home to stand trial, thus
dooming the last great cast of Athenian imperialism—the hubris of which
is supposed to be one of the targets of the *Trojan Women* (Ehrenberg
298-302).

Surely politics as a distinct and pervasive, probably dominating, force preempts religion through these years when classical tragedy flourishes. Ritual remains a factor, but mainly when it is an instrument of ideology and outright power moves. We should remind ourselves that the Periclean state *paid* Athenians to attend tragedies: "The introduction of the *theorikon* (two obols for visiting the theatre during the great festivals) was very popular; if Pericles introduced it, it reveals his shrewdness as well as the people's love for tragedy and comedy" (Ehrenberg 248). It is hard to imagine these shrewdly state-financed audiences responding to symbolic actions represented in tragedies as if they had authentic ritualistic value. It is equally hard to see a politically subsidized tragedian doing otherwise than a modern commercially or governmentally supported artist, whose mise-en-scène, theatrical or cinematic, might exploit ritual values, for good or bad ends (the American Western or Riefenstahl's "documentaries" come to mind), but never exactly rehearse them for themselves. Athenian tragedies, in short, because of their technical sophistication and highly charged political milieux, had to be self-conscious commentaries on any ritual elements possibly involved. The extroverted kind of tragedy, such as the *Persians*, "for which Pericles trained the chorus" (Lesky 61), would verge on propaganda; the introverted, such as *Philoctetes*, would be virtually identical with what we now tacitly designate as "high art," or self-referential expression; and trilogies such as the *Oresteia* would perfectly synthesize propaganda and high art.

Tragedies are supposed to be mythic even more than ritualistic. As Charles Segal asserts in *Tragedy and Civilization*, "Tragedy is the form of myth which explores the ultimate impossibility of mediation by accepting the contradiction between the basic polarities that human existence confronts" (21). Yet myth as a nonmediating albeit somehow mediating structure situating itself between Lévi-Straussian polarities such as nature/culture could not successfully resolve any instance of tragic agon—Segal's paradoxical "impossibility/accepting" conjuncture notwithstanding.

It is this insistence on some sort of resolution—achieved, according to Segal, by "accepting" tragedy's exposure of the "impossibility" of mediating the "basic polarities" it dramatizes—that is unacceptably contradictory in views of tragedy emphasizing its mythic nature and functionality. By contrast, tragedy itself is antimythic. It rubs our noses in what we cannot accept: for example, that civilization constantly breaks down. We cannot have our tragic and resolve it, or sustain its polarities through myth, too. The actions of tragedies are one-way.

Yet critics who admit this deadly destructiveness of tragic action typically proceed to a next step wherein the audience is distanced from tragedy's unacceptable truths by "the magic circle of the orchestra" (Segal 51), by Aristotelian catharsis, by a paradoxical "negation of civilization" that is really "a profoundly civilizing experience" (48). It finally "somehow' enhances our sense of life" (48). However, tragedy, unlike myth, as Barthes points out, is upsetting and not enhancing: "'The myth . . . starts from contradictions and tends progressively toward their mediation; tragedy, on the contrary, refuses the mediation, keeps the conflict open'" (qtd. in Segal 51; oddly, Segal quotes this with approval). One cannot, or should not, denature negations by converting them into unified poles or mere obverses of positivities; a tragedy *really* negates in its action, unlike myth, the circuitry of which subsumes opposing forces in creating a current of tensions. Tragic action ends in destruction—of many different antagonistic elements, depending on the tragedy. Its mathematics are coldly analytic, precluding transcendence by absorption of conflicts in an ever-larger totality.

Instead, the solutions of tragedy—solutions, not resolutions—are stark reminders that power determines the outcomes of heroism or civilizational order, by virtue of itself alone. In "The Algebra of Literature: The Wolf's Game," Serres offers a relevant lesson from La Fontaine as explication of Western scientific texts' modus operandi: "The reason of the strongest is always the best" (276). His conclusion, "Western man is a wolf of science" (276), is inescapable once we see that "science is a game, an infinite game, in which we always win" (268). Similarly, I shall argue of tragedy that it is an equation between the tragically appropriate and power. We simply lose to this algebra even if we win:

> But the lust for power never dies—
> men cannot have enough.
> No one will lift a hand to send it
> from his door, to give it warning,
> "Power, never come again!"[2]

This power achieves the denouements of tragic actions as does a sword; the Gordian knots are cut because they cannot be untied. Myth is infinitely accommodating. Tragedy is abrupt, ruthless. Rousseau, in his attack on spectacles, correctly diagnosed the corruption of theater, indeed of all culture, when he decried the hypocrisy of immorally enjoyed representations of immorality pretending to remedy morals. Yet an even more serious hypocrisy attaches perennially to tragedy. Although Hume, however wrongheadedly, noted that the mimesis of pain in tragedies causes pleasure only because the audience can savor its own freedom from the particular instance being represented, most other theoreticians of tragedy have been even less clear-eyed. For it remains hypocritical to point to the suffering depicted in tragedies and claim that ultimately, through ritual and myth, it alleviates suffering in the polis or even enhances the civilized community. Comedy may perform that function, if indirectly, through relief. If anything can be said about the relation between tragedy and suffering, it is the truism that tragedy rehearses the pathos to instill an answering pathos.

A tragic sufferer always loses. One might cite the exceptions, such as Orestes and Oedipus, but it is only the trilogy form's extension of the action to a religiously or historically apprehended future that makes them appear to be long-run winners. While the hero's or heroine's sufferings, even the torment of Prometheus, may cease ultimately, the rule is that he or she endures some significant degree of pathos, usually to the point of forfeiting life or falling short of all that makes life worthwhile, namely, justice. Besides, the victors in tragedy never compromise; they negotiate to their own advantage from positions of strength: Orestes is backed by Athene in the *Eumenides*, for example; Medea is supported by the Sun; and in *Philoctetes*, Odysseus is ordered by Zeus-backed Agamemnon to retrieve the bowman. When the name of the game is winning or losing, there are no polarities, thus neither mediation nor resolution: a wrestling match or a bout of wits may be refereed—for example, by Apollo in the *Eumenides* and by Neoptolemus in *Philoctetes*—but neither can be said to be mediated. The possibilities of tragedy are victory, defeat, or draw, but no real synthesis abrogating or transcending the inherently agonistic nature of the struggle. Power—not myth, any more than ritual—makes "the hard, historical actuality of Greek tragedy" (Benjamin 103). And the proper dramatic plots rendering the historical agon imitated hinge on aggressive solutions: deception, as by Odysseus in *Philoctetes;* evasion, as by Apollo in the *Eumenides;* suppression, as by Zeus in *Prometheus Bound;* repression, as by Athene in concert with the Furies in the *Eumenides;* obliteration, as by Dionysus and his maenads in the *Bacchae;* and homicidal madness, as in *Heracles.*

Still another approach to defining tragedy as a genre requires uncovering original models. The lyric and tragedy for sixth- and fifth-century Greeks were popularly esteemed products of *techne,* to be displayed, judged, and awarded honors or material prizes at Olympia and other festivals from Corinth to Athens. Accordingly, Aristotle's paradigm for making *(poesis),* applied throughout the *Poetics,* is the same one he discusses at length in Book Beta of the *Physics:* "art" is knowledge of how things have been produced, whether the health known to the physician, the building known to the builder, or the tragedy known to the tragedian. The earliest extant tragedies of Aeschylus bespeak his knowledge of the historical tragedies of Phrynichus, fragments of which lead us back still farther in our search for original models. Eventually, however, we draw a blank. The models and blueprints Aeschylus followed no longer exist independently of their incorporation in his surviving dramas. The archaeology of the parts of tragedy that Aristotle initiated remains likely: choral odes are probably earlier, peripeties later. But the plan that first generated the *techne* for Aeschylus to know remains mysterious. A modern archaeologist may be able to reconstruct a house from the traces of threshold or foundation stone, but Aeschylus would have needed more than a choral ode to draft the *Persians*.

We could, and should, search in the opposite direction and extrapolate what tragedy is from what it has become since Aeschylus, Sophocles, and Euripides. But all that is attainable is what tragedy has become—the trouble with dialectic. We get Senecan reading dramas, Christian Passions, medieval romances, Marlovian and Shakespearean historical tragedies, Jacobean revenge tragedies, Racinian case studies, *drame bourgeois*, Romantic ballet and opera, and novels and tales galore. All of these are tragic. However, none are tragedies except by association, by inclusion in categories abstracted from Aeschylus, Sophocles, and Euripides. Not even Aeschylus or Sophocles could have known anything so pure as tragedy. Yet the term sticks fast, apparently indissoluble: "For even if there were no such things as the pure tragedy or the pure comic drama which could be named after them, these ideas can still survive" (Benjamin 44).

Finally, lacking full, clear, or stable references, we could look for referentiality itself, the *vraisemblable*. However, Polonius's admirable scheme still applies: for life is tragico-comical-satirical-lyrical-pastoral. That is, it is no more essentially tragic than it is anything else. Indeed, life has never conformed with any of these genres. *They*, however, may be bent to life's protean shapes, a procedure presumably ideal for a realist aesthetic. But with tragedy the result is either soap opera or newspaper mayhem, both of which modern genres are not so contemptible as even their addicts confess, yet they remain equally distant from the most "aesthetic" of all literary genres.

We are left with the texts, and they take us down many roads; moreover, Aristotle's "road from Athens to Thebes" may not necessarily turn out to be the same as "the road from Thebes to Athens" (*Aristotle's Physics* 45). For the vectors of generic meaning can frustrate, perhaps cancel directionality itself. There are, however, discernible markers that proffer minimal information about where we might be and where we will probably end up within individual tragedies. These are not anything so intelligible as themes. Aristotle was right, after all, about the formal nature of these guideposts. The readability of tragedy according to his theoretical map depends above all else on the sequence of imitative actions reflected (episodes) and refracted (peripeties) by plots. Strictly semantic meanings do not adhere to these markers, as they do to Aristotle's "diction," that is, speeches and their figures, or even to his "character," daimon as one's "lot" combined with *arete*, consistent practice of excellence. But they more or less precisely indicate how we can go about composing our meanings. If, as travelers, we ask, when lost, "Where are we?" rather than "What does this place mean?" so, as readers, who are always lost until we find ourselves, we need to ask, "Where is this tragedy going?" not "What does this signify?" A tragedy's action, then, will be thought of, in its formal aspect at least, as Aristotle's dual telos of motive and end. This telos is rarely explicit, and it blurs the contemporary distinction between overall paradigm and sequential syntagm. Yet it is often more easily tracked by analyzing the latter, which corresponds to the diachronic nature of plots.

Persians: Tragedy of Battle Victory

Violence and order are the two most immediately intelligible non-thematic, teleological marks for starting well and arriving at the end of the *Persians*, which is now fairly solidly established as the first of Aeschylus's extant tragedies. If Athenian patriotism is the explicit goal and original inspiration of this tragedy, Scaliger's inversion of Aristotle is apt: "Wherefore action is, as it were, the pattern [or example] or medium [strictly, 'means'] in a plot [story], emotion [response] its end. But in civil life action is the end, and emotion its form" (qtd. in Benjamin 99). The victorious realization of Themistocles' strategic program at Salamis was the action inaugurating the maturity of Athenian civil life. And Aeschylus wrote his tragedy, with the fullest historical account we have of the naval battle itself serving as its centerpiece (the Messenger's report to the Persian court), to articulate the emotion representing the form of that violence, which form became the action of his plot.

The drama recapitulates the violence of history. And it does not stop at recapitulation via the Messenger to the Persian capital. The emotions roused in the Greeks by history are perceived by Aeschylus, the maker, as coextensive with the new form of their life. By contrast, Xerxes, witnessing from his hilltop vantage the disaster wrought at Salamis upon his armada, loses form, becomes a non-emperor, his very principle as absolute ruler annihilated. He first appears, haggard from retreat, toward the end of the tragedy. Xerxes *is* the end, the final spectacle of defeat, the cadence to the courtiers' worry, his mother's dream, the Messenger's news, the spirit of Darius's retrospective prophecy: "See, here, these rags, the remnants / Of royal robes I wore; / This quiver for my arrows" (*Persians*, lines 1119-21). In the resulting historical vacuum the Athenians inherit the power: to defeat an absolute ruler in one definitive stroke is *to be* the new power.

Therefore, the *Persians* is a tragedy imitating the civil action of victory in that it transforms this violence of history into an emotion of power—this new genre's proper end. In short, Aeschylus makes an imitation of an action by the same means the Athenian *thetes* used to make their history, that is, in Serres's terms, by inserting their local identity, the Greek *polis*, into Xerxes' global *ens*, the Empire. The insertion is accomplished by means, simply, of violence: "Violence is one of the two or three tools that permit us to insert the local into the global, to force it to express the universal law, to make reality ultimately rational."[3] No wonder, then, that Aeschylus, the official founder of tragedy, thought of himself at the very end of his life as above all a victorious hoplite: "Under this monument lies Aeschylus the Athenian, Euphorion's son, who died in the wheatlands of Gela. The grove of Marathon with its glories can speak of his valor in battle. The long-haired Persian remembers and can speak of it too" (qtd. in Lattimore 1). His final word neither demeans nor subordinates the words he crafted as a competitor, and usual victor, at tragedy festivals: Aeschylus the tragedian *is* Aeschylus the soldier. Their end was one and the same—power: power as the end of civil life, power as the emotional end of his plots.

Violence of battle, then, marks the true action of this first tragedy. It also marks the true action of epic, however. Where does the difference reside? If we realize that Aeschylus's concentration in the plot of the *Persians* is on the response to defeat in Persia, an answer may be possible. Homer's *Iliad*, while emphasizing the Greeks, also celebrates the values of Troy, particularly the doomed heroism of Hector. Homer's epic evenhandedness makes for an effect of grandeur that derives its force from the way he transforms the locality of the action of the Trojan War into the universality of all wars of ambition. War poets today still frequently think of the characteristic violence of the *Iliad*. Yet they never think of the *Persians;* they could not make the defeat of Xerxes their paradigm were the tragedy even better known.

The point is that Aeschylus is not evenhanded, although compassion for the vanquished Persians and empathy for an absolute ruler whose very being is canceled by Salamis are undeniable effects of the dramatic poet's focus. Aeschylus is celebrating the violence that has made him a Greek, the violence that creates by destroying. Persia's powerlessness against a few Athenian ships is Greece's power. Traditionally, the Greeks became Greek probably for the first time through this power displacement of 480. To make the same point less obliquely, the *Iliad* is an epic because it does not fasten on the formation of new identity through war. The *Persians*, however, is a tragedy precisely because it dwells on the horror of the defeated as a perfect reflection of the joy of the victor.

To apply Hegel's Lord and Bondsman metaphor, Aeschylus knows that the essence of victory is not realized until the loser recognizes the winner as his subduer: thus "The long-haired Persian remembers / . . ." of the epitaph. The negation of the foe is then felt (emotion) by the victor as the negation of his fear of losing his life, a liberating emotion because the victor's life is released from his bondage to fear itself. To stare the vanquished in the eye, even fictionally as Aeschylus does by concentrating on Xerxes' collapse and the Persians' consternation, is to live for the first time with full consciousness of one's life as separate, as one's own.

This reflective quality of the action makes the *Persians* a voyeuristic experience, just as did the quality of tragedy's original format during the time of Peisistratus's dramatic-lyric competitions: The audience attending the spectacle imbibed a new sense of their unity as audience through the enjoyment of a unique privilege—"This is for us, for we sit as ultimate judges of this contest enacted before our eyes; we are the winners." Moreover, from Peisistratus to Euripides, tragic art, lyric or dramatic, occupies a ground beyond the vicarious and just short of the physical; even in its interior sense tragedy remains a competition just like chariot racing or wrestling. The chorus in Aeschylus's *Libation Bearers* comments, "so we / can watch him surge at the last turn, / storming for the goal" (lines 788-90, Fagles); in the same drama Electra asks, "And who outwrestles death—what third last fall?" (line 343, Fagles). The status of "attendance" as a format alone grants power, the power of superior vantage. Xerxes has been toppled from his "high hill"; now Athenians witness his humiliating plummet, and from their own hill, the hillside of the Dionysian amphitheater. In the aesthetic texture of Aeschylus's *Persians,* the intensity of connection between history and play explains the priority of the visual. For the *Persians* is a public pageant of topical figures, exotic colors, solemn dispositions, and, most important, words that can be seen: "Their whole fleet hove clear into view; their right wing / first, in precise order" (lines 397-98). It is there, in the Athenian audience's subjective capacity— aroused by the emotion effected by the aesthetic action of the *Persians*—to see themselves reflected in their victim's eye, glazed over by the shocking totality of his loss, that "they" become a polis instead of individual citizens, families, tribes. Xerxes, on the other hand, *is* Persia as an absolutist state; after Xerxes nothing can ensue but *le déluge.* Thus Aeschylus contrasts his stunned isolation in defeat with the Athenians' newfound collectivity. Xerxes is shown as a solitary, without an army (he bears an empty quiver), and without his mother attending (she exited earlier, like the spirit of his father, Darius). Only the chorus remains to meet him, and with badgering questions instead of support:

> XERXES: See, here these rags, the remnants
> Of royal robes I wore;
> This quiver for my arrows—

> CHORUS: Is this your kingly treasure
> Saved from so vast a store? [lines 1019-23]

The emotional end of Aeschylus's first tragedy, then, is political form: the new order of collective identity. And the means to this civil form is, following Scaliger, the aesthetic action of power expressed as violent action producing victory. Consequently, the birth of tragedy, so far as the *Persians* allows us to surmise, is neither darkly residual Dionysian rituals nor mediating myth. It is, instead, the deliberate, public, open-air celebration of winning in a violent martial contest between the will of an Eros-driven Eastern potentate full to bursting with globality and the will of what has become through violent conflict a distinctive Western collectivity of independent localities. The tonality of epic is antithetical to the exultation Aeschylus inculcates in his audience by a combination of simple means, each of which elaborates the pathos of individualized subjects. One of these means, discussed above, is the ceremonial intensity of focus on the subjective experience of the enemy's defeat—an intensity producing recognition on the audience's part of itself as victor.

Another technique is brevity of action. This is especially significant in contrast with epic's length: for over the long term Homeric objectivity toward war prevails; the short term belongs to tragedy's framing of immediate pathos. This inherent subjectivity of formal brevity "performs," or fulfills, the audience's equation of Xerxes' downfall with their own historical origination. It must also be remembered how artificially it does this: objectively speaking, this experience is possible for the Greeks only, and for the Athenians only temporarily, because Persia will remain a threat to them, until Sparta succeeds in employing Persian help against Athens in the last Peloponnesian War, and to the rest of the eastern Mediterranean, until Alexander. Subjectivity has, besides, all along served as Aeschylus's nonpropagandistic means in the *Persians* to instill Athenians with an immediate grasp of their new identity. For only through his intent gaze into the solitary suffering of Xerxes as single man, who yet is all of Persia in his status, can Aeschylus generate the Athenian *feeling* of what it means to have a self. Epic scope would only diminish Xerxes' pathos, which would then degenerate into the anguish and terminal horror of one great loser among myriad others throughout history. Since Xerxes, in his aesthetic as well as his historical identity, is both all and one, in vanquishing him the Greeks—each participant, like Aeschylus himself, and each polis resisting Persia—can attain a delirious sense of freedom that is virtually personal and not only collective. This effect depends on Aeschylus's rendering of all Persia's collapse within the unitary dimension of the singular yet grandiose persona of Xerxes. Salamis was a victory over a man, not an abstraction, and it was in turn wrought by a few men like Aeschylus himself under the leadership of unique Athenian personalities such as Themistocles. Agamemnon, returned home in the *Oresteia,* will later declare himself conqueror of Troy by drawing the same rhetorical opposition between the individual as war chief leading other independent men and the individual as despot—Agamemnon as Argive king as opposed to Agamemnon as satrap.

What begins to come to light with the *Persians* is that early Aeschylus is as brutal, in his concentration on force as the telos and transparent technique of tragedy, as late Euripides. Or early Shakespeare: the apprentice Elizabethan playwright—not long after the defeat, by the English, of another armada—followed true to Aeschylean form by baptizing his own career in the fires of patriotic ferocity, especially the Talbot sections of *Henry VI.* Granted, the *Persians* is probably not Aeschylus's very first tragedy; only an extremely small percentage of his works have survived. But it is now fairly certainly established as the earliest of the seven we know in their complete state, and it probably shows where he was coming from as starkly as his epitaph at Gela shows where he concluded. This may seem a rather blunt account of the real origin of such a complex, high art as Greek tragedy. Critics and historians alike seem anxious to hurry past this earliest of Aeschylus's extant efforts, as if a patriotic play could not represent authentic tragic values: the *Persians* as spectacle or mere pageant. Yet the straightforward conjunction of violence and the subjective experience of the new order of collective identity effected by the *Persians* explains more of the action and emotion, civil or aesthetic, in the other tragedies of Aeschylus, and of those by Sophocles and Euripides, more cogently than any other etiology. In a true account of tragedy's generic beginnings, the violence of history and the power of tragedy converge on the axis of a new order of Athenian identity:

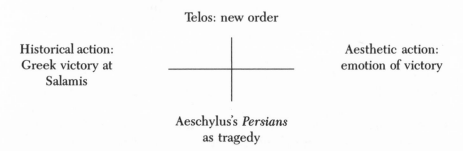

Telos: new order

Historical action: Aesthetic action:
Greek victory at   emotion of victory
Salamis

Aeschylus's *Persians*
as tragedy

Perhaps it is obvious at this point, but Aeschylus's tragedy is already beyond good and evil. There is no morality to be extracted from the

Persians. Nor is Xerxes made to appear to the Athenians as guilty of hubris. If he were, he would have to be judgable as one starting as their equal yet puffing himself up beyond the proper limits for all mortals, however magnificent their station. However, Xerxes is not supposed to be even conceivable as an equal: as Persia incarnate, his true status is superior, an absolute eminence this side of the transcendent. It would be folly for the Athenians to see Xerxes as morally exemplary of the folly of overstepping bounds. He is, as emperor of Persia, by definition an overstepper, a boundless crystallization of Persia's boundlessness. Thus Aeschylus is careful to show the allegations made by Xerxes' mother, Atossa, and his father, Darius, of their son's folly as dramatic ironies shaping Xerxes as victim. It would be futile for Aeschylus to glorify the Athenians' victory if Xerxes were brought down either by a flaw within his nature or by some punitive agency other than themselves. Thus Xerxes is an object of derision when he still cannot acknowledge that mere Greeks have brought him down. Persians, not the Athenian hoplites in their circle—understood both tactically, as the naval encirclement at Salamis, and theatrically, as the Dionysian amphitheater—are the ones who credit some other factor besides the violence of surprise attack for his defeat. First Xerxes' mother cites a transcendent force: "Oh, what malign Power so deceived our Persian hopes? / My son, marching to taste the sweetness of revenge / On Athens, found it bitter" (*Persians*, lines 471-73). The ghost of Xerxes' father, Darius, a veteran of an earlier unsuccessful invasion of Attica, in 490, is more practical in appraising his son's defeat. The debacle follows logically and logistically from the un-Persian emphasis on naval means and the Hellenes' agricultural poverty, which made sparse scavenging for the cumbersome Persian land forces and forced them to overextend their supply lines:

> Even if your force be twice as great,
> Never set arms in motion against Hellene soil.
> You cannot win; the land itself fights on their side.
>
> . . . .
>
> Their soil is lean, and kills
> With famine any force of more than moderate size.
> [lines 783-85, 787-88]

While Darius does conclude, "The just reward of pride and godless insolence" (line 808), the mundane and specific analysis preparing the audience for it suggests that the conclusion's main purpose is not to cite hubris but to provide weighty cadence to the great spirit's judgment of his son's debacle.

Certainly the devastated Xerxes himself, on first appearing in the
spectacle, blames anything he can rather than hubris: "Weep for the
deadly doom that Fate / Has launched against me unforeseen" (lines
899-900). Instead of admitting to overweening pride as his virtuous vice—
which is a close definition of what Aristotle's *Poetics* really signifies by
hubris, and then apropos of Sophocles, not Aeschylus—Xerxes himself
points to a likelier cause, when he betrays his youthful shame in a self-
pitying lamentation. He gains thereby from the victorious auditors the
kind of pity they might be expected to bestow on an inexperienced but
talented chariot racer. The lamentation falls far short of his father's ghostly
solemnity: "Behold me, theme for sorrow, / A loathed and piteous outcast, /
Born to destroy my race" (lines 932-34). Aeschylus's effect here is entirely
human. Young Xerxes is no hubristic hero; he lacks the capaciousness,
having room in his stripling, characteristically hyperbolic judgment as
young emperor for little more than a glimmer that he has mucked up,
"Born to destroy my race." After all, were he really like the potentate's role
he plays, the Athenians could not see how they could have defeated him so
utterly as they did; Marathon, the culmination of his father's expedition
(Aeschylus was there, too), was a much closer confrontation than Salamis.
At the same time, were Xerxes less than the inexperienced son trying to
fulfill what he thinks to be his father's wish, the Athenians could not enjoy
their reputation as realistic opportunists rather than mighty equals to
Persia. Hubris in the role Xerxes is given by the shrewd Aeschylus would
spoil the audience's fun, and a tragedy that is no fun is no game, admitting
win and loss, at all. Above all, Aeschylus wishes to avoid rather than allege
hubris. His task is to make a politically symbolic presentation of a historical
action, not to intone moral warnings. As we shall see, the *Oresteia*, as well,
ends on this same kind of supramoral, fully political upbeat.

Moral psychology is not the source of this early Aeschylean tragedy of
direct, unadulterated, victorious power. Instead, an Athenian clarity of historical vision combined with the flush of unexpected success provides Aeschylus
with a very different source of effect, one that is as mathematical and physical
as it is political: the nature of Salamis as a battle. The Messenger's detailed
description of the naval victory itself is at the heart of this first tragedy. The
requisite picture Aeschylus must create in the Athenians' imagination is
perfectly coincident with the picture the Messenger must create in his Persian
courtiers' inner eye to make his otherwise incredible announcement of defeat
genuinely credible news. The dramatic technique is brilliant, a meticulous
rendering of the where and when of the ships' clashing:

> And soon
> Their whole fleet hove clear into view; their right wing first,

> In precise order, next their whole array came on,
> And at that instant a great shout beat on our ears:
> "Forward, you sons of Hellas! Set your country free!"
> [lines 396-400]

Naval battle in this instance is not only historically determining but also aesthetically appropriate. For Aeschylus symbolically casts Persia's downfall as an effect of its mistake in bridging the Hellespont: "Our bound of empire, spanned / By boats from land to land" (lines 131-32). The mistake lies in Persia's land-bound identity protruding itself over the strait separating Asia from Thrace. Now that Salamis has proved it to them, the Athenians' own identity is with the sea. Unlike Persia with its land mass, Athens finds its proper space for deploying its power, its political *Lebensraum*, in the Mediterranean, inclusive of all the minor seas. Aeschylus goes so far in this tragic pageant as to ignore strict history, by conflating Salamis and Plataea, for the sake of glorifying Athens over the other participating poleis. No marvel is it, then, that Persian archers and horsemen prove futile before Nature's revulsion against Xerxes' bridge: "He would wrest Nature, turn sea into land, manacle / A strait with iron, to make a highway for his troops" (lines 750-51). Again, it is not that Persia really is presumptuous, guilty of hubris, but that, after they have surprised themselves with the good fortune of their foresight at Salamis, the Athenians can now, through the magic of retrospection, regard the Persians' venture across the water as a violation of nature. National identities thrive on such lore, and literature freely exploits its possibilities: Napoleon could conquer all that was "properly" European, but not the mystical spaces and hyperborean winters of Mother Russia; the redcoats could control their Empire by sea, but a protracted land war in colonial North America they were not "meant" to win. The *Persians* is a tragedy fusing not moral philosophy with religious dread, but political message—power exchange —and patriotic feeling—the new order of Athenian solidarity.

Eros, not hubris, fits the tragic geometry of Persia's fortunate fall. The dream related by the emperor's mother, Atossa, is just the right piece for Aeschylus to cover any lack of ultimate human motive force behind Xerxes' mistaken attempt to absorb, to pacify, to cancel the disharmony caused by the very existence of Greece:

> Listen: two women, finely dressed,
> One in the Persian style, the other Dorian,
> Appeared to me, flawless in beauty, and in gait
> And stature far excelling women of our day.
> Sisters of one race, each had her inheritance,

> One Greece, the other Asia. And, it seemed, these two
> Provoked each other to a quarrel; and my son
> Restrained and tamed them, yoked them to his chariot,
> And fastened harness on their necks. [lines 179-87]

The dream vision offers Aeschylus's audience another picture, one matching in its intensity of allusion the Messenger's report, which, although a
historical document, also possesses the visionary quality. Further, the
picture's buried narrative, its easily accessible latency, delineates a Xerxes
who *restores* to unity a duality that is fated to split by the already developed individuation of one of the sisters. Thus Eros controls Persia's
historical task, which is to overwhelm disparity through a kind of love not
dissimilar to that famously figured by Plato, who also imaged love, in the
Phaedrus, in terms of a charioteer reining in a dark horse of passion and a
white horse of friendship. But how does this political mission of love, as it is
figured by Atossa's dream, assume a shape realistic enough to serve as a
plausible explanation Aeschylus might offer his heroic Athenians?

The Messenger's battle scene—the other, even more central picture—provides Aeschylus with the requisite geometry to offset and deter
this Persian historical love. The vast Persian fleet is represented as chasing
the small Athenian detachment of ships at Salamis, only to be surprised by
their "precise order" and their cry, "Set your country free!"

> All night long the captains kept
> Their whole force cruising to and fro across the strait.
> Now night was fading; still the Hellenes showed no sign
> Of trying to sail out unnoticed; till at last
> Over the earth shone the white horses of the day,
> Filling the air with beauty. Then from the Hellene ships
> Rose like a song of joy the piercing battle-cry,
> And from the island crags echoed an answering shout.
>
> The Persians knew their error; fear gripped every man.
> They were not fugitives who sang that terrifying
> Paean, but Hellenes charging with courageous hearts
> To battle . . .
> . . . and soon
> Their whole fleet hove clear into view; their right wing first,
> In precise order . . . [lines 384-98]

What this stirring yet beautiful *tableau vivant* diachronically realizes is
Athenian violence, in the service of locality and rationality, opposing itself
to Persian violence, expressing globality and erotic distension. Again, as

Serres states: "Violence is one of the two or three tools that permit us to insert the local into the global, to force it to express the universal law, to make reality ultimately rational. In fact, as in geometry, what passes for a universal globality is only an inordinately distended [local] variety. Representation is nothing but this distension, swelling, or inflation. One can still say to those who are too violent: you are ignorant of, you are forgetting geometry" (qtd. in Harari and Bell xxvii n.).

The Persian rowers and soldiers, "keeping course / As they were ordered" (lines 383-84), have forgotten geometry, of which they are suddenly reminded by the Athenians hoving "clear into view." For this conflict is between an engulfing global violence and an integral, local violence that forces the birth of rationality. The Persian fleet is so swollen that its massively loving violence falls in on itself, allowing the clean order of Athenian rationality, with its naval geometry of envelopment, to penetrate and annihilate[4]:

> At first by its huge impetus
> Our fleet withstood them. But soon, in that narrow space,
> Our ships were jammed in hundreds; none could help another.
> They rammed each other with their prows of bronze; and some
> Were stripped of every oar. Meanwhile the enemy
> Came round us in a ring and charged. [lines 408-13]

From this distension issues excess, the excess of imperial *Eros*. Athenian civilization will itself undergo similar distension in the not-so-distant future, when Alcibiades leads his armada in encroachment against an independent Syracuse. Athenian victory is a rational consummation of encircling, ramming, stripping, and impaling. Into this amorphous Persian excess the Greek violence inserts its precise order, restoring geometry and establishing political integrity. Finally the *Persians* defines initial Aeschylean tragedy as a matter of *geometria*, not *sophrosyne*. This is tragedy of passion, but of passion the violence of which is order because its aim is jubilation at the triumph of the rational over the erotic: a classical tragedy, indeed. Certainly a far cry from the Nietzschean "Dionysian," an even farther cry from moral acceptance of the permanently unacceptable. But the geometry of the *Persians* is still the violent order advocated, in a judicial rather than naval context, by the mature and complete Aeschylus of the *Eumenides*.

Eumenides: Tragedy of State Victory

Violence and order are easily discernible guideposts to the action of the earliest play we have from Aeschylus; they would have been as impossible

for his Athenian auditors to miss as they are for Latin American readers and
South African audiences today. Yet violence and order do not control the
semantic components of the *Persians*. They remain nonthematic instiga-
tions of certain responses and cannot be read as summations of the diachronic episodes such as Atossa's dream vision or the Messenger's report.
In this patriotic tragedy, probably produced in 472, eight years after the
event it imitates, Aeschylus exploits the *dynamis* between illusion and
history, between dramatic emotion and civil action, entirely within the
framework of a single play. The diachronic is not overwhelmed by anything
definable as paradigmatic, such as the new order of collective Athenian
identity. Instead, the paradigm is given, already in the air: it is the
historical flush of victory still being savored by Athens. Then, through the
aesthetic action culminating in the purely visualized naval battle, the
paradigm of victory unfolds in such a way as to stoke the emotions of the
victors to their highest pitch. When they subside, at the point when
Xerxes appears an utterly stripped and reduced victim, a precipitate is left:
the order of a new identity, product of violence.

The distance between the starting and finishing marks in the *Oresteia*,
thus the tension of the tragic race to be run, is still greater than it is in the
Persians. One reason is that Aeschylus's masterwork, and his finale—it was
produced in 458, two years before Aeschylus died—stands as a full trilogy;
Proteus, a satyr play parodying the trilogy, has not survived. Consequently,
the violence of the *Oresteia*'s first play, *Agamemnon*, has the true effect of
violence—obscurity. We feel the compounded violence of Thyestes'
curse, the Trojan War of ten years' duration, and the portentous return of
the conqueror to his impatient anti-Penelope the way it is felt by the
chorus of aristocrat elders. Confused, we cannot foresee, and we dread
seeing, any pat order in either the events—the fall of Troy, signaled by
Clytaemnestra's fires, for example—or our responses to these events—for
instance, our hesitancy to trust this passionate woman. The two teleological markers of violence and order in the *Oresteia* are clearly visible
only at the moment of matricide, in the *Libation Bearers:* that "innocent
murder" (line 830, Lattimore) of his mother by the son of the father she
murdered, by the son whose matricide is also suicide, requires a new order
now that the order of the family has collapsed.

This new order is fully articulated by the third play, the *Eumenides*.
Yet Aeschylus's mastery of the diachronic through the entirety of the
Oresteia, his perfect timing, is not an automatic function of the natural
sequence beginning-middle-end of the trilogy format. *Prometheus
Bound*, produced sometime between the *Persians* and the *Oresteia*,[5] is
also, like the *Eumenides*, part of a trilogy—the first instead of the last,
however, and the only part extant in complete form. Moreover, *Pro-

metheus Bound presents the same direction, from violence to order, as both the *Persians* and the *Oresteia*. Yet *Prometheus Bound* differs from both the earliest and last tragedies in its complete lack of diachronicity. It starts, proceeds, and concludes all within the paradigm of victory. Prometheus himself represents this paradigm; he is equally signifier and signified. "Prometheus" the name means forethought, prophecy of the orderly end of salvation from the vantage of the violent onset of suffering. As such, especially in his immobility, pinned by Zeus to the rock "forever," Prometheus exists in the play only as words, his prophetic speeches to the sympathetic chorus of Oceanus's daughters and to Io, another myth figure, who signifies the eventual deliverance of Prometheus by her own and Zeus's descendant, Heracles. With its minimum of dialectic, the tragedy is really a lyric, not an imitation of an action at all. Undoubtedly this primacy of the lyric is why mainly poets and not dramatists have been perennially attracted to the possibilities of Prometheus unbound.

The point of a comparison between this earlier play and the *Eumenides* in particular as well as the entire *Oresteia* is that past and future, the version of the violence-order diachronic markers in *Prometheus Bound,* are converted into the paradigm of victory by being conflated into "the triumph of time" itself. Past and future become *aspects* of a collapsed equation: the past (suffering) equals the future (deliverance). Out of this suffering, caused by the demonstration of Zeus's power in Prometheus's pathos and the invasion of this power in Io's strange, prolonged trial, will come, inevitably, salvation and new order. Xerxes, in the *Persians*, is an actor on the historical stage of Athenian victory. But Prometheus is a symbol on the plane of mythic verbalization. The action of his agon is prophecy, the foreseeing of deliverance by Heracles: "Learn it as truth: it shall be" (line 760). Unlike a similar agonistic foreseer, Cassandra in *Agamemnon,* Prometheus is allotted the hero's role and, since he is a Titan, fails to be either a genuine sufferer or a catalyst to disaster, except mythically in his defiance of Zeus by giving man fire and hope. Instead of inspiring his auditors, the chorus, to either action or insight, he constantly tells them to cease offering to help lest they get caught up in Zeus's further violence against him.

Such conflation of past and future into a verbalizing symbol of victory is precisely what Aeschylus avoids in the *Oresteia*. While the paradigm of victory oversaturates *Prometheus Bound,* which implodes into nothing but meaning, in the *Eumenides* the same paradigm has to be worked out by reason, or Persuasion in the context of the court trial, then both wrested from and restored to the realm of the biological, or the Furies. Therefore, only at the very conclusion to the *Eumenides* can we see the teleological markers of violence and order for what they mean: the diachronic extension from a past mired in blood into the future of a progressive Athenian civilization.

What accounts, then, for this difference in the direction indicated by the markers in *Prometheus Bound* and the *Eumenides*—from mythic symbol to meaning in the earlier tragedy, from the violence of matricide to the order of progress in the later? Prometheus is an image of progressive power; thus his existence in a mythic nonaction is equivalent to prophecy, the imaging in words of what will ensue. Orestes, however, as mortal, is a medium, or agent, of power. This humanly realized power converges with that of the Olympian gods in the *Libation Bearers* and the *Eumenides*. Furthermore, Orestes as son of both a yet-unavenged father and an equally unavenged mother, is also a medium of the Furies' power. The site where the powers of the sky, backing the human agency of a hero, and the powers of the earth, urging the biological power of a mother, intersect is Athens as "victor city" (*Eumenides*, line 926, Fagles). Put another way, the action of the *Eumenides*, directionally marked by violence and order, is the intersecting of two convergent hierarchies, Olympian deities plus Orestes the prince representing the king Agamemnon, and one divergent subarchy, the Furies—at the place and time of Athens as a democracy dominated, but only superficially, by the aristocratic values of the pristine Areopagus.

Tragedy in the *Eumenides* is a distribution of power, logically through a paradigm of victory—previously established in *Libation Bearers* through Orestes' "I have won" (line 1017, Lattimore)—but diachronically through a circuitry directing three distinct kinds of power across a political structure. This energy system eventually activates Aeschylus's conceptual design for a politics of prevalence based on a justice of reciprocity. But the original energy feeding into the *Eumenides* is the matricidal violence of the *Libation Bearers*. Orestes, propelled by his own revenge yet also coerced by Apollo, who proves later to be serving Zeus's principle of patriarchal-monarchical rule, forces a crisis in the familial and political orders of Argos: in killing his mother the hero effectively cancels the House of Atreus. For in ridding it of his usurper mother he is not only smashing the remnant of her paramour's *tyrannis*—Aegisthus's status in the palace entirely depends on Clytaemnestra's personal energy and official authority as queen—but also annulling his own status as son. Henceforth Orestes' only identity is that of political heir. He is almost newborn as a matricide, like his eventual presiding judge in the *Eumenides*, the motherless Athena, who issued from the head of her father, Zeus.

Another result of matricide in the House of Atreus is that the cycle of blood for blood is both fulfilled and, though we are not allowed to see it until the *Eumenides*, terminated by being added to a new geometry of justice. It needs to be emphasized, however, that the cyclical kind of evil cursing Argos as a precivilized kingdom in *Agamemnon* and the *Libation Bearers* is the positive *ground,* supporting values one might call "the tragic," which underlies—like the earth spirits, the Furies— the consummately civilized polis of Athens in the *Eumenides.* "Tragedy," on the other hand, is what the third play attempts to substitute for "the tragic" action, extending from the fall of Troy to the execution avenging the murder of Troy's conqueror in the first two plays. Tragedy in the *Eumenides* will stop the tragic cycle, but it will not, cannot, eliminate it. Instead, the two hierarchies of Olympian and human power will, in a great ideological act of illusionism, appropriate the subarchy of the blood-for-blood Furies. And the two winning powers will depend, ultimately, on nothing but their power to do so.

Clearly, the pervasiveness of Zeus in the *Oresteia* and, through his intermediary Apollo, in the *Eumenides* reveals his function as the ultimate power base on which any new order must be firmly founded. Despite this pervasiveness, Aeschylus is not building only on myth, as he did in *Prometheus Bound.* To avoid the weakness of action afflicting the earlier tragedy, he makes the Zeus-Apollo hierarchy at the outset of the *Eumenides* converge with the power hierarchies of Orestes, sole remnant of the family rule typifying the precivilized Argos, and of Athens the "victor city," with its characteristic institution, the Areopagus, and its patron goddess, Athena.

Family, in both the narrow sense of household (*oikos*) and the larger sense of clan (*genos*), is the focus of *Agamemnon* and the *Libation Bearers.* Argos is for Aeschylus not only the historical ally of Athens on the Peloponnesus, but also a phase of social organization, a semibarbaric, transitional site, with Athens rising beyond the temporal horizon. Orestes, fleeing madness, his own and the sociopolitical madness of Argos, and arriving eventually at Athens after undergoing ritual purification at Delphi, crosses more than a geographical threshold. Having once again, after returning to kill Clytaemnestra, fallen to the status of outlaw, Orestes has really gained freedom from a social state based on exclusively family-centered law, the *lex talionis.* But as an outlaw for matricide in avenging his father's murder, he is also an anomaly, as much an agent of the family-based justice he leaves behind in fleeing Argos as a symbol of transition to freedom. If the court trial at Athens results in the exoneration of Orestes, it cannot cancel his status as agent for an earlier mode of justice. Unlike the fast-and-loose Olympians, Orestes effects his fate through irreversible deeds, however justifiable according to family-based law, however aided and abetted by the gods' power. He is, in other words, *bound* to his life, as son, as son of the king, as executioner for self and Argos. Orestes is a locus classicus of anomalous transitional man: a revolutionary cannot be a child of the revolution; he will always remain an extension, a negating extension but an extension nonetheless, of the ancien régime. Only through self-destruction does he break through—this is the literary reason for the matricide. Orestes' real purification was not the Apollonian rite, but rather his act of violence in obliterating the semicivilized family. But of course such absolution *is* guilt, and the guilt will obtrude as he attempts to pass over the bridge to the future.

Once his trial is underway, Orestes himself dwindles to insignificance, much like a first-generation revolutionary. What he signifies overwhelms his fictive actuality: he beomes the question of Orestes. The family law he both substantiates and annuls in the act of "innocent murder" also puts him beyond the jurisdiction of that more advanced polis he is about to enter, Athens. So why does Apollo send him to Athena's temple in the first place? Any exoneration to be performed at Athens will not stick to a revolutionary Argive from the Bronze Age. And how can Aeschylus effect a transition from the *lex talionis* to any higher mode of justice if his transitional agent is himself stuck in time?

Aeschylus is frank in the answers provided by the *Eumenides*. The hierarchy of family power must be bent into convergence with the hierarchy of Athenian civil power, so that Orestes will receive relevant judgment at the Acropolis and at the Hill of Ares. This convergence is not possible in history, where one stage is replaced by a more advanced stage only through breaks, irreversible actions, once-and-for-all deaths, and disastrous obliterations, not through anything so retroactive and fictive as transition or convergence. Yet Aeschylus displays his sleight of hand instead of concealing it; the *Eumenides* may be the most honest of all works presuming to treat historical change. It is not the honesty of *Agamemnon*, where Clytaemnestra does not even break stride to decide not to cover up her savagery, from either the public or the private eye: her penultimate remark to Aegisthus in the first play, "You and I have power now" (line 1707, Fagles), flies well beyond honesty. Nor is it the honesty of the *Libation Bearers*, where the brother lays it on the line: "Now force *clash* with force—right with right!" (line 448, Fagles), and the sister intones with barely controlled delirium, "O Persephone, give us power— lovely, gorgeous power!" (line 477, Fagles). The honesty Aeschylus evinces in the *Eumenides* is a matter of ideologically flexible focus. Just as Orestes dissolves into the *Oresteia*, into the tragedy "on" Orestes, so, too, does the hero as fulfiller of the law of familial curse unobtrusively yet detectably recede into the category of occasion for the full display of rule by law in the Athenian state. This political telos is the underlying motive for the change of scene between Argos and Athens. Categories shift, from family to city-state, or, following Aristotle's *Politics*, from the genetic basis of the state, the *oikos*, to the logically prior ground of all social life, the polis.

The Furies are drawn into the political configuration Athens-Athena: the advanced polis as site of justice, the patroness deity as presiding judge. The machinery for resolving the question of Orestes is firmly in place, the hierarchies of mythic and civic power now having attracted nature's subarchy into this new force field—a force field that will produce a different sense of justice from any prevailing before. Only one element remains absent: the citizens who after all are the polis. Now that he must introduce a real civic institution, and not mere symbolic representations of political reality, Aeschylus has to be even more adroit than he has been in making the Furies amenable to entering into a dialectical situation with Athena-Orestes-Apollo.

One misperception of the role played by the Areopagus in the *Eumenides* is that Aeschylus is endorsing a reactionary, pro-nobility politics by putting at center stage the high council, which, since Solon, was composed of lifelong members who had held the archonship, whether the office of polemarch or one of the other kinds of archonship. Elders of leading *gene* who had led the polis to its advanced position are, after all, as retirees, the appropriate community members for judging the case of Orestes, which is really the case of breaking from the precivilized past. In fact, by 458, when the *Oresteia* was produced for the first time, the Areopagus, though still the deciding tribunal in cases of homicide, was no longer a solid center of aristocratic political activity.[6] Nobles such as Cimon had to dirty their hands along with their pro-*demos* rivals by adopting democratic power techniques. Between Aeschylus's audience and the council's members intruded sufficient political distance to make the original Areopagus convened by Athena in the dramatic action seem symbolic rather than immediate. The institution is not so symbolic as the mythical figure of Athena and not so imbued with the values of the legendary past as Orestes, but sufficiently so in both respects to serve as a body of founding-father citizens possessing the necessary detachment and venerableness for a momentous, specifically judicial matter. The Areopagus is selected to provide civic support for Athena as presiding judge because, unlike the *demos* in its assembly, it can mediate, just as in our own time elder-statesmen diplomats mediate international issues of peace and war although the popular Congress has final power to ratify or dissolve treaties and sole power to declare war.

If Aeschylus has proper aesthetic and political reasons for introducing the Areopagus as his representative Athenian institution, he also proceeds to prove he is not lending factional significance to his selection, by removing the Areopagus to the background very shortly after he puts it in the limelight, just as he has managed the figure of Orestes earlier in the *Eumenides*. For no sooner does Athena summon the high council than they express their futility by balloting a deadlock. They are also entirely silent figures throughout their appearance, as befits symbols with historical presence but little else, especially when they share the scene with colorful mythical figures the likes of Athena and the Furies.

If they prove futile, at least in terms of their actual balloting and their silence, why has Athena convened them in the first place? Paradoxically she announces that "a case of murder" is "too large a matter, / some may think, for mortal men to judge" (lines 484-85, Fagles) in preparation for her decision to bring in the Areopagus. Even more paradoxically, especially since her greatest opposition comes from the Furies, whom she has earlier finessed into agreeing to her presiding in Orestes' case, she herself passes off her own newly recognized power: "But by all rights not even I should decide / a case of murder—murder whets the passions" (lines 486-87, Fagles). At the same time she freely discloses her bias toward a purified, suppliant Orestes: "If you are innocent, I'd adopt you for my city" (line 490, Fagles). And if Athena has already proven herself a better mediator between Mount Olympus and earth than Apollo, why should she then admit she cannot mediate at all? "So it stands. A crisis either way. / Embrace the one? Expel the other? It defeats me" (lines 495-96, Fagles). With this seemingly candid avowal, Athena swears in the Areopagus:

> But since the matter comes to rest on us,
> I will appoint the judges of manslaughter,
> swear them in, and found a tribunal here
> for all time to come. [lines 497-500, Fagles]

Surely Aeschylus does not write a mere "account of the foundation of _____." here. For before Orestes can be judged, all the power hierarchies, plus the Furies, that he has taken such pains to align and configure specifically to make a judgment indeed have to demonstrate their ability to produce one. Yet Aeschylus undercuts, even cancels, the cumulative power he assembles. Certainly Aeschylus is careful to mark the artifice of his courtroom drama. However, beyond the honesty of self-revelation lies another possibility: perhaps the upshot of the *Eumenides* is not justice, after all, but political power in the name of progress.

In summation to this point: Although Orestes has undergone ritual absolution at Delphi, deservedly so since Apollo has "ordered" him to kill Clytaemnestra, he is still guilty of premeditated matricide, and he admits it. The state-based Draconian laws on homicide still apply in the Athens of

Aeschylus[7] (who is already anachronistic in juxtaposing the Areopagus with Mycenean Agamemnon). Even if the state laws against homicide cannot be said to apply clearly within the *Oresteia*, the Furies still hold their "Privilege primeval" (lines 393-94, *Eumenides*, Lattimore). And family-based justice coexisted with state homicide law from as early as the late seventh century to long after Solon, through the fifth century in Athens: "Since the shedding of blood was still considered a family affair, the prosecution had to be initiated by the kin of the victim" (Fine 190). Athena, as the highest symbol of the Athenian political unconscious, entered once Orestes beseeched her from her temple on the Acropolis, as he was instructed to do by Apollo. Thus the Olympian power hierarchy, backing the political aspect, if not the traditional family aspect, of the blood-for-blood justice performed by the last of his family of Argive rulers, converges with the civic power hierarchy. This convergence is represented by Orestes' transition from Argos—where no political order is left once the successor to Agamemnon's throne is again driven, this time by the Furies alone, into exile—to Athens, where the political order is stable. Once the subarchy of nature's justice, the Furies, consents to be included in the political configuration newly established in response to the ultimate "question of Orestes," Athena, whose Olympian power is combined with her maximum mediatory effectuality as a female Apollo, relinquishes her control over the configuration. She does so admitting that "the case of murder" in this instance is not only beyond mortal capacity to judge but also antithetical to her nature as Athenian protectress. But then, apparently to buttress the civic power hierarchy's role in the configuration, she summons the Areopagus, who then nullify their already somewhat dubious effectuality by becoming a hung jury. Technically, Orestes is exonerated because in a five-five split decision, the verdict automatically goes for the defendant. Therefore, the entire reason, presumably, for gathering together all the powers—Olympian, familial, civic, earthly—namely, justice, is contradicted by their openly forecast inability and actual failure to pronounce a judgment. Consequently, the only likely promise of justice reverts to the Furies.

Now comes the moment of overt triumph of political power in the *Eumenides*, a power that has become a composite of Athenian symbols (Athena and Apollo) and civic structures (Athens as site, the Areopagus as institution). Athena does not really break the tie: the deadlock in the Areopagus's balloting is itself the reason for Orestes' acquittal. Athena's ballot is, like herself, politically symbolic; it imbues Orestes' technical exoneration with the significance of Olympian endorsement. Her grounds for intruding when she does not have to are transparently political. Representing Athens, the "victor city," she will not rest satisfied with the technicality as the basis of Orestes' freedom. She wants Orestes to *win*, to be a real victor because of power and not a formal victor by default:

> My work is here, to render the final judgment.
> Orestes, I will cast my lot for you.
> No mother gave me birth.
> I honour the male, in all things but marriage.
> Yes, with all my heart I am my Father's child.
> I cannot set more store by the woman's death—
> she killed her husband, guardian of their house.
> Even if the vote is equal, Orestes wins. [lines 749-56, Fagles]

The form of this speech is carefully judicial. With "My work is here," she speaks as an elected Athenian official, as it were: she has been appealed to for civic action. With "No mother gave me birth," she speaks as an Olympian, and reaffirms what Apollo has proved earlier, against the Furies, by exhibiting Athena in the midst of courtroom give-and-take: "The *man* is the source of life—the one who mounts" (line 669, Fagles). Whether Athenians, even the men, believed what Apollo claims is doubtful; whether Aeschylus really believed what his character Apollo says is even doubtful. The important point for the developing action of the *Eumenides* is that Athena's emphasis on her birth and Apollo's rhetoric furnish ammunition for the Olympian contest with the Furies that is beginning to surface. The question of Orestes is an occasion for this highest and deepest struggle. In declaring herself for Orestes the way she does, Athena proves the Furies have her constant attention. They, it bears repeating, are the only resort for justice once Orestes is freed by technical default. Thus when Athena diplomatically inserts "in all things but marriage" but continues to mention that she is her "Father's child," "honour[s] the male," and therefore "cannot set more store by the woman's death"— when she so explicitly shapes her preballoting declaration this way, Athena is formally declaring, for her father, war against the Furies.

Now it is an open and absolute power struggle between Zeus and earth, between the omnipotent Olympian and the permanently privileged Furies. These so-far well-behaved earth spirits understand the issue perfectly. As soon as Orestes exits in triumph, followed by Apollo, the Furies go straight to the heart of the matter and fire the first salvo in defiance. It is aimed not at Athena, a goddess to them and a self-reflecting symbol to citizens, but at Athens, the advanced civilization that is slipping beyond their grasp:

> You, you younger gods! you have ridden down
> the ancient laws, wrenched them from my grasp—

and I, robbed of my birthright, suffering, great with wrath,
I loose my poison over the soil, aieee!— [lines 792-95, Fagles]

Aeschylus puts his audience in an odd position here. The Furies are presented not only as victims of Olympian trickery, but also as the sole source of genuine justice. Viewers attending *Agamemnon*, then the *Libation Bearers*, and now the *Eumenides* have never been led to doubt the Furies' claims, however much Aeschylus has allayed their terrors through comic techniques. The right side, however, as it appears to them, is presented as losing. Yet they have been led into cheering on Athena and Apollo in their contest with the Furies over Orestes. Why does the patriotic author of the *Persians* and the revolutionary ally of Prometheus against Zeus put his community in such a quandary? Does he wish them to experience either a mythic or a ritualist suspension-resolution through immersion in terror and pity or through the magic of Dionysian ecstasy?

On the contrary, the *Eumenides* at this juncture is just beginning to take shape as tragedy. Tragedy becomes the appropriation of the tragic for the purpose of ideological justification of state power. The tragic, in distinction, is nothing mysterious; it is what all Athenians would recognize as an appropriate label for the cyclical conception of evil that is controlled by fate and revolves endlessly through reprisal, the only justice:

FURIES: You will learn it all,
    young daughter of Zeus, cut to a few words.
    We are the everlasting children of the Night.
    Deep in the halls of Earth they call us Curses.
ATHENA: Now I know your birth, your rightful name—
FURIES: But not our powers, and you will learn them quickly.
ATHENA: I can accept the facts, just tell them clearly.
FURIES: Destroyers of life: we drive them from their houses.
ATHENA: And the murderer's flight, where does it all end?
FURIES: Where there is no joy, the word is never used.
    [lines 426-35, Fagles]

The clarity of this exchange is the same Aeschylean clarity of report encountered in the *Persians;* the context then was naval victory, the context now, justice. Aeschylus knew the one from experience, and he casts no doubt on the nature of justice in his last work.

The *Oresteia* does not question what it assumes; it does not ask, "What is justice?" Instead, the question Aeschylean tragedy poses is, "Who wins?" To provide an answer through dramatic action, tragedy keeps to *recognition* of true justice but proceeds to insist on a *redefinition*. What is wanted is not a substitution of mercy or compassion or wisdom or the mystery of it all for justice. A redefinition is required by the winning side, Athena-Athens, to vindicate its power and educate the citizenry concerning what it will *call* justice now that it is victorious. The finale of the *Eumenides* redefines justice as the principle of reciprocity. The Furies' justice, which is nature's, thus inevitable, affirms the principle of reprisal. When applied, the principle of reprisal means an endless cycle of blood for blood. That is true justice, otherwise it would not be recognized by victims' families as the only justice.

But if justice as reprisal is cyclical, how does a polis advance into the future? How does one, following the vector of Orestes, leave Argos and proceed to Athens? Clearly the Furies are "the mind of the past" (*Eumenides*, line 838, Lattimore), [8] a proud label they first announce shortly after Athena's declaration of war. All time to them, since it is cyclical, is past. So any redefinition of the Furies' justice as reprisal will require successfully expanding the sense of time that conditions justice taken as a historical and no longer simply natural fact. All through the *Eumenides* the Athenian polis has appeared as the future contrasted with the precivilized Argos. When a historical Athenian institution like the Areopagus, though, proves unable to dispense justice in the question of Orestes, Aeschylus has exploited the potency of Athena as mythic identity of the polis to shield the council's actual futility from the audience's critical gaze, for the sake of their patriotic sensibility. Now, upon the technical acquittal of Orestes and Athena's declaration of Orestes as victor, a declaration based on the supreme power assertion of Zeus's will, Athens the shining example of what civilization could be and, within the scope of prophecy at the end of the *Eumenides*, will be—the historical state itself—comes to the fore.

To accomplish this shift from attention to the past to the prospect of future Athenian power, Aeschylus must arrange things with almost ludicrous care. When we see the *Eumenides* turn from a context of justice to a question of political fortune, we can deduce why Orestes has been exonerated by the technicality of a tie in the balloting. Athena's tie-breaking ballot was not, as we have seen, necessary to acquit Orestes; it was a purely symbolic gesture, the addition of mythical value. But it plays a very practical part in Aeschylus's design, by allowing Olympian power to attach itself to a figure, Orestes, who is nothing but an occasion for Athenian self-justification. Therefore, Orestes must not have tainted Athens in its handling of his case. Acquittal by default means Athens has avoided judgment, like Athena earlier in her turn to the Areopagus; Aeschylus shows Athens operating as a site where something historically necessary happens, yet, as it were, automatically, without the implication of civic power. Orestes is not *judged*. The deadlock in the Areopagus does not make him innocent, but rather makes him appear innocent from a specifically Athenian political perspective: Athena declares, "The man goes free, / cleared of the charge of blood. The lots are equal" (lines 766-67, Fagles). Already absolved by Apollo so he would not pollute the Athenian complex of Olympian and civic power, Orestes was, is, and shall be forever guilty. But he will never again stand charged with matricide because Athens has served as the place in time where he magically enters the future—specifically, the future of permanent alliance between Athens and Argos. This temporal place, moreover, escapes infection because of the hung jury: the Areopagus has not decided the question of Orestes. Since it does not, Athena's predetermined decision for Orestes is also free of any contact with Orestes' guilt. Her ballot is not necessary; the Athenian civic machinery locks; and Orestes returns, duly processed and cleared of his crime yet never judged, to complete the historical arc between the past and the future. Most important, Orestes will carry with him the official stamp of Athena's Olympian power blessing.

First it is necessary to unveil the process whereby Athena demythifies herself, revealing her blessing's true worth: outright superiority of potential power. Athens is shown to be directly threatened as a result of Athena's ballot; the Furies, as fertility spirits and biological guardians of sexual reproduction, will blast Attica's agriculture and vitiate Athenians' offspring: "Poison to match my grief comes pouring out my heart, / cursing the land to burn it sterile and now / rising up from its roots a cancer blasting leaf and child" (lines 796-98, Fagles). This fate indeed would be only just, for the Furies' justice is prior to any other. It is nature's biological justice the Olympians have cheated and insulted. If Athena should argue, as she does not, that the future is also natural, for otherwise there would be no time at all, the Furies' answer is built into their nature: justice is conditioned only by the past. What grows out of the soil depends utterly on that soil, as even the chorus of Argive elders recognized in *Agamemnon:*

> The truth stands ever beside God's throne
> eternal: he who has wrought shall pay; that is law.
> Then who shall tear the curse from their blood?
> The seed is stiffened to ruin. [lines 1563-66, Lattimore]

Yet Orestes is that very seed, the last of the House of Atreus, given Apollo's view that only the male is the source of life. And Olympian power behind the front of Athenian power sends him back to Argos not only processed and cleared but victorious, presumably to lead Argos out of the night into the day of Athenian-style progress.

Briefly, the winning Olympian side will not *start* by proving its qualifications to inherit the future. Athena will not, in other words, justify her victory by redefining justice, then show how Athens will prosper if it abides by the new definition, which will embrace the future as its condition, thus overriding the past of the Furies' biological justice. Just the opposite: Athena, like the Furies, will abide by her own nature and *start* from might, then move on to right. An Olympian specially invested with her father's omnipotence, she will fire her first salvo against the Furies by threatening them with Zeus's lightning bolts:

> You have your power,
> you are goddesses—but not to turn
> on the world of men and ravage it past cure.
> I put my trust in Zeus and . . . must I add this?
> I am the only god who knows the keys
> to the armoury where his lightning-bolt is sealed.
> No need of that, not here. [lines 833-39, Fagles]

Power is the name of the game in this tragedy. Any new definition of justice for establishing a new historical order of prosperity and peace will be based on the deliberate direction of this power—violence—for certain ends. Violence and order are the alpha and omega of the *Oresteia,* just as they are in the *Persians.* The Furies know well what the power of those lightning bolts from Mount Olympus would be if directed at them: with these same weapons Zeus quelled those other children of earth, the Titans, including Prometheus, to gain the very Olympian power Athena now aims their way. Their justice is first endangered not by the prospect of redefinition but by the threat of obliteration. The Just itself may survive transcendentally, but many agents of justice have been exterminated in the past: "the gods so hard to wrestle down / obliterate us all?" (line 855, Fagles). Yet any new conception of justice that could possibly be erected from this adamant base would be false, not passable as justice, because law established exclusively on power is not law but interest. Therefore, if Athena concocts a new justice, it will be through an ideological process furthering the interests of those among the violent who may win.

What are Athena's interests but Athens' survival, progress, and preeminence among rivals—what goes without question today as the pursuit of legitimate national self-interest? Legitimacy aside, the *Eumenides* is an Athenian tragedy, concluding a trilogy that moves from a state destroying itself to a state expanding and vindicating itself. This movement is characterized by a shift from family-based justice of blood for blood (or its historical variant, the equivalency of blood price) to state-generated justice of law and official procedures. Yet the action of the entire trilogy shows the Furies to possess the only genuine justice, the primordial justice of nature, and they are overpowered by the supernatural Olympian desire to assert its own new order by strengthening its earthly city so it will inherit a future of peace and plenty. The victor city, in short, has its future to protect. Athens is already erected on a firm foundation of political power, a foundation demonstrated within the *Oresteia* by Athena's collection of the spoils of Greek war in Troy and easily deducible from the Athenian audience's consciousness of its own historical successes against Persia and its resulting preeminence among all the Greek poleis. Nevertheless, the city needs the kind of guardian spirit that represents some power prior to historical good fortune. Athens needs the Furies, just as Athena, for a different immediate purpose, needed their consent to preside in the question of Orestes. The favor of the Olympian gods expresses Athenian good fortune in the power games of war and competition. But a future of equally good or even better fortune requires a *ground*, a natural base to support the political foundation already in place and supplement the supernatural favor. Thus, to allay their fury and spare Athens from their retaliation, Athena invites the earth spirits to make Athens their home:

> If you leave for an alien land and alien people,
> you will come to love this land, I promise you.
> As time flows on, the honours flow through all
> my citizens, and you, throned in honour
> before the house of Erectheus, will harvest
> more from men and women moving in solemn file
> than you can win throughout the mortal world.
>
> . . . .
>
> This is the life I offer, it is yours to take.
> Do great things, feel greatness, greatly honoured.
> Share this country cherished by the gods.
> [lines 860-78, Fagles]

The Furies cannot accede to Athena and maintain their identity, yet if they wish to avoid the fate of other children of earth they must accede. When they do, the action of the *Eumenides* becomes verbal commentary. Our attention is distracted from the action of the Furies' acceptance to the *meaning* of this impossible final shift: from the only justice the tragedy demonstrates, to either its protagonists or its audience, to the sudden and inexplicable relenting experienced by this justice, embodied in the Furies, before its desire for a permanent historical niche. Now the audience must interpret what is *said*, lyrically. Thus the tragic action begins to be propagandistic Persuasion, the verbal action of which is to result in a name change: henceforth justice will be "gracious," or "kindly" (Eumenides), instead of "furious." Aesthetically, this jump from Aristotle's action to diction marks the appropriate jump from the tragic, now left behind by the negating Furies' unaccountable acceptance, to tragedy, the fulfillment of the paradigm of political victory:

> ATHENA: And I,
> in the trials of war where fighters burn for fame,
> will never endure the overthrow of Athens—
> all will praise her, victor city, pride of man.
> [lines 923-26, Fagles]

However, once they undergo their name change, the Furies will also, as their old furious selves, settle into the deepest structure of Athenian civic life. Athena above, the Eumenides below, will provide roof and foundation for Athens, with the Areopagus holding sway in between, surrounded by the columns of the city's martial power. Each will take up position on the appropriate hill: the Furies under the Acropolis, the Areopagus on the Hill of Ares, Athena in her temple atop the Acropolis, monument to Olympian favor toward the "pride of man," which lives out its civilizational destiny of unfolding power and glory. These hills will both define the city's limits *and* set its perspective culminating in imperial power.

How, finally, has this fantasia developed through the jump from the tragic to tragedy as paradigm of victory? Where is justice? In the ground, as always, but now with a specific locus under Athens. When is justice? In the past, for it is still "the mind of the past"; but the Furies are now the Eumenides, ensuring the future of Athens. How did justice break away from the tragic cycle repeating the past and adhere to the political good fortune of Athens? Justice is justice, the power of deeds done requiring their consequences; it cannot change, although it can assume another name.

The lyrical words composing the end of the *Eumenides* furnish a gloss for what has happened to justice. The Furies of earth are nature's justice, the only entirely reliable, that is, inevitable, justice there is, ever has been, or ever will be. Athena's persuasive paean redefines this biological justice, but, amazingly, her words do not change its power by expressing the convergence of her own Olympian powers and her city's, powers making right on the forge of might: "these upright men, this breed fought free of grief" (line 922, Fagles). No, Athena's words will tell the Furies they are no longer nature's, down in the earth, but raised up, "goddesses of

Fate!" (line 972, Fagles): "All realms exalt you highest of the gods" (line 978, Fagles). However, Athena means this only in an encomiastic sense. Her formal speech assigning their new role to the Furies again plants them deep:

> I enthrone these strong, implacable spirits here
> and root them in our soil.
>   Theirs,
> theirs to rule the lives of men,
> it is their fated power.
> But he who has never felt their weight,
> or known the blows of life and how they fall,
> the crimes of his fathers hale him towards their bar,
> and there for all his boasts—destruction
> silent, majestic in anger,
> crushes him to dust. [lines 940-48, Fagles]

Thus Athena rewrites the job description of justice in Athens. This she does not by changing justice, but by adding to the old component certain new components of its definition. The old component is exclusively biological: agriculture and sexual reproduction with its social effectuality the function of the family. Unless justice is done, the crops will rot, babies will be deformed, and families will turn on themselves. The new component of the definition of justice is legal: the procedures and rituals ensuring the regulation and extension of the power of the state. Unless justice is done, the state will not work, anarchy will endanger the welfare of all, and other city-states will either attack with impunity or break their alliances because of loss of confidence. Thus the Furies, as the Eumenides, will, following Athena's redefinition, underwrite and protect future Athenian biology by means of capital punishment. According to our original terms of analysis, then, the Furies will enhance Athenian life at its very roots by virtue of death. They will buttress civic order by means of unerringly directed violence: "There are times when fear is good. / It must keep its watchful place / at the heart's controls" (lines 517-19, Lattimore). The fulsome-appearing "gracious ones" will perform a state function that the beautiful Athena, an unnatural sky god intellectually sprung from Zeus's brain, cannot: terror. Terror is redefined as creative and positive, a pervasive goad to citizens to respect the sanctity of life or suffer the curse of nature and the reprisal of law combined. Athens cannot but endure and prevail.

Because it is so self-consciously ideological, the Aeschylean way of tragedy becomes a historical scheme. It may take the form of war-crime "theater trials" that redefine the historical constant of genocide as an unnatural act requiring instinctive revulsion. It may appear in the stark form of revolutionary terrorism directed by the stateless in the name of their future against the sanctioned force of established states protecting their past. Or it may assume the guise of feminist redefinition of rape. From today's vantage Aeschylean tragedy as such may even have a future: in the Middle East, in Argentina and Chile, as well as in the more recently decolonialized cultures of the Third World. The Aeschylean sense of history's process of self-naturalization, perhaps in the modern form of Marx's critique of Hegelian right, can certainly serve the oppressed as they seek to redefine justice by converting hard-won laws and political gains into natural rights. Yet these groups can adopt Aeschylus only if they, too, aim for and sustain a politics of prevalence and avoid the Euripidean politics of loss, which has almost equated itself with tragedy since the mid–nineteenth century.

So far my account has kept close to the action of the *Eumenides* up to the Furies' acquiescence, and to its words after the redefinition of justice signified by the change of name from Furies to Eumenides. Perhaps this account is too close to give an edge to the difference between the Aeschylus who originated tragedy as a genre that distributes power—through the political paradigm of victory to actions and words marking the violent hammering-out of order—and the Aeschylus universally acclaimed for his final balance, synthesis, equilibrium, regeneration, self-fulfillment, and humanistic theodicy. The difference between all that these terms convey and what Aeschylus's imitative actions and lyrical words do is absolute. Tragedy is a ludic presentation of winning, drawing, and losing. Aeschylean tragedy is the action and celebration of Athens the victor city. Nothing else, and that is much.

If we draw back from the text of the *Eumenides*, the theoretical difference may be more visible. The correct term for what happens to the Furies is the political term "appropriation," not the Hegelian "synthesis." In the *Eumenides*, Athens is ideologically fortified for the future by the appropriation of the natural justice of the past and the infusion of that justice into its structural ground: the logical-legal category is joined to the biological-agricultural. Through such an act of appropriation, Aeschylus's Athens grows as historically omnipotent as Zeus and the Fates are mythically. Seen this way, the telos of the *Eumenides* is what Habermas calls "the fantasy of hope" (288).

It is a tough, sagacious, and subtle ideological fantasy, however. Nature and law are neither synthesized nor equilibrated; justice remains unchanged; civilization is not regenerated; and the artful Aeschylus does not practice obfuscation. Instead, what happens in the *Eumenides* when the Furies are appropriated by Athens upon their accepting Athena's extortive offer is that the only true justice, which *is* reprisal, is *added to*—not combined organically or synthesized or mechanically balanced with—the new component of respectable civic power. The sum of Aeschylus's arithmetic is the conception of *reciprocity*, as Aristotle defines it in the *Nicomachean Ethics:*

> But in associations that are based on mutual exchange, the just in this sense constitutes the bond that holds the association together, that is, reciprocity in terms of a proportion and not in terms of exact equality in the return. For it is the reciprocal return of what is proportional (to what one has received) that holds the state together. People seek either to requite evil with evil—for otherwise their relation is regarded as that of slaves—or good with good, for otherwise there is no mutual contribution. And it is by their mutual contribution that men are held together. [124]

Justice in the *Oresteia*, like naval battle in the *Persians*, is a matter of geometry—proportion—as well as addition. By inviting the Furies to take up their home in Athens, Athena is reciprocating the benefice the Furies will bestow on Athenians with their terror, and by accepting her offer the Furies are reciprocating the respect Athena grants them in recognizing the city's need for terror: as natural reprisal, the Furies bring their principle of evil for evil, while the Olympian offer extends good for the good the terror brings. Mutual exchange, divine favor for furious grace and death for purposes of life, is the proportionality wrought by Aeschylus in the *Eumenides*, the tragic action and lyric words of which serve to shape a revolutionary literary work that is perfectly "median": "For the proportional is median, and the just is proportional" (*Nicomachean Ethics* 119).

Philoctetes: Tragedy of Stalemate

In Sophocles, tragedy as a configuration of political power issues not in Aeschylean victory, but in a stasis representing perfect suspension between historical force and personal integrity. In Aeschylus, both early and late, fate is a clear, often obvious shape of the politics of prevalence. Thus dramatic action, as the aesthetic imitation of historical or historylike action, and the arrangement of the imitative episodes, or plot, retain their formal priority over character and diction-plus-thought.[9] Both of these, the hero and the words written and spoken to articulate the hero's relation to the action, are strictly means to realizing the plot. In Sophocles, who serves as Aristotle's primary model in the *Poetics*, the action so exactly corresponds with the practice of the hero's or heroine's virtue, construed as Aristotelian functional excellence, that character seems to be fate. Antigone, Electra, and Philoctetes are all, following Aristotle still, entirely functional, designed solely to realize the actions of their respective plots. Justice is both motive and objective in the case of these actions. It appears, then, paradoxically, as if Sophocles is offering character studies of tragic human nature in terms of justice, while he is actually doing just the opposite. These heroic figures are complete instances of functional excellence (*arete*) in the action of achieving the final cause, justice for the polis. The efficient cause is injustice in the context of the political family of rulers; the formal cause is revenge, or political justice experienced partially, by the agent of the telos. Similarly subordinated to achieving justice is the heroic character's diction-thought. Thus love of brother in respect for *themis*, or traditional justice, particularly familial, expresses Antigone's pathos. Hatred of mother expresses Electra's virtuous martyrdom to the woman's way of inflicting torture on the guilty (her anguished moaning drives Clytaemnestra to distraction) and to the exigencies of preparing for her brother's masculine-style execution of justice ("It is not words that now / are the issue," Orestes tells Aegisthus, *Electra*, lines 1491-92). And *Philoctetes*, articulating a life of pure pain through a heroic plot the action of which is nothing but pathos—which is also the hero's form—is a tragedy of history's overcoming of the individual, who resists even in the act of personal obedience to destiny.

In other words, Sophoclean character is also plot, but plot that, while still logically prior to character and diction-thought, is completely apprehended through the hero's words. These words express a kind of character that itself becomes the site where power is deployed by history: higher justice is realized in Thebes through Antigone's body; justice is performed in Mycenae by Electra's words and their fruition in Orestes' act; and justice is dissolved on Lemnos by a reaction within the character of Philoctetes between his experience of the injustice of pain and the historical *ananke*. There is no wall between person and history, inner and outer, in Sophocles. The Aristotelian categories of causation, the Aristotelian ethical definition of *arete* as functional excellence, and the Aristotelian aesthetic categories are all seamlessly joined in the fateful figures of Sophoclean heroism.

Sophocles' way with character is obvious from a comparison with Aeschylus, whose *Prometheus Bound* is his sole work to conflate character and action so completely. It is equally evident from a comparison with Euripides, whose sense of the contingency of life does not allow the exclusivity of focus on character that marks all of Sophocles' actions. And it consistently typifies Sophocles' work throughout his career—early works, such as *Antigone* (produced ca. 441); middle-period works, such as *Oedi-*

pus Tyrannus (ca. 426); and late works, notably *Oedipus at Colonus* (produced posthumously, probably between 403 and 401), *Electra* (between 426 and 413), and *Philoctetes* (408), written during the last two decades of Sophocles' ninety-year life. But only in *Philoctetes* does this character-as-action or action-as-character become explicitly the sole sustained subject of Sophocles' formal interest as he plays out his distinctive version of the tragic game, which is aimed no longer at Aeschylean winning but at stalemate. Thus, too, does *Philoctetes* provide clear evidence for the theory that tragedy is a specifically political genre, and that genre as such is power. For Sophocles' most intense mimesis of heroic character turns out not to resist, by upholding man's singularity, a conception of historical power but, instead, to reinforce the "innerness" of what is typically considered alien to personal identity, namely history itself. However existential its emphasis, *Philoctetes*, immune to ontology and psychoanalysis alike, is no existentialist drama. It remains perhaps the most completely *and* most sensitively historical of all history plays, Shakespeare's included.

In *Antigone* the stalemate issues from the clash between character and state. The illumination from this clash is blinding because Antigone stands out starkly, the very style of tragic character as it is most commonly perceived; from the perspective of plot, her angularity strikes across the monolith of Creon's state and shows up the amorphous noncharacter of the Theban chorus. Entirely within her virtue of integrity, at the level of words expressing character, Antigone reigns supreme as a site where the martyr's role is placed by the heroine's act of will on the soft base of a lonely girl's capacity for love, which is also her city's best promise. Creon's state, whether considered as his empty imposition of will—the sacrilegious edict—or as a structure in itself, without him—at the end, when he is discredited as ruler—the state itself, in contrast with the site where it deploys its power in Antigone's character, retains the unchanging passive status of history. The paradox is clear: she *acts* and suffers; the state *wills* against her, its ruler falls, and it, as the people in their collectivity, merely endures. Vulnerable, Antigone functions as a principle of iron; apparently invulnerable, the state in its true malleability either expends itself in futility (Creon) or, merely receptive and reactive, says sensitive things but never intervenes (the chorus). The power of the state, which is to maintain or at least stand for justice, resides entirely within the dimension of the ravaged character-site of Antigone herself, while the merely empowered Creon—especially as he is described by Haemon—commits injustice, thus ravaging himself as state power misapplied.

Notwithstanding these paradoxical exchanges of power between character and state, the two remain formally distinct. Sophocles in this early tragedy is above all else fixed on expressing the hideous ironies produced by the intersection of Antigone and Creon/chorus. In *Oedipus Tyrannus* and *Oedipus at Colonus*, the same duality leaves intact both heroic character values, on the one hand—Oedipus abdicating from political power, Oedipus elevated to political spirit—and history as the category of valuelessness, on the other—Thebes inherited by Eteocles and Polyneices, then defaulting to Creon. But in *Philoctetes* the hero *is* this duality of character and history: Philoctetes' character unifies stinking wound, which prohibits him from making it to Troy ten years earlier, with victorious bow, the agency of which is destined to bring Troy down in the imminent future. Pathos is unified with historical functionality, character *is* action. *Oedipus at Colonus* represents this impossible unity impossibly, through religious projection. *Philoctetes*, however, renders this impossibility entirely within the limits of history; the tragedy as action defines itself wholly, from beginning to end, within the one character of the wounded bowman, a character-site in complete isolation that becomes an entire world containing the antitheses of passive personal suffering and active historical triumph. Odysseus and Neoptolemus do not force Philoctetes to be this impossible character-as-action, self-world; they are mere agents, one efficient, the other compassionate, of his destiny, which they are scheduled to deliver on destined time. Electra's character may be said to approximate Philoctetes', but in *Electra* the suffering heroine needs her brother to complete the historical triumph of justice; in *Philoctetes*, however, it is the historical triumph of the Greeks at Troy that needs the suffering bowman. Thus in *Philoctetes* we cannot celebrate the heroic character in distinction from the reality of history, as we are allowed to do while following Antigone to her vindication only after death, or Oedipus to his eventual symbolification, which takes him beyond a declining history. We must, instead, acknowledge both the extreme inner dimension of Philoctetes' pathos and the extreme outer dimension of his victorious historical appointment at one and the same time within one and the same character.

Truly, character is fate in *Philoctetes*, but not in the ordinary, and nonsensical, interpretation of character as the cause of fate. Instead of the single paradigm of power, which is Athens as victor city in the *Oresteia*— and instead of what would be rendered, according to the simplistic equation of character and fate, as nothing more than the incomprehensible moral formula "suffering equals triumph"—in *Philoctetes* there are two paradigms of power in one character-as-action: self and history. Neither self nor history wins, neither character nor action loses. Therefore, in *Philoctetes*, Sophocles finds the form that perfectly fits the tragedy of stalemate, which provides the tragic content of all his plays.

But how is stalemate, which is the final form of the action, also stalemate at the level of content? By applying the hypothetical scheme of tragedy as a competitive game admitting win, loss, or draw, we can trace the various fortunes of the different powers in conflict through *Antigone, Electra,* and *Philoctetes.* Sophocles is blindingly clear in *Antigone* concerning the win and loss columns of each power, from god to heroine. Each power wins no more than it loses. The gods can be said to win their vindication, but they lose—of course, not really, for they are gods—the life of their vindicator. Creon loses his power in winning his point, by asserting this same power beyond the interests of the state and against religiously backed, family-based law *(themis).* Antigone wins a moral victory at the expense of her life, which is the only source of morality (Haemon, the only other moral agent, her fiancé and sole defender, must commit himself to what his bride has become, death itself). Symbolically, she wins at the expense of life itself as a human order. For, as promised bride, she will end her unfortunate family instead of beginning another. And the people win only as losers: they survive.

The win and loss columns balance out to a blank neutrality. The game of power dissolves when winning and losing cancel one another. But Sophoclean tragedy possesses action; its neutralizing distribution of power is this action. Therefore, a play like *Antigone* does work as a tragedy, and the game is presented. Yet it is present only in dissolution, an endgame clearing the board of all the pieces, black and white, losers and winners alike. That this game structure inheres in the Sophoclean endgame is what keeps *Antigone* generic. What makes it a tragedy, in other words, is that it discloses the pure structure that genre certainly is in the case of tragedy, yet that may seem to have disintegrated in tragedy of stalemate. Sophocles' tragedies in particular draw attention to the equation of genre with game because they freeze the game at its end by neutralizing victory and defeat.

In *Electra,* a sister tragedy to the earlier *Antigone,* the neutralizing action of offsetting wins and losses finds its primary formal outlet in the characters of the elder surviving daughter and the sole heir of Agamemnon. However, unlike Antigone, who relents yet follows through to her fate, Electra experiences at no time in the course of the plot, from her prolonged wait for Orestes to her eager participation in the tactical planning once he arrives, any resistance whatsoever to her functionality. She acknowledges the cost of her virtue flatly, without plea for pity:

> I have awaited him always
> sadly, unweariedly,
> till I'm past childbearing,

> till I am past marriage,
> always to my own ruin. [lines 163-65]

And unlike Antigone when she applies to Ismene for help, Electra, confronted by her craven sister Chrysothemis, acts out a rhetorical design to clarify the issue and stimulate herself to renewed effort. But she does not at all voice a plea: "You have said nothing unexpected. Well / I knew you would reject what I proposed" (lines 1017-18). Electra is nothing but her *arete*, which is what enables her to bide her time as the embodied memory of injustice against the father in the palace of her mother and her usurping lover, until Orestes comes to perform the requisite justice. When her brother returns from exile, he appears a thoroughly trained agent of the plan wrought by his tutor, Paedagogus, a character who is also appropriately streamlined, even in name, to his role. Both brother and sister, then, perfectly fit their action; indeed, *Electra* is the one tragedy that may fully exemplify Aristotle's famous claim that there could be tragedy with no character and no diction-thought, just plot. For the characters of Electra and Orestes disclose no pressure exerted on their identities by their functional excellence. In fact, they may be said to lack that most personal of the virtues, self-control (*sophrosyne*), for there is nothing in them to control. Moreover, their diction-thought is as subordinated to their virtue as their virtue to the action of justice.

The revolt of the flesh, along with its curbing by the will for the sake of both personal and historical integrity—the expansion of *arete* to the point of tragic stalemate between desire and act—is present in both *Antigone* and the late tragedy, *Philoctetes*, though in different forms, but lacking in *Electra*. Thus the stalemate in Sophocles' version of the House of Atreus legend is a different kind of stalemate, aesthetic rather than existential. Instead of embodying a standoff between humanity as vulnerability and the human agency of historical justice, Electra and Orestes have been honed down to edges of the action. Their characters are reduced to their functional excellence (and that more narrowly defined than Aristotle would allow), so that their humanity perfectly meshes with their effectuality. Their integrity is undeniable, and it is not inhumane; but it is one-dimensional, not full. They win through, like their counterparts in Aeschylus and Euripides, but they lose the most requisite element of their status as imitations of historical identities, which must be both active and passive—namely, their very imitative quality. Unreal even as shadows, Electra and Orestes do not pay with their lives in the plot; they cannot die, as Antigone dreads and Philoctetes desires. And they cannot live, triumphantly as in Aeschylus or emptily as in Euripides, both of whom stick to the problematic survival of the brother and sister avengers built into the legend imitated. For Electra's and Orestes' characters are sheer means to the telos of their plot. When the plot ends, they cannot be the victors they teleologically must be according to Aeschylus, because their characters are nothing but the means to the end of victory. This zero degree of character in *Electra* is in strict accordance with the Aristotelian dictum: plot wins, character loses. It loses by evading the very purpose of plot, which is to realize itself not only through its means, but also, in proportional return, *for* its means. Thus *Electra* becomes a tragedy of aesthetic stalemate. The paradigm of victory has no inheritors either within or beyond the actions.

Philoctetes is Sophocles' most daring tragedy of stalemate because it ventures beyond both the aesthetic neutrality of *Electra* and the neutralization of winning and losing forces in *Antigone*. Formally, the character of Philoctetes is like those of Antigone and Electra: he, too, is a seeker of justice. But the arena where he struggles toward his telos, where his virtuous functional excellence fully displays itself, is the world of his pain. Power is deployed politically upon Antigone, and causes her pain. Electra is the medium of the demand of Agamemnon's pain for justice. In Philoctetes as hero, though, the rotting, snakebitten foot, physical pain in its categorical, inexplicable self, wrestles the political stratagems deployed by history's agents, Odysseus and Neoptolemus, to a draw.

These two Greek heroes need him—so Helenus, the captured Trojan prophet, has foretold—for history. Philoctetes' bow will bring down Troy. It is written that way. And only Philoctetes can wield that weapon because Heracles has entrusted it to him alone. But the crucial hero at the end of history's Trojan War subplot has been forced by history itself to drop out of history, his own and his comrades': Odysseus had abandoned Philoctetes on Lemnos when Agamemnon set course for Troy ten years earlier. The bowman's wound had too noxious a stench for him to be allowed to proceed to his destiny. Subsequently, Philoctetes acquired another destiny, the destiny that takes apparent priority over historical history, and that is the destiny of pain. Philoctetes is bare human agency itself; with his hand he shoots Heracles' bow, with his foot he suffers. His pathos is not the potential of suffering epitomized by the epic Achilles with his vulnerable foot, but the suffering of suffering. This is more than a metaphor Sophocles plays with. Electra, expressing her father's urgency for justice, is herself nothing but a metaphor, as the aesthetic character reduced to her virtue, which ironically consists exclusively of her diction-thought, her reminding words. But Philoctetes' urgency on the uninhabited island of Lemnos is that of a character isolated from history, isolated from human society itself, from home, father, and comrades, isolated from words themselves, which screaming has preempted. He is also isolated because of this pain. The other Greeks on his ship could not tolerate his cries, which stopped their rites and confused their sense of mission. In *Philoctetes* individual pain automatically isolates the sufferer; the power it wields ruthlessly cuts off the infected one from others. This Philoctetes on his island with his specifically located wound yet another island on the world of his body, this character *is* pain, a concentrated torture that is so specific it seems the effect of malevolence.

Thus the tragic hero's integrity in this play will be a composite of his pain, his virtue as a bowman, and his historical mission: sufferer's foot, warrior's hand, and history's hero are all encompassed within this one character. Philoctetes is more than a character-site like Antigone, whereon the political game is played out to its stalemate. And he is more than a pure medium or means to the end. Philoctetes, who is his pain, is also the essence of stalemate. The forces of history that abandoned him will reconverge on Lemnos, in the guises of Odysseus and Neoptolemus, son of Achilles. They have been delegated to retrieve the bowman by the Atridae, who, frustrated by their ten years' effort, believe the prophecy of Helenus signifies imminent breakthrough. Yet the means to Troy's overthrow, Philoctetes, hates the sons of Atreus and particularly Odysseus, their agent now as he was in the past, when the afflicted bowman was abandoned. Philoctetes still possesses Heracles' bow, and survives on the birds it brings down; if he crosses paths again with Odysseus, he will not hesitate to aim it against his betrayer. Philoctetes will not consent to a plea to rejoin the Greeks, and he will certainly not deliver this consent to Odysseus as their agent. However, he does fall victim to Neoptolemus's practice of Odysseus's ruse and lets Neoptolemus take his bow. Yet he extracts a promise from the compassionate younger Greek serving as front for the wary Odysseus, who remains hidden from his old victim, a promise to take him back home, to Oeta, sacred to Heracles. So the man isolated by his pain reestablishes his connection with humanity in trusting Neoptolemus and depending on him to fulfill his promise. Neoptolemus discloses his part in the ruse to his quarry, confessing, "All is disgust when one leaves his own nature / and does things that misfit it" (lines 902-3).[10] Nevertheless the younger hero falls a casualty to his youth and fails to help Philoctetes escape the net that Odysseus, returning, successfully casts in his proper victor's determination "to win" (line 1052). The hunter's success, though, is not enough for Odysseus, who adds another ruse, this one in the form of an apparent concession to Philoctetes: "What I seek in everything is to win / except in your regard: I willingly yield to you now" (lines 1052-53). For Odysseus, following his own virtue of craftiness, knows that a merely coerced, physically retrieved bowman will not perform in keeping with his functional excellence, which is to ply Heracles' bow victoriously. If

Philoctetes is returned, delivered to his destiny at Troy on schedule, he still will not function properly unless he himself wills to take up his bow, which Odysseus threatens to entrust to Teucer. Odysseus's new ruse also fails: when he and Neoptolemus leave, once more abandoning Philoctetes, the now weaponless bowman decides on suicide. Neoptolemus, now a man like his father Achilles, defies Odysseus: "Nor shall I yield to force," he declares (line 1252). He saves Philoctetes from suicide by returning his bow. Thus Sophocles reasserts the equation of bowman and bow. But the bowman's virtue remains a nonfunctioning part of his identity so long as Philoctetes continues to refuse Neoptolemus's exhortation to take up his weapon and voluntarily accompany the Greeks to Troy. Although acquiring the stature of a man in defying Odysseus, so that he now encounters Philoctetes man to man, friend to friend, Neoptolemus remains an impatient boy in his inability to understand why Philoctetes insists on remaining on Lemnos despite the offer of a cure by Asclepius and despite the *ananke* of history:

> The fortunes that the Gods give to us men
> we must bear under necessity.
> But men that cling wilfully to their sufferings
> as you do, no one may forgive nor pity.
> Your anger has made a savage of you. You will not
> accept advice, although the friend advises
> in pure goodheartedness. [lines 1317-23]

Neoptolemus may be right about his own heart. But he is wrong about Philoctetes, whose deepest pulse is his experience of unjust pain. The bowman's hand is restored to its proper function when Neoptolemus returns Heracles' bow to Philoctetes. It is the bowman's foot the young son of Achilles cannot comprehend. For he thinks it can be cured—indeed history says it will be. What Neoptolemus fails to see, however, is that Philoctetes' virtue will be only half restored when his hand's agency is restored and his foot cured. The infected snakebite, according to Philoctetes' Aristotelian philosophy of pain, has become more than a physical, thus curable, phenomenon, more than a mere efficient cause. It caused "the sting of wrongs past," but it was also the reason and occasion for Odysseus and the Greeks' betrayal of him. In short, the corrupted foot originally separated the bowman from men, and to a man once betrayed, as for one isolated by constant pain through no fault of one's own, the human bond has been broken for good. The man of pain can no longer be a man among men:

> Eyes of mine, that have seen all, can you endure
> to see me living with my murderers,
> the sons of Atreus? With cursed Odysseus?
> It is not the sting of wrongs past
> but what I must look for in wrongs to come.
> Men whose wit has been mother of villainy once
> have learned from it to be evil in all things. [lines 1355-61]

Although he cannot fathom the depth of the bowman's distrust, Neoptolemus can act for him, from the heart. He consents to take Philoctetes home, not to Troy; and the two, both of whom are scheduled to be heroes, are on their way to being men.

But now another man appears, who was also more than a hero yet less than a full god—Heracles himself, whose bow Philoctetes must not use only to survive, by killing birds for food on Lemnos, or to defend himself and Neoptolemus from vengeful Greeks, but use to *win*. Heracles has to appear because neither the formal cause of love, the pain of Philoctetes constituting his bare integrity as a man alone, nor the love produced, the friendship of Philoctetes and Neoptolemus, will meet the ultimate criterion of Sophoclean heroism. Heracles himself is the only source of this something more that is required of Philoctetes, for Heracles' story is a story of a particular kind of victory, the victory won through suffering:

> Let me reveal to you my own story first,
> let me show the tasks and sufferings that were mine,
> and, at the last, the winning of deathless merit.
> All this you can see in me now.
> All this must be your suffering too,
> the winning of a life to an end in glory,
> out of this suffering. Go with this to Troy.
> [lines 1418-24]

To an order like this, direct from the source of Philoctetes' power and identity as a bowman, and from a glory already achieved through comparable suffering, there is no answer from the sufferer stranded on Lemnos, just obedience, the obedience of action: "Voice that stirs my yearning when I hear, / form lost for so long, / I shall not disobey" (lines 1445-47). Neoptolemus and Philoctetes will proceed on their way as fast friends, but not as homecomers. Now they will be the heroes they are; "like twin lions hunting together, / he shall guard you, you him" (line 1437).

But Philoctetes does answer as well as obey Heracles. His "I shall not disobey" is the single most important utterance in the whole tragedy. It is a well deliberated answer, forthright yet at the same time reserved. It is not just an executant's signification of already settled action because its double-negative form demonstrates Philoctetes' conscious partitioning of the obedience of action, which is external, from internal obedience of thought. The distinction is clearer in a more drawn-out and literal translation. The Greek is as follows: "οὐκ απιθησω τοῖς σοῖς υνθοις," "ouk apitheso tois sois mythois." Literally this means "I shall not disobey your/your words [in my thoughts]" (my translation from Webster's Greek). The positive "to obey" would be merely "πειθοναι." The phrase "in my thoughts" is added to pull out the internalization of meaning suggested by the conjunction of "not disobey" and "your words." A not-disobedient response to words is a calculative, differentiated response. It is mentalized by being doubly distantiated; Philoctetes' assent is thereby placed directly over the abyss of the dissent marked off from the realm of the mental. The only possible "place" for this dissent to occur, then, is the realm of the physical: Philoctetes' foot, his pain. "I shall obey" would be simple positivity, action already begun, the promise that cannot be broken, the intention coextensive with the act—it would be the soldier's sign, not that of the man of pain. In distinction, Philoctetes' "I shall not disobey"—or "I will not disobey your words," in the better translation by Robert Torrance (91)—emphasizes the formality and distance that would characterize an introverted sufferer's compliance rather than an extroverted hero's eagerness. It is an answer in contradistinction to a salute because it expressively displays full human integrity. This is the integrity of pathos stalemated by action, of overwhelming pain overwhelmed in turn by glory, of identity seized yet not absorbed by history, of Heraclean deed outlasting yet not supplanting the suffering doer. Like Zeno's arrow, the bowman himself is both stopped and in flight when he says, "I shall not disobey your words in my thoughts"—which becomes the quintessential Sophoclean rendering of the tragedy of stalemate.

However, does Sophocles mean by Heracles' "the winning of a life to an end in glory, / out of this suffering" what Aeschylus means in the *Eumenides* when he has Olympian assertions of the necessity of historical progress and victory overwhelm the injustice of matricide and the very spirits of justice, the Furies? Will the injustice of Philoctetes' original suffering from the bite and the added injustice of his fellows be suppressed, repressed into the past, like Orestes' murder of his mother and Athena's triumphant appropriation of the "mind of the past?" Will the personal identity of Philoctetes the isolated sufferer be obliterated by the historical identity of Philoctetes the victor of Troy, the way the identity of Orestes the wronged son is erased by that of Orestes King of Argos and the

way the Furies are coerced into becoming the "gracious ones?" Will
Sophocles break out of the stalemate depicted in *Antigone* and *Electra?*

The answer in *Philoctetes* is a quiet "No." Sophocles remains true to
his tragedy of stalemate, stops short of transforming it into Aeschylean
tragedy of victory. For the deepest chord of Philoctetes' tragic identity as
hero-sufferer is a discord, the dissonance of life and death, of heroic
fulfillment in deeds of glory and the obliteration of glory in death. This
clash of elements at the deepest stratum of his character is precisely what
Philoctetes points to by refusing to be cured and delivered on schedule to
his heroic destiny. His wound, his pain, significantly afflicting his *foot,* is
the bedrock of his nature.[11] When Odysseus and Neoptolemus offer him
deliverance from his pain, Philoctetes understands they are demanding
that he abandon his own truest self, just as Odysseus had unjustly abandoned him because of this wound in the first place. Left behind by history
ten years before, Philoctetes had to be reborn, acquire a new identity. The
reason for his comrades' leaving him then became the formal cause of this
new self, the self that had to be conceived in the pain cursing him.
Philoctetes' pathos is this new identity, appropriate to the man surviving
alone on Lemnos, where the heroic identity has no place. Pain as the
source of new identity is equated by Philoctetes' inexorable logic of pain
with death, for pain points toward death—the release not of escape but of
culmination, of rejoining the ultimate source of all identity, the dead
father. For all fathers are the death wrought by time, precedence itself. In
the grip of his worst attack, Philoctetes, insisting on suicide, spells out his
most intimate character in extremis:

> PHILOCTETES: A sword, if you have got one,
>   or an ax or some weapon—give it me!
> CHORUS: What would you do with it?
> PHILOCTETES: Head and foot,
>   head and foot, all of me, I would cut with my own hand.
>   My mind is set on death, on death, I tell you.
> CHORUS: Why this?
> PHILOCTETES: I would go seek my father.
> CHORUS: Where?
> PHILOCTETES: In the house of death.
>   He is no longer in the light.
>   City of my fathers, would I could see you.
>   I who left your holy streams,
>   to go help the Greeks, my enemies,
>   and now am nothing any more. [lines 1204-18]

Thus the question of injustice in *Philoctetes* dissolves into the greater issue of identity, its sources and consequences. The "god" Chryse as serpent bites Philoctetes; the corrupted wound tortures him and leads his fellows to abandon him on Lemnos to a life re-created by nature's *ananke*, by the pain of an isolated survivor. But it is a life blessed by its curse, for the curse points to the reestablished identity of *physis* through reunion with the father in "the house of death." Philoctetes cannot commit the injustice of abandoning this identity, developed over ten years on Lemnos. To do so would be to commit more than spiritual suicide; it would be to violate the very source of life by breaking the negating umbilical cord, father-death-pain-self.

Yet Odysseus and Neoptolemus's insistent offer to Philoctetes of cure, deliverance, and fulfillment of historical *ananke* would amount to just this abandonment. Philoctetes can willingly violate his nature no more than the young Neoptolemus can renounce his father, Achilles, or the cunning veteran Odysseus can shake the paternity of Sisyphus. Philoctetes' world is another world, as tangential to history as uninhabited Lemnos is, lying offshore from the Troad. Philoctetes' cave is clearly a man's dwelling place, but barely: "He makes his bed without neighbors" (line 183). Later, when Neoptolemus repeats the offer of deliverance for the last time, Philoctetes, the man already destroyed by the daimon of his pain, knows the youth's gentlest persuasion means an even worse devastation than that wrought by his foot. For if he allows himself to be persuaded after resisting coercion, he will not only be separating from his pathos, he will be assenting of his own free will to being someone other than he knows himself to be:

> NEOPTOLEMUS: Be easy. I would only have you listen.
> PHILOCTETES: I am afraid of that.
> I heard you before, and they were good words, too.
> But they destroyed me when I listened. [lines 1266-69]

Words are for the history makers, men and women active in that other world of achievement, which is possible only in freedom from pain. As Odysseus puts it with the steely self-assurance of the unscathed, "I see / that everywhere among the race of men / it is the tongue that wins and not the deed" (lines 98-99). Words destroy identity; they are for the book of glory recording all the wins. Pain creates identity, it is meant only for the "cave that shared my watches" (line 1452).

Philoctetes on Lemnos maintains the loser's integrity of pain. Odysseus obtrudes on this cul-de-sac that interrupts the Greeks' progress along the high road to Troy, and he introduces the ruthless freshness of a winner.

But not even Odysseus's craft can extract Philoctetes from his lair in the
womb of nature as experience, the world of pain, and redeliver him to the
life of historical triumph. The one life makes no sense alongside the other;
it is as if Lemnos is a fold in the map of history, a crease hiding the archer
from both his destined targets and his deliverers. However, the friendship
elicited from Neoptolemus by Philoctetes' desperate longing for home,
while it falls short of repositioning the hero on his track to Troy, at least
reties the social bond. Finally, Heracles, also both a legendary winner and
a man of pain, traces the arc of victory for Philoctetes by describing the
completed trajectory of the Greeks' attempt of glory. Completion of the
trajectory requires the proper use of the proper tool—Heracles' bow—in
the proper place at the proper time, and by the proper bowman:

> Troy you shall take.
> You shall win the prize of valor from the army
> and shall send the spoils to your home,
> to your father Poias, and the land of your fathers, Oeta.
> From the spoils of the campaign you must dedicate
> some, on my pyre, in memory of my bow. [lines 1427-32]

Philoctetes responds, "I shall not disobey" (line 1447). Why will he
not? He has overridden Odysseus's guile and withstood Neoptolemus's
love. Is his integrity of pain finally overridden by his suddenly awakened
identity as hero? "Voice that stirs my yearning when I hear, / form lost for so
long" (lines 1448-49). Heracles is no highest-echelon Olympian, like Athena or Apollo in the *Eumenides*. Yet he is as fully a demigod as any, since his
descent is direct from Zeus, and, according to Aeschylus in *Prometheus
Bound*, even his mortal lineage goes back five generations to Io, another
woman of many targeted by Zeus. Like Aeschylus's Apollo and Athena,
however, Heracles does say, "I come / to tell you of the plans of Zeus for
you" (lines 1414-15). But it is his own, human hero's story of the "winning of
a life to an end in glory / out of this suffering" (lines 1423-24) that seems to
stir Philoctetes to take up Heracles' bow, now of necessity his, and proceed with Neoptolemus to his cure, and to his target: "Paris, the cause of all
this evil, you shall kill / with the bow that was mine" (lines 1426-27).
    The distinction between Philoctetes' virtue and his pathos, rather the
distinction between his *arete* construed specifically as *hexis* (his bowman's
skill, which ensures survival) and his most fundamental *physis* as man of
pain, is as ineradicable a distinction as that between victory and justice in
the *Eumenides*. Heracles, however, appears—like Theseus at the end of
Oedipus at Colonus—primarily as an exemplar of man *making* himself a
"god," a process that can end in victory but only through suffering. In

Aeschylus the civilization, Athens, not the hero Orestes, claims the spoils of victory, which can never quite hide the stain of the history of heroic winning through that precedes the achievement. Sophocles, like Aeschylus, grants history its *ananke*, the Greeks their glory. Unlike Aeschylean victories, though, the victories of Heracles and Philoctetes, entirely necessitated by history, do not offset the heroes' sacrifices, the pathos of men of pain. Philoctetes' pain, unlike his *arete*, cannot be reduced to the means, character, serving the end, glory. When Sophocles tried the Aeschylean force play in *Electra*, and made his characters coincide utterly with their fate, there was no victor left to claim the victory, but only the stalemate of aesthetic self-cancellation.

The conclusion of *Philoctetes* replaces the stalemate of external forces, characteristic of *Antigone*, and the stalemate of perfection, characteristic of *Electra*, with his most cunning and compassionate stalemate, that of stasis completely within the figure of suffering historical agent. The paradox is almost as impossible as it would be if Christ, as Son of Man and Son of God, were unable to transcend the paradox of His two natures. Love, created from the bowman's pain and the compassion of Neoptolemus, is no more a transcendent value in *Philoctetes* than it is in *Antigone* when the chorus intones its awesome power. Heraclean heroism is the crux of Sophocles' tragic matter in *Philoctetes*, as it will be in Euripides' *Heracles*.[12] Accordingly, the stasis, the civil war raging within implied by the hero's ambivalent "I shall not disobey," grants the god-backed historical realm and the pain-wracked human realm exact parity of value. Philoctetes *will* go to Troy and enter the book of deeds as it is already written by *ananke*. But Philoctetes will also stay, in secret obedience to the law of his wound. His bow will strike, but the Heraclean hero's heart, his *physis*, will remain stricken, crawling through the cave home on "sea-encircled" Lemnos. Philoctetes at the last is a man dragged into heroism by his *arete*, specifically by his *hexis*, which has also preserved him for history. But his integrity—as man of pain connected with the ground of experience by his foot, not his arm—statically, by definition of pathos, remains imbued with the beauty of a stalemate that outshines the radiance of glory. This stalemate also offsets the triumph of transcendence with the regret of breaking away from *physis*, a regret expressed in the plea "Blame me not":

> Lemnos, I call upon you:
> Farewell, cave that shared my watches,
> nymphs of the meadow and the stream,
> the deep male growl of the sea-lashed headland
> where often, in my niche within the rock,
> my head was wet with fine spray,

where many a time in answer to my crying
in the storm of my sorrow the Hermes mountain sent its echo!
Now springs and Lycian well, I am leaving you,
leaving you.
I had never hoped for this.
Farewell Lemnos, sea-encircled,
blame me not but send me on my way
with a fair voyage to where a great destiny
carries me, and the judgment of friends and the
all-conquering
Spirit who has brought this to pass. [lines 1451-68]

Medea: Tragedy of Winner-Lose-All

In the conventional, narrow sense of "political," perhaps only Aeschylus would qualify as a political tragedian, for his explicit program of Athenian power provides the firmest structure of his tragedies, especially his earliest, the *Persians*, and his last, the *Eumenides*. Yet Sophocles was himself an influential factor in aristocratic politics as the Athenian conflict with Sparta deepened. Furthermore the performance of his earlier plays contemporaneously with Aeschylus's *Persians* during the epoch of Themistocles drew upon responses and probably even attitudes that were civic in the political sense as well as the festive: "When Sophocles in his first appearance in the contest of tragedies in the spring of 468 was competing with Aeschylus, the feelings of the spectators were running high. Consequently the archon, Apsephion (469/8), instead of appointing the judges by lot in the usual way, prevailed upon Cimon and his fellow generals, when they entered the theatre, to act as judges. This occasion became famous, and some scholars claim that it reflects the glamor of Cimon's recent great victory [Eurymedon]" (Fine 348). More important, however, in *Antigone, Electra,* and *Philoctetes,* none of which is set in Athens or is even characterized by such intrusions of encomiastic fervor concerning Athens as the famous choral ode in Euripides' *Medea*, Sophocles transmutes the political into the historical, which is more general. Although of the three tragedies only *Antigone* formally pits the individual against the state as institution, Electra and Orestes' struggle against their mother is, to Sophocles as to Aeschylus, mandated by the imperatives of justice, both familial and political. *Philoctetes,* with its Trojan War context, of course is the most abstracted from current history of the three plays, yet it stands, along with *Oedipus at Colonus*, as Sophocles' most "Tolstoyan" deliberation on the relation between inner self and historical *ananke*.

With Euripides, politics can be accommodated by critical theory, whether it is construed as a narrow, even topical, matter—such as the condemnation of Athenian imperialism in the *Trojan Women*—or as a broad, pervasive concern—such as the clash between state power as such and the irrational in the *Bacchae*. What is really most political in Euripides, however, is neither Aristophanic-style current events nor late Sophoclean meditation on history. Instead, the genuinely political in Euripides is a formal phenomenon. The deus ex machina, for which Euripides is notorious, is actually his strongest, most successful ploy as a tragedian. I should like to argue that the theatrical device of breaking into tragic action from realms beyond, historical or religious, is in fact the single most powerful element of the Euripidean way of imitating historical action, as well as the element most relevant to the telos of his characteristic plot.

Because it is not compatible with organicism, because it is radically different from consistent character, coherent psychology and Aristotelian "diction," the deus ex machina works, imitatively, precisely the way history works: it breaks into lives, obliterating them, justifying them, determining them, bending them this way and that. Actually Euripides is like, not unlike, both Sophocles and Aeschylus in his application of the historical to the personal via the obtrusive "machine." Only the vision of Heracles at the end of *Philoctetes* can produce Sophocles' telos of permanent irresolution, of stalemate between the bowman's pain and his historical destiny. And only Athena's hint about her father's lightning bolts forces the Furies to become the Eumenides. The deeper reason all three tragedians resort to the deus ex machina for effecting the ends of their actions is that it already *means* those ends. The machine is in itself a paradigm, and it operates in Euripides the way victory does in Aeschylus. A proper designation for this formal ploy, which is really a paradigm that cuts across and through the action, would be "overdetermination": it is excessively effectual, both on the natural level by its nonrational violence and on the aesthetic level by its violation of expectation.

For Medea to escape to promised sanctuary in Athens by means of the power of her grandfather the Sun indicates that overdetermination perfectly renders the way history works—with shocking indifference to morality, psychological consistency, or even sense. When Dionysus himself enters the historical realm of Pentheus, we are indeed *in* the action of Euripides' last tragedy. When in *Electra* the Dioscuri impose, through senseless historical effectuality, the justification of Electra and Orestes' matricide on these unheroic, inchoate, guilty, yet accidentally effectual characters, the nature of the demigod twins as surprise interrupters is the very point. No human reference can vindicate the bloody yet hardly intrepid brother and sister; only a nonhuman reference can, and properly speaking that is no reference at all. In *Heracles,* Euripides' clearest and most moving attempt to realize the contingency and anarchy of the personal, the historical, and the religious, the inexplicability of Heracles' horrible madness can be rendered no more logically than by the machine of Hera, Iris, and Madness's drastic intrusion.

Thus defined as overdetermination, the formal, inorganic deus ex machina, while all along a key device for both Aeschylus and Sophocles in their best works, becomes the overt signature of Euripidean tragedy, from *Medea* through the *Bacchae.* Only when the disorder of Euripidean character and expression is stricken by the sudden jolt of the machine does Euripides' peculiar sense of the political come clear. As for Aeschylus and the late Sophocles, the political becomes the power of history, but in Euripides the political is backed by brutal religious energies, and not just awesomely inscrutable ones: Medea's Sun grandfather with his grisly "treasures," the absent Apollo, who commands Orestes to kill his mother, and Hera's viceroy Iris, who visits Heracles with madness, are no longer the same kind of god as Athena was in bending justice to her will or Zeus in sending Heracles to Philoctetes. These "gods" of Euripides are really just symbols of how things happen to people, how history as a ferociously unprincipled principle breaks them to its will and imposes sense and justice senselessly and unjustly.

The deus ex machina breaks in because that is what history does in Euripides. Aesthetically it is a vehicle transparent to the very meaning it conveys: that *outside* forces, irrational, nonhuman in origin and agency, yet utterly human at the same time, make people do what they do and determine the value of what will ensue. "It" is always bigger than "they" in Euripides. If he were to work toward this meaning through character, as Sophocles is critically acclaimed for doing, he would not be able to get beyond either Aeschylean political order or Sophoclean character that all but equals fate. So in a very different way from his predecessor, Aeschylus, and his competitor, Sophocles, Euripides realizes genre as power by making tragedies the sheer formal operation of which signifies nothing else than the political "cut," the edge of history as a power slicing cleanly through the deepest insides of people.

Both political order and character streamlined to fit fate are products of tragic action determined *from within,* by its motive impulse and goal: victory in Aeschylus, stalemate in Sophocles. But the Euripidean version of the generic game of tragedy is about neither winning nor drawing. Instead, it is a game in which potential and actual winners lose everything. If triumph or deadlock were the outcome of the Euripidean game, and if it were structured by intently teleological action, as in Aeschylus, or by consistent characterization, as in Sophocles, we would have a *Medea* or *Heracles* that was determined, ordered internally from beginning to end by its own logic. However, Euripides' game possesses the illogic of perpetual and absolute loss, a sense of which numbs or hyper-enlivens his players instead of moving them to the ambivalent action with regret of a Philoctetes or the humble pride of an Orestes such as Aeschylus depicts. Therefore, only by overdetermining the dramatic action, by breaking into it, and only by violating consistent characterization, by showing its ultimate incoherence, even its madness, can Euripides realize the nature of the tragic game of winners who lose all. To achieve this end of ends he needs specifically to go *outside* his actions to deliver the abrupt destructive blows of history, the rationale of deus ex machina exploited for all it is worth: "Jason batters at the doors. Medea appears above the roof, sitting / in a chariot drawn by dragons, with the bodies of the two children / beside her" (*Medea*, lines 1317-19). This *coup de théâtre* simply, as a matter of miraculous "fact," takes the end-of-the-road heroine par excellence way beyond our sense of proper end, to a blazing prospect of consumption at the heart of the Sun. The effect of this spectacle is distinct from that of any that would be possible from character or speech, or even action. Indeed, Medea's iconographic appearance "above the roof" both exhausts the action and nullifies all the words that have, throughout, whirled the characters about in a vortex of empty recriminations.

The image struck by stage direction alone smashes the verbal structure of the play to bits. At the end of this scene, Jason is left, characteristically, speechifying into the void that has been magically wrought by his barbaric wife's capacity for ultimate act. The Sophists' *pharmakon*, words as remedy, has made a flurry of preparations, but not for the alleviation of woe or prevention of disaster.[13] The preparation has been for nothing but the cessation of words necessitated by this consummate spectacle.

It is one of tragedy's greatest shocks: the Sun descending to save his granddaughter from just reprisal for the deed she displays openly, vauntingly—the murder of her two sons, whose bodies are both really and iconographically slumped over the chariot's sides. Euripides manages the appearance of this machine in such a way, sudden, instantaneous, that we are compelled to turn our attention away from the place from which the Sun's chariot has descended, toward the direction in which the passenger will go, ascendant, leaving behind a world she has transformed into an abattoir. Seneca is clearly the inheritor of Euripides' Medean mode. Medea has displayed bravado: "To such a life glory belongs," she declaimed when she settled once for all on killing her own children (line 808). She has also confessed; when Jason asked, "And you murdered them?" she replied, "Yes, Jason, to break your heart" (lines 1397-98). In her stunning suspension between the two, up becomes down and down becomes up. The murderess has her apotheosis, and Jason, the hapless husband-hero, garrulous to the last, makes a fool of himself spewing a self-justifying and self-pitying speech from below into the airless, scorching vacuum of the Sun. "During this speech the chariot has moved out of sight" is Euripides' final stage direction (line 1416).

Yet all this effect is not for the sake of making a conceptual point, as it is, for instance, when Aeschylus manages Athena's arm-twisting maneuver to elevate those underground spirits, the Furies, to the position of officially revered goddesses secured within the Athenian power structure. Medea's perverse apotheosis is neither the logical end of *virtù*, glory deserved for attaining the goal of her political revenge against Jason, nor the natural result of her tremendous passion and pride, which are related and proportional if not overlapping: "Let them understand / I am of a different kind: dangerous to my enemies, / Loyal to my friends. To such a life glory belongs" (lines 806-8). Thus the first problem is to find out why the political trajectory of her revengeful scheming is not enough to determine the arrival of the Sun's chariot, which is thus pure *éblouissement*. The second problem is to discover why the obvious explanation of her conclusive "glory," namely, her heroic passion itself, also fails to account for the perverse conjuncture of damnation and blessing in the iconic machine. If we uncover these two gaps in the structure of Euripides' deus ex machina—and it is a structure: one reads Euripides backwards from the machine—we will see not the puzzling, even failed tragic craftsman, but a deeply original and probably unsurpassed approach to the making of tragedies.

Medea is no hypocrite. To achieve her end, she had to be willing from the initiation of her plan to pay the price of her sons. So she tells Jason the truth from the chariot, the iconic splendor of which does not obscure this plain rendering of the economics of her revenge. No reckless revenger, Medea deliberates, engaging in what Aristotle terms *proairesis*, or forechoice. As Aristotle points out in the *Ethics*, one deliberates concerning means, not ends. Thus when she seems to retract her plan, she is not emoting; she is considering the sharpness of her pain as a gauge of the effectiveness of her intended means.

When the chorus reminds her of the pain she will inflict on herself, Medea acquires not only an external gauge but a sureness of purpose that can come only after she has disentangled herself from her self-justifying rhetoric. Pietro Pucci is wrong when he explains Euripides' sophistical rhetoric in *Medea* as a "disseminating" process (84, 119, 154-59, 229n). In fact, Euripides shows Medea using rhetoric deliberatively, to move beyond rhetoric to her achievement, victorious revenge. The procedure is one of closing down verbal apertures, not of opening them up, so that they will gradually focus on the act itself. Medea is no model Sophist; on the contrary, she follows Socrates' good rhetorical model as Plato sketches it out in the *Phaedrus*. To arrive at the truth through division, tossing out the seeming to get to the real: what else is this than Medea's own method of employing words to grow sure of the right plan, to move through words to action? She rhetorizes to the end of not having to rhetorize any more, the same way Hamlet does, although his revenge is simply just and Medea's is both just and monstrous, like Clytaemnestra's in Aeschylus: "Let be. Until it is done words are unnecessary" (*Medea*, line 817).

Yet why are we still not prepared for the Euripidean surprise of the Sun's chariot "machine?" Character, plot, character's diction (planning and testing) all move with the aesthetic inevitability of "probabilities," an inevitability that imitates in the Aristotelian manner the fatefulness of history seen as retrospective cause and effect. Even the murdered sons are *in* the chariot, the draped corpses realizing, in an extreme bodily icon, Medea's initial prospectus of "my darling children's blood" (line 795). Why is Euripides not content with Sophoclean seamlessness?

The answer requires going beyond Euripides as a formalist, even though he is, like Aeschylus and Sophocles, a complete master of means-to-ends relations, as I could argue by pointing not only to *Medea* but also to such representative yet individuated works as *Hippolytus*, *Electra*, *Heracles*, and the *Bacchae*. Euripides' deus ex machina is a ubiquitous formalist structure that can float: it can appear at the end, as in *Medea* and *Electra*, or toward the beginning, as in the *Bacchae*, or at both, as in *Hippolytus*, or in the middle, as in *Heracles*. Such versatility can be explained only with reference to something beyond structure. This something is not referential verisimilitude. Euripides is not really the father of a kind of psychological realism that many find rather "modern." Nor is it a function of linguistic dissemination. Euripides concentrates linguistic powers, riding down hard on signifiers that tend to slide away from his heroine's telos. It is probably the fixedness of this telos in Euripides, an almost obsessive intensity of movement to the end, that does not allow Euripides to merge unobtrusively with his ultimate goals the way Aeschylus does with his paradigmatic victory or Sophocles with his delicate yet rigid stalemates. The fixedness of this telos requires us to add another conceptual category, one adequate to going beyond the telos. Neither "paradigm of victory" nor "stalemate" will suffice to explain Euripidean tragedy, wherein the scheduled, or apparently fated, winner loses everything: the extreme tragedy of unexpected and immeasurable loss. For why does Medea, apotheosized in the Sun's chariot, not achieve victory, and why is she and not Jason, her victim, the loser? Why do Orestes and Electra lose the triumph of their overcoming of their own reluctance, first his then hers, to kill their mother, a victory underwritten yet condemned by those representatives of Zeus, the Dioscuri? Why can Hippolytus not win even a genuine moral victory when, technically vindicated and outrageously forgiving, he lies dying in his father's arms? Or why do Phaedra and Hippolytus, who do win the ultimate points for Aphrodite and Artemis respectively, not receive anything but indifference and neglect from their feuding goddesses until it is too late? Or, most significant of all, why does the very incarnation of masterful winning through, Heracles, lose all that is dearest to him through no fault of his own, indeed through the very source of his power, Zeus's paternity, which impels the jealous Hera to turn Heracles' arrows against his own sons and wife?

By consistently selecting big winners for his exemplars of total loss, Euripides points an accusing finger at the gods, particularly Zeus himself. Behind the final ironies in these tragic actions of winners losing all lies the Euripidean categorical imperative of religious despair. This is a categorical imperative, for if something on Olympus is all wrong, everything on earth will inevitably follow suit. Moreover, everything down here among men will be messed up when the gods take to fixing it up with their violence. Euripides is no agnostic, no atheist; on the contrary, the actions of his tragedies are puppet shows, the machinelike effect of which originates in overdetermination by irresponsible gods who are free to act because Zeus acts only sporadically, arbitrarily, and inscrutably. Euripides as puppet-master inserts his dei ex machina to parody the willfulness of an omnipotent god whose power resembles a universal vacuum of power, letting anything happen that will. The Euripidean surprise is the truest effect of the absence of any predictability, any justice, any reason—any concern—on the part of gods, who cannot, as Heracles suggests to Theseus, really *be* gods if they behave the way they do. The devastation he has just wrought at Hera's "tyrannical" instigation lends Heracles' "if truly god" reply the status of far-reaching critique:

> THESEUS: No man lives unscathed by chance;
>   Nor, if we may believe the poets, does any god.
>   Have not gods joined in lawless love among themselves?
>   Dishonoured fatherhood with chains to gain a throne?
>   Yet they live in Olympus; and if they have sinned
>   They are not inconsolable. What's your defence
>   If you, a man, cry against fate, while gods do not?
> HERACLES: What you say of the gods is hardly relevant.
>   I don't believe gods tolerate unlawful love.

> Those tales of chainings are unworthy. I never did
> And never will accept them; nor that any god
> Is tyrant of another. A god, if truly god,
> Needs nothing. Those are poets' lamentable myths.
> [*Heracles*, lines 1314-26, Vellacott].

Heracles is saying, with an appalling simplicity matching the total destruction caused by Hera's vengefulness, that the gods Theseus is talking about are not worthy of being gods. If they were, there would be no God. Euripides presses the the negative verge of monotheism in Heracles' religious despair over Olympian godlessness, much the same way Seneca will later base his tragedies on what amounts for a first-century Roman to an absence of love, love such as would emerge historically only through Christianity.

The category, then, that is most appropriate to Euripides' tragic puppetry of winners whose losses are shockingly total is religious despair, despair that the gods are not gods yet are always dropping down arbitrarily on human beings, whether on the just, as in *Heracles;* the unjust, as in *Medea;* or both, as in *Hippolytus.* Still, a truer perspective on the ultimate purport of the deus ex machina is the human perspective, from below Olympus. Although we admire Medea's flaunting her gruesome victory from her grandfather the Sun's chariot, our experience places us alongside Jason, however contemptible we may find him because we identify with the heroine's superior, rather supreme, position. And from Jason's perspective we must acknowledge the truth of what he says to Medea: "You suffer too; my loss is yours no less" (line 1361). Indeed, Medea is the winner only because her loss, as mother of the sons she kills, is greater than the father's, whose vanity has tempted the fateful retaliatory force that is his barbarian wife. The surprise wrought by the descent of the Sun's chariot to extricate the monstrous granddaughter from the framework of justice is the surprise that Medea's victory is at the expense of her best self, or selves.

The deus ex machina concluding *Medea* simply renders the unexpected effect of divine intervention in the human terms of a woman whose pathos as a mother, exploited by her own plan of mastery over herself, puts her beyond the pale of justice, beyond ordinary humanity, yet entirely within the range of ordinary anguish. The godlessness of the Euripidean gods becomes a manifestation of the inhumanity of the human. The two realms are identical. The gods, as Heracles puts it, cannot be God because they are too human, while the most human of women acts inhumanly as a god. The result is the same whether the gods descend to a mortal level or a human being violates her humanity to become a god: victory costs total loss, loss of supramortal status by the Sun, who saves a criminal, and loss of human status by Medea, who is saved for her perverted humanity as woman and mother by being apotheosized.

Euripidean tragedy thus presents the prospect of victory under total eclipse. The terrors of history as the power differential are given free play by Euripides, who no longer uses power as Aeschylus always attempted to do, no longer presumes to deal with it as Sophocles did. Euripides' spectacles are opened wide to what Aeschylus's Argive elders see so clearly in *Agamemnon:*

> But the lust for power never dies—
>   men cannot have enough.
> No one will lift a hand to send it
> From his door, to give it warning,
> "Power, never come again!" [lines 1355-59, Fagles]

CHAPTER THREE

Tragic Genre

Historically, tragedy proper originally was, and continued to be through the 1830s, with Büchner, a form of live mimesis, or theater. This aspect of the genre is not merely formal: tragedy was a public occasion for the Athenians, and spectacle in itself suggested to Renaissance Christian audiences that this world is just a stage. Moreover, the primacy of the electronically "live" visual media of film and television in the postindustrial West is now essential to any adequate understanding of how, since the French Revolution, history itself has become spectacle, and images have become historical. Tragedy as a genre, as Aristotle first noted, cannot be reduced to a verbal or literary medium. Euripides' spectacular staging in *Medea* (albeit deplored by Aristotle) bears a semantic weight without which his elaborate rhetorical structures would collapse upon themselves, just as a visual shot or montage sequence in *Potemkin* or *Arsenal*, rather than any subtitle, clearly makes revolutionary history a tragedy of winning. Formally speaking, then, tragedy must be *witnessed*. This is the real reason Oedipus blinds himself; thereby he enters a nontragic post-Oedipus world when Sophocles wishes to terminate *Oedipus Tyrannus* and commence the "literary" *Oedipus at Colonus*. It is the real reason Medea deliberately appears, exultant over her own tragedy; thereby she is witnessed by all as a veritable icon of tragedy.

Three times, however, tragedy virtually disappeared as a genre of public display, to emerge transformed into a mode, "the tragic." Seneca wrote literary tragedies designed to ornament moral perceptions rather than execute actions. In the late Middle Ages, aside from the inherent tragedy of the Mass (the Passion ritualized) and the publicly performed mystery cycles (the Passion historicized), literary narrative, particularly the romance, wrought new modal configurations of the tragic. During the nineteenth century new genres began to proliferate, all of which could register the tragic mode: the historical novel developed by Scott, well-made French melodrama, all grand opera (not only Wagner), Romantic ballet, and the novella form of fabular tale practiced by Kleist, Büchner, Stendhal, Flaubert, Tolstoy, and Mann.

Each of these times when tragedy subsided as a form and the tragic mode accelerated in development was characterized by an interiorization of culture, whether caused by a Roman crisis in the judicial soul, by a natural inward tendency of Christian culture, or by the advent of bourgeois industrialism with its own privatistic, consumerist cultural preferences and technological innovations. Elitism of various kinds attends such instances of interiorized culture: Seneca, the disillusioned bureaucrat, wrote for an inner circle of powerful Romans acquainted with Greek culture. Clerics and courtiers wrote and read multiple redactions of romance that pose sophisticated problems of Christian psychology and politics. Middle-class families ingested and continue to ingest mass-distributed fiction at home or pay to see the latest hit in melodrama, opera, or ballet—all of which, to sustain themselves, had to be, by the 1830s, profitable ventures like other businesses.

Tragedy as public spectacle thus can be seen generally to require a whole community of all the classes—unless it becomes an exotic museum attraction, as happened to classical tragedy during the early nineteenth century—while the tragic modes generally survive through their appeal to particular coteries and classes. Furthermore, history as the arena of agon is always paramount in public tragedy, while in the tragic mode it is a setting, or backdrop—still significant, as in Kleist's *Michael Kohlhaas* or Tolstoy's novellas—against which an interiorized soul's agon takes place: Ravenswood and Lucy's or Tristan and Isolde's tragic loves; Ivan Ilyich's and Aschenbach's solitary tragic deaths. Philoctetes' pain is equally and interdependently physical and historical, while Ivan Ilyich's is relevant to his family and society only as a negative critique of their essential indifference.

Still another formal principle pervading far more tragedies than is usually acknowledged is the deus ex machina. It is not Euripides alone who relies on this principle. Aeschylus needs to bring in Athena and the entire Olympian apparatus to resolve the *Oresteia*; and Sophocles, who is not so pure an organicist as Aristotle would have him, introduces Heracles' spirit at the end of *Philoctetes*. Later tragedies and tragic modes employ Athenian-style machines for a variety of ends: the Aeschylean style, to signify theological justification as a mystery beyond doctrinal interpretation of the right or true (the potion in Beroul's medieval romance, *Tristan*); the Sophoclean style, to bridge history and the individual (battle victory for a psychological renovation leading to a metahistorical triumph in Heinrich von Kleist's *Prince Friedrich of Homburg*); or the Euripidean style, to destroy (the guillotine in Georg Büchner's *Danton's Death*). Indeed, deus ex machina as a formal imperative is present even if not overt in all tragedies. For, finally, it is what marks actions as paradigmatically tragic, in that they are out of the agonists' control. Thus the invisible *machine infernale* maintains winning/losing/stalemating as a system beyond values of moral good and evil.

If tragedies can be said to have precise content, it is the content of forms of power themselves. There are three kinds of tragedy, in terms of content, each of which originated with the Greeks and extended through the early modern period of European literature, to at least Tolstoy and Ibsen. Aeschylean tragedy celebrates victory or envisions its prospect: Shakespeare's histories,[1] Calderón's *Life Is a Dream*, and Kleist's *Prince Friedrich of Homburg*. The Sophoclean kind of tragedy of stalemate, in which heroic integrity is stressed whether the hero or heroine dies or survives: Schiller's *Mary Stuart* and *Don Carlos*, or in the tragic mode, Tolstoy's *The Death of Ivan Ilyich* and Mann's *Death in Venice*. Euripidean tragedy shows the winner losing all, whether for good or bad: Seneca, all of Shakespeare's tragedies, Jacobean revenge tragedy, seventeenth-century *Trauerspiele*, Racine, Büchner's *Danton's Death*, and nearly all that has been referred to as "tragic" in drama since Ibsen and Strindberg. If these are the possible outcomes of tragedy, then tragedy as a genre is a game. Whether this game at all corresponds with or refers directly to the nature of life as it is distinct from history is endlessly debatable. Perhaps the life-originated actions imitated by tragic plots are, even for the West, only apparently agonistic. Perhaps winning and losing, thus stalemating as well, are false categories, as is suggested by certain currents of contemporary feminist thought. Certainly, however, the inception of tragedy in Greece and the continuity of the three kinds presuppose the context of political-athletic contest.

To this day, competitive sport remains the most authentic ghost, or simulacrum, of tragedy. In two contemporary sports particularly, tragic content clearly betrays itself in athletic actions that have been abstracted to repetitive forms allowing ever-progressive physical refinements: boxing and football. Boxing is our version of the Greeks' wrestling, which for Aeschylus served as a prime metaphor for tragic struggle. Boxing is a nonmoral agon: one is "for" both boxers or else "it's no match." As men, boxers are first mutually necessary, however much one may be favored, because they are equally indispensable to the fight itself, or action. (This indicates why professional wrestling is always farce in genre, for the fan willfully sees the one opponent as evil incarnate, the other as unalloyed good.) Thus, if the fight is not fixed, either opponent may be the victor, justly and to the satisfaction of those attending. The only bad fight is one in which the victory is undeserved, irrespective of any perceived or projected ethical valorizations, one in which the best man does not win. Excellence in boxing is a neutral function of technique, power, and courage. Medieval trial by combat also simulated this tragic primacy of technique and technical *arete*, or professional *virtù*, over social ethics. Physical force is the necessary clarifying praxis antecedent to any ethical end, and it directly signifies divine favor or disfavor with utter disregard for the social good. Like tragedy, this fighting game is prerational dispersal of power, brutal, technical, absolute.

Football expresses the same tragic agon as boxing, but more impurely because the nature of team sports allows a greater role to contingency— referees' calls, increased probability of error in execution, the weather. Yet the outcome of a football game allows the uncompromising schematics of victory/loss/tie to strike cleanly through the confusion. Despite or perhaps even because of the total secularization of physical competition, including the "noncommercial" Olympics, contemporary sport produces the only genuinely collective passion of which technologized cultures are capable; in this respect even war is no match for sport as the ghost of the tragic game.

The only way for tragedy to evade its power dispersal while keeping within the structures of game is for tragedy to dissolve into tragic mode. Except for Seneca, who is only proto-Christian in his reading tragedies, the reason the mode departs from the straight teleological path of tragedy as a genre, classical or postclassical, is that it is a specifically Christian phenomenon. The tragic modes of medieval romance and nineteenth-century grand opera, for example, explode into Christian deliverance from the mundane.

Tragic genre, then, is agon itself. It is not essentially between particularized opposed values such as "ours" and "theirs" (*Persians*), good and evil (*Hamlet*), love and hate (*Hippolytus*), good and good (*Oresteia* or *Life Is a Dream*), bad and bad (*Medea* or *'Tis Pity She's a Whore*), individual and state (*Antigone* or *Danton's Death*), self and history (*Philoctetes* or *Prince Friedrich of Homburg*). All these oppositions are occasions, not grounds, of tragedy. Nor is tragedy based on just any conflict, but only those admitting of victory, loss, or stalemate. For instance, some historical and many personal conflicts may simply dissipate, come to nought. The agency of time in reality dulls, unlike aesthetic "stage" time, which whets the edges of conflicts. It would be hard to imagine a dissipated conflict as the basis of tragic action. This is one reason most twentieth-century "tragedies" are in content as well as in form really instances of the tragic mode: Kafka's *In the Penal Colony, The Great Wall of China, The Burrow*; Beckett's *Waiting for Godot*; Mann's *Doctor Faustus*. It should be noted as well that Sophoclean stalemate is entirely different from dissipated conflict: Philoctetes' "I shall not disobey" is a perfectly suspended, ultrasharp paradox, not a victory and not a loss—and not an eroded or evaded or transcended conflict.

Nor can tragedy as a genre issue in just any kind of victory, loss, or stalemate. The tragic duck tears and hedgehog agonists in Giraudoux's *Electra* notwithstanding, a cock fight can be tragic no more than war: the one lies beneath the categories, the other beyond. Tragedy is a human game, not for real. And within the confines of the game, conflicts may be either solved (victory in Aeschylus), suspended (stalemate in *Antigone* and *Philoctetes*), or winner-loses-all (Euripides).

Tragedy is beyond good and evil, although it may employ moral categories in its superstructure as counters in the game. The ground of tragedy may indeed be amoral: Büchner's tragedy *Danton's Death* is revolutionary history, nothing more and nothing less. Tragedy may be immoral, as in Euripides' *Medea,* the immorality of which was discerned by Aristotle; Euripides' *Electra*; Jacobean tragedies; and, from one point of view, the tragic modes of Seneca and Beroul, the earliest of the medieval *Tristan* romancers. Or it may be moral, as in *Antigone, Heracles,* and, in the tragic mode, Seneca and Beroul, from another point of view. Moreover, some tragedies may be both moral and immoral at the same time, yet not amoral: *Eumenides* and *Life Is a Dream* are of this type.

But tragedy is always an imitation of political-historical actions, which, according to Scaliger, are cast into "forms" of emotion (qtd. in Benjamin 99). Works in the tragic mode retain, though as background instead of foreground, this political-historical first dimension: Ivan Ilyich's death is itself a critique of bureaucratism in its substitution of empty formalism for the substance of life and death. At his most personal, Euripides is completely political, which fact shows that the Athenian consciousness could accommodate both dimensions while experiencing little or no abstraction. In *Heracles* the hero's "self"-destruction, that is the destruction of his family as what constitutes both himself and the basis of the civilization he achieves, *is* Athens's destruction of itself when it turns to the madness of imperialism, which is the expression of power for power's sake alone.

Deaths abound in tragedies, yet often it is the death of others besides the hero or heroine that is typical, through the imitation wars, revenges, matricides, suicides, and slaughters of innocents that frame the agon. The hero and heroine may themselves both live and prosper: Orestes, Electra, Kleist's Prince Friedrich, Calderón's Segismundo. The hero may also both live and suffer in defeat, as does Heracles, or suffer then live in triumph-in-loss, as Philoctetes, or loss-in-triumph, as Medea. The heroine or hero may die, of course. But heroism itself may not even be necessary to tragedy; heroism is absent from Ford's *'Tis Pity She's a Whore* and Euripides' *Hippolytus,* as well as Seneca's *Phaedra* in the tragic mode.

Another supposedly essential ingredient of tragedy, poetic justice, may be completely lacking, as in *Medea* (in Medea's case if not Jason's) or Euripides' *Electra* and *Heracles,* or it may be the chief product forged out of the agon, as in Aeschylus. The soured Roman, Seneca, throws justice out as a lost cause. And Beroul denatures it through a Christian exchange of justice for love, Christianity's own justice. Büchner simply does not see it: only one's "nature" matters.

Still another misconception is that tragedy and Christianity are incompatible. Yet the Passion itself is tragic, perhaps even a tragedy. And there are secularized Christian tragedies: Calderón, the English Jacobeans, Corneille, and Racine. It is also a misconception that tragedy is an abiding or permanent genre verging on a deep civilizational structure; such a view fails to see that its lapses from the history of culture are, in a sense, more revealing than its continuity. For tragedy can flourish, to be sure; it did in fifth-century Athens; sixteenth- and seventeenth-century Spain, England, and France; and post-Revolutionary Germany. But it can wane as well, either subsiding into nondramatic modes, such as romance in the Middle Ages, or proliferating into very different alternative mimetic genres, such as opera, ballet, and film in the nineteenth and twentieth centuries. Both tragedy and the tragic modes can also decline to the point of virtual demise, as now. All in all, the periods when tragedy proper thrived were very short, tragic modalism developed very irregularly, and many other genres and modes have shown themselves to be hardier, less dependent on just the right cultural conditions.

However, it remains a necessity to conclude that tragedy *is* a bona fide genre. This truth is most easily perceived when tragedy is contrasted with the tragic modes. Tragedy, on the one hand, figurally *disperses* political power, according to such conflictual schemes as self versus other or others, even gods, or self versus self. The tragic modes, on the other hand, *take power away* from the agonists and, by extension, from others, substituting knowledge or enlightenment instead. When the enemy loses as in Aeschylus, or when the hero loses his or her life. yet wins integrity, as in Sophocles, or when the winner loses all, as in Euripides, the prospect is power, the game is public, the consequences are historical, the audience's experience is of communal strengthening. That is tragic genre proper. But when the enemy is oneself "outside" history, as in Büchner's *Lenz* or Dostoyevsky's *Notes from Underground,* or when the agonist's achievement of integrity is almost totally private as in *The Death of Ivan Ilyich,* or when the winner's victory is indistinguishable from his loss, as in *Death in Venice,* then the prospect is powerlessness, the game's spell is broken by naturalism, the consequences are merely psychological, and the reader's experience is of alienating knowledge. That is tragic modalism in the novella.

The difference between tragic genre and mode is internal as well as contrastive, for it lies in a difference of medium. Tragedy proper is "said" while tragic modes are sung, danced (pace Nietzsche), expressed in forms other than spoken or declaimed words, such as music, choreography, or omniscient indirect narration. From the Messenger's report on Salamis in the *Persians* to the obsessive discussions among actual revolutionaries in *Danton's Death*, tragedy is the preeminently verbal mimetic genre. Comedy, dependent on timing and mistiming, is closer to dance than tragedy. There may be entirely adequate comedy without words—witness the supremacy of comedy during the silent film era—but silent tragedy, notwithstanding dumbshows, is artificial, empty gesticulation. Ballet and opera can manage tragic modalism, but not even *Tristan und Isolde* or *Giselle* is a tragedy. The very disparateness of words and music introduces into the action ambiguities that contradict the stark clarities of structure mandated by tragedy. The music will always "soar," will always carry the audience permanently away from the action, back, inward, into the music itself—this is the "formal" reason Nietzsche broke with Wagner and Pound failed to incise Attic outlines onto opera. Not even the Büchner of Berg's *Wozzeck*, which as a play is proper tragedy, can cut through the self-sufficient ambiguity of the music; and though Kurt Weill's anti-operatic musical aesthetic applied to Brecht can generate aesthetically self-sufficient parody, it falls well short of tragedy. Ballet more closely approximates at least the form of tragedy, but it does so in the manner of athletic agons such as boxing. By simulating tragic conflicts in the physical movements of disparate bodies in space, ballet can ape tragic teleology, but the victory, loss, or stalemate it can suggest retains the ghostly status of suggestion.

Only film, of all the contemporary mimetic media, can cope with the verbality of tragedy. It is a popular medium of great historical and political power, as Eisenstein and Dovzhenko were deliriously aware earlier in this century. But the film medium is fatally superficial. Its oneiric qualities undercut its power of relatively direct mimesis: *Alexander Nevsky* is no *Prince Friedrich of Homburg* because the dreamlike naturalism of its visual dimension raises the element of spectacle above and beyond the action. Aristotle always deplored this capacity of spectacle to override, even usurp, the action borne by plot and *dianoia* and diction. Film automatically converts tragedies into hallucinations. This is the reason Dovzhenko abandoned cinema, first by refusing to violate the reality of suffering required by his wartime assignment to shoot documentary pictures of Nazi barbarities, then by returning to literature, which can always get beyond the visual because it never has to start with the visual.[2] On the other hand, the novella's purism as a verbal medium, compared with the kind of verbality in tragedy or with the kinds in Senecan reading tragedy and opera, not only prevents it from being tragedy but also confines it within the specific limits of a tragic mode. For the problem with the novella is the opposite of that with film. The novella's gain in intimacy, especially through indirect narration, keeps it private, ahistorical, completely lacking in the qualities of public display that overwhelm the inherently spectacular film medium, where even extreme close-ups inflate the real to the superreal.

This discussion of important generic implications of difference in medium, however, demonstrates the final inadequacy of developing generic traces as characteristics of medium. Tragedy is more than direct mimesis, after all, and it is something other than its elaborateness of forms or its ethical, religious, and cultural diversity of content. As power distribution according to configurations of victory, loss, and stalemate, tragedy is primarily agonistic action as such. It is power dispersal for its own sake. Thus it does not matter whether the outcome is precisely victory, loss, or stalemate. All three are tragic insofar as outcome itself is the point—and not the visualization or verbalization, not the Sophoclean or Euripidean "despair" at love's and friendship's inability to compensate for absolute injustice, not any conceivable moral meaning or tragic wisdom, not annihilation or Nietzchean collapse of individuation into the Mother of Being (*The Birth of Tragedy*, Section 16).

Tragedy is really, *as* outcome, a kind of epic. It certainly came out of epic, genetically, as both the *Persians* and the *Poetics* suggest. However, it is epic carved down in time—to an entire morning for one trilogy plus parody in Aristotle's time,[3] then to an "evening" later—to concentrate on the action's teleology. Tragic action is goal-intent. No Homeric wandering or delay is permitted, just the appallingly straight and narrow way toward victory, loss, or draw. Though they abound in classical tragedy, no Aristotelian reversals *(peripeteia)* are *required* of tragedy as a genre, neither from good fortune to bad nor from bad to good. Good fortune may turn with the tide ultimately, after generations of struggle, as in the *Oresteia*. Yet bad fortune may announce itself from the very outset, with the action proceeding down a perfectly straight track, as in *Antigone* and *Hippolytus*. Beyond fortune, the moral good may straightway win out, as in Sophocles' *Electra*, or it may be equally straightway doomed, as in *Medea*. Or there may be no moral dimension to the outcome at all, as in the stately linearity of the *Persians* or the stark rush of disaster in *Danton's Death*. Metaphysically, justice may serve as an elusive ideal at the beginning as well as the end of the action, as in Greek tragedy, or, transmogrified into love, justice may become a certainty of faith that is virtually preestablished in the subjective response, as in Christian tragedy. Chance may directly rend human designs, as in Euripides, or, transformed into indirect providence, uphold and vindicate them, as in Calderón. Fate may pit individual against history throughout the action, from beginning through middle to end, as in *Philoctetes*, or it may create the individual out of history in ways perhaps obscured yet traceable from the beginning, as in *Prince Friedrich of Homburg*.

Does the law of tragic genre, then, consist simply in the *purposiveness* of Aristotle's "action," its teleological movement from motive (beginning) through episodes (middle) to outcome (end)? Rather than its purposiveness, the *contest* infusing the action with the potential of victory, loss, or stalemate is the thing. Yet this essence lacks all content, as I have argued. Instead, the ground of tragic genre is contest *as* law, the tautology of tragic action as such. Thus, too, is the power of tragedy always political, in the sense of power deployed in history toward outcome. Tragic action as such is the inevitability of strife, individuation in the world necessitated by disparateness in space and time, the opposite of Nietzsche's Dionysian collapse into the Mother of Being. This law of contest between concrete disparates, not between moral or metaphysical or even formal occasions and abstractions, is the generic imperative that indeed makes tragedy a *kind* of epic and not simply an outgrowth of epic. Tragedy is, then, short epic.

Moreover, contest as the law of tragic action as such is the armature of comedy and all other action genres as well. The difference between tragedy, which may be understood as genre itself or as the purest manifestation of genre among all the directly mimetic action genres, and epic, comedy, opera, or ballet lies not in medium nor even in form. Instead, the difference lies in the *selection of outcomes*, with its final cause in power itself and efficient cause in the creative imagination of the maker and consumer.[4] Homer's epic includes all three issues of tragic action—victory, loss, and stalemate—and each receives fairly equivalent aesthetic emphasis. Thus the *Iliad* produces the victory of the Greeks; several losses of the equally worthy Trojans (they are not denigrated for the Greeks' sake as the Persians are in Aeschylus), as well as the losses of the individual agonists, Hector and Achilles; and the stalemate of history as time passing. Unlike the *Oresteia*, with its history of progressive victory; unlike *Philoctetes*, with its "victory" of progressive history stalemated by the struggle between hero and destiny; and unlike *Medea* and *Heracles* with their regressive victories of nature collapsing into divinity collapsing into history over the progressive protagonists, the *Iliad* remains unaltered in its historical direction by the end of the epic action. The *Odyssey* also includes a full complement of tragic outcomes: Odysseus's victory over the suitors, his loss of his comrades, and the stalemate of history's stasis, as in the *Iliad*.

Comedy and the separate action genres that may assume the comic mode as well as the tragic, such as French melodrama, ballet, and opera, always of course issue only in victory. This is the victory of either nature plus reason attuned to nature (Aristophanic and Roman comedy, farce, Shakespearean romantic comedy, Molièresque comedy), or nature plus transcendent faith (tragicomedy, as in *The Winter's Tale*), or bourgeois sentiment (melodrama), or religiosity fused with sensuality and *l'art pour l'art* (opera and ballet). Comedy admits of no uncompensated or untranscended loss, and stalemate would stifle both the *rire* and the *sourire*. Besides, stalemate would contradict the formal object of comedy, which is relief from tension, while tragic stalemate is the acutest pitch of tension. If the generic law of tragedy requires one of the three outcomes, it may be *any* one. But comedy is ultraselective: *only* victory is allowed.

Thus tragedy falls midway between epic's all-inclusiveness of outcomes and comedy's exclusiveness. In quantitative terms, then, tragedy's power is not so massive as epic's, but because of its concentration in any one of the three outcomes, it is more effective aesthetically and more affective psychologically. Thus Aristotle can be accounted for, who claims the superiority of tragedy over epic; and his insistence on catharsis could be redefended by arguing that tragedy's solutions are total, as outcomes, while comedy's resolutions merely defer or repress the terror and pity. Comedy is indeed light, but in a quantitative rather than moral or spiritual or metaphysical sense.

Power dispersal as the non-essence substance of the law of genre not only provides a matrix establishing a simple, nongenetic relation among the action genres. It also suggests that tragedy is the only pure genre, with epic assuming the status of the progenitor genre, and comedy, that of specialized genre. Consequently, the theory of tragedy both leads to the theory of epic and covers the theory of comedy. One might then well abandon the attempt to contrast epic with tragedy and instead explore the hermeneutic problems posed by the ending of the *Iliad*, for example, namely the presence of Achilles' and Hector's tragedies as they evolve *within* the epic. Equally sensible would be an approach to comedy that would get underneath the exclusive teleology of victory and the aesthetic form of release, to what might be called the tragic substrata—the absences of loss (cancelled) and stalemate (deferred or bypassed). Certainly comedies such as the *Clouds*, *Twelfth Night*, Molière's *Don Juan* and *Le Malade imaginaire*, and Beaumarchais's *Le Mariage de Figaro* would benefit from this approach, as would modernist works supposedly in the comic mode, such as Beckett's novels and plays, Musil's *The Man without Qualities*, *Ulysses,* and *The Metamorphosis.*

Most important, though, the notion of generic power dispersal can lay a bridge between literature and aesthetics on the one hand and cultural history on the other. The results of this spanning conception could go well beyond the usual, fairly obvious correlations of the vulgar, or sociological, Marxist critique rightly scorned by Lukács. It could be more precise in its hermeneutics than Foucault's power-knowledge nexus, as well as less exclusively cognitive in its insights. It could avoid the utopian New Left implications of Habermas's critique of ideology, which articulates cultural "fantasies of hope" (288). And it could fulfill the scenario set by Fredric Jameson for a complete Marxist dialectics of culture. For genre, tragic genre above all, would be the required nonessentializing mediatory tool for understanding society's own power configurations of victory, loss, and stalemate: "The strategic value of generic concepts for Marxism clearly lies in the mediatory function of the notion of a genre, which allows the coordination of immanent formal analysis of the individual text with the twin diachronic perspective of the history of forms and the evolution of social life" (Jameson 105). But I shall delay development of this general theory of genre until the concluding chapter.

CHAPTER FOUR

Satires

POLONIUS: What do you read, my lord?

HAMLET: Words, words, words.

POLONIUS: What is the matter, my lord?

HAMLET: Between who?

POLONIUS: I mean the matter that you read, my lord.

HAMLET: Slanders, sir; for the satirical rogue says here that old men
   have gray beards, that their faces are wrinkled, their eyes purging
   thick amber and plum-tree gum, and that they have a plentiful lack
   of wit, together with most weak hams. All which, sir, though I
   powerfully and potently believe, yet I hold it not honesty to have
   it thus set down; for you yourself, sir, should be old as I am if,
   like a crab, you could go backward.

POLONIUS: [Aside.] Though this be madness, yet there is method in't.
   Will you walk out of the air, my lord?

HAMLET: Into my grave?

POLONIUS: Indeed, that's out of the air. [Aside.] How pregnant sometimes
   his replies are! A happiness that often madness hits on, which reason and
   sanity could not so prosperously be delivered of. [*Hamlet* 2.2. 190-209]

When Hamlet answers Polonius's question with "words, words, words," he
demonstrates with some knowingness the slippery seminature of satire.
Tragedy's action is constituted by history's own specifically political action,
the power differential expressible as the threefold possibility of the historical world: victory, loss, stalemate. Satire, properly speaking, has no
action, just signifiers—words. These words have their bite, their edges,
yet these edges lack the sharpness of mimetic-political action. Instead,
they possess intention, or aim. Hamlet the satirist rhetorizes until Hamlet
the tragic hero kills. He is Sophocles' Electra and Orestes combined: the
satirist denounces, sometimes like Electra under a frail cover of irony,
biding time for the hero, who will act, like Orestes.

Accordingly, the directionality of satiric "words, words, words" is dual, indeed split. While the target remains the same, namely Polonius, one satiric intention is to criticize, to evaluate him rationally, the other to luxuriate in the irony inhering in the words. Thus Hamlet's satire obliquely takes the measure of the obnoxiously rheumy old courtier, whose "weak hams" are the result of a lifetime of bending ingratiatingly to political power. Yet as Hamlet's satiric mirror reflects the Polonian type for those who "read," it also reflects back upon its own verbal nature: Hamlet the rhetorician goes where his ironies will; some of them hit their target, others are transformed into ludic elaboration. Polonius the fool, unable to see though he senses Hamlet's satire, is still no idiot: there *is* method in the madness. He himself responds, albeit ignorantly, to the "happiness that often madness hits on." That is, Polonius as "reader" interrupting Hamlet "reading" acknowledges the rhetorical capacity of language, its gesturalism. Satire *means* to criticize, to aim reason at targets; but in the very act of critique, satire wanders its own verbalizing way—"Words, words, words." Were Hamlet here not the complete satirist, Polonius would not be uncertain whether he really is the target. Thus Hamlet's words strike without the victim's knowing what is hitting him, only *that* it hits.

Where, then, does all this mad method lead? Hamlet the ironist guards himself against exposure as a planner of revenge-justice, and he makes a foolish if cunning enemy uncomfortable. Yet, mainly, Hamlet reveals the futility of satire with its split rhetorical directionality: words cannot achieve the finality of action, whether it be winning, losing, or stalemating. What can achieve this finality in *Hamlet*? Only the grave. But that is the destination of the tragic Hamlet, not the satirist, and, too, the destination of Polonius the butt. Perhaps, though, we can pull up somewhat shy of Hamlet's ultimate end and focus on what he *does* achieve, or fail to achieve, as a satirist, one whose madness-feigning "reason and sanity" both "deliver" their critique and miss their target altogether.

First of all, this seemingly necessary self-contradictory movement of satire suggests that standard notions of genre itself are futile. At the least these notions must be adjusted before they will fit genres that lack the coherence of tragedy, with its definitive movement toward outcome. If genre possesses a definable nature, then it may well be that an elusive genre such as satire may not after all be a genre. So have many literary historians been tempted to conclude. If, however, the indefinability of genre is accepted, the case of satire may in fact indicate that we should consider genre as a thoroughly historical phenomenon. If genre is power, always inconstant, stabler or less stable, it becomes perfectly responsive to the contradiction in satire between its rational aims and its instrumental yet independent ironies.

Indeed, all satire is a sensitive litmus for genre as power. For unlike tragedy's operation, satire's is unstable, only semigeneric. It is not anti-generic, because satire's instability does not mean generic self-cancellation; nor do its contradictions call into question the concept of genre as such. A kind that is only a semigenre, satire after all *works* by being self-contradictory. Something at the historical core of this genre accounts for this irony of satiric irony, as it is grotesquely evident in the satiric traditions, both literary and oral, of the oppressed. Irish satirists from Swift to Shaw and Joyce in the very process of getting even with the British both reveal and maintain their humiliating situation of powerlessness. Similarly, American blacks "puttin' on ole massa" display and in displaying underwrite the master's continuing power over them. This dominance forces the dominated to adopt satiric irony as their last defense: this is the reason why George Jackson, in *Soledad Brother,* declares—"tragically"—for dangerous straight talk, spurning irony and the other inmates' safely covert wiseacre language. Satire as an unstable semigenre both empowered and entrapped by "words, words, words" dramatically figures the frustration of being less powerful than one wishes to be—Hamlet's frustration at being able to do no more than amuse himself shadowboxing with Polonius the appendage, when his desire is to kill the real power, Claudius. Definitely the theory of genre must accommodate this historically problematic modus operandi of satire.

The set of operations in both Augustan verse *satura* and Menippean prose narrative *satura* shows, in midwork, a marked shift into modes of other genres, particularly tragedy (Juvenal and, later, Swift) and the novel (Petronius and, later, Cervantes and Twain). The reason for this instability is that satiric deployments of power are hampered by their dependence on rationality. As such, they prove unable to resolve dilemmas caused by the genre's concern with matters of morality, society, taste, and religion as they are *rationally perceived* rather than *politically engaged.* Ironies are the result of rational-satiric critiques, which want definitive outcomes yet cannot get them because the discursive formation appropriate to critique is rhetorical-evaluative instead of mimetic-political. Hamlet's satire merely covers him, but his mousetrap tragedy fully activates his plan for justice. Outcomes are the result of political-tragic actions, which "do" rather than "want," whatever the moral, social, or religious concerns may be.[1]

Satire thus resides at a kind of midpoint along the range of genres conceived as varying configurations of power. A semigenre, this originally Roman genre never can resolve the problems it apprehends rhetorically, according to standards of rational evaluation. Typically it turns away from gestural critique to assume a more completely ironic stance. This specifically satiric irony is a matter of "words, words, words" aimed at discrepancies between equally verbal values and rationales, while tragic irony discloses the abyss between these verbalisms and what happens. Satiric irony ends up either leaning back toward the nonevaluative and absolute solutions of action-based tragedy, or turning forward toward the developmental ontology fully possible only in the realist novel of the eighteenth and nineteenth centuries, and later, in the self-conscious fiction of the twentieth century. Or satiric irony may yearn entirely away, toward the freedom from all rational rule that has always been possible through fantasy, as in the second half of *Don Quixote.*

At this point, however, especially since my focus in this chapter is on satires as they have evolved historically, I need to dig around the undeniably earthy roots of satire, instead of luxuriating in the prospects the case of satire affords the theory of both genre itself and the range of genres. For indeed satires compose one of the traditional kinds. Yet it remains the least reputable, probably because satiric techniques are patently reductive: low gestures impugn and revile those who are unjustly high and secure. So satire's ill repute as a genre itself becomes satiric: Why crudely and cruelly deplore crudity and cruelty unless they do adhere to the target? Satire, in other words, can never exactly be wrong. It reduces the already reduced, or a least the reducible. True enough, any particular satire may in fact be libelous or may be judged to be erroneous. But the peculiar power of genre to waive factuality is nowhere more clearly evinced than in satire, the genre commonly acknowledged to be either altogether nonfictional— especially by its really intended targets—or closer to the factual realm, in its topicality, than any other. Satire may occasionally be proved a function of a distortion in the satirist's nature, such as Swift's scopophilia or Juvenal's sour grapes as a member of the rentier class. It may be easily demonstrated to be wrong in particulars of reference, as is the depiction of Royal Society empiricism in Book III of *Gulliver's Travels.* It may be charged with self-contradictoriness, such as that characterizing Twain's attitude toward technology and technocracy in *A Connecticut Yankee.* Nevertheless, the satiric flash of illumination, however arbitrary or garish, permanently prints its negative on the reader's inner eye. Once satirized, a target can never thereafter appear free from suspicion or completely conceal the scars. Genre triumphs over strict justice in satire, which combines the scurrility of rumor with the intrinsic authority of literature.

Thus satire consists in literary strategies for gaining moral, social, religious, or political ascendancy by reasoned demonstration that its high targets really are what they have been from the start—low. If the literary genres are discursive configurations of power, satire is the selection of necessarily rational means for attaining symbolic superiority over its targets. For only rationality can display this kind of ascendancy. The exercise of superior power with little or no regard for rationality, as happens in tragic mimesis for example, can result in win-loss-draw configurations. But since the power differential in itself, which tragedy purely mimes in its action, has nothing to do with rationality but only with power, reasoned proof that high really is low becomes the specialty of a genre that is rhetorical rather than mimetic in its operations. Through reason, rhetoric can ascribe the *values* of high and low to undeserved victories, as in Swift's attack on Marlborough; to losses, as in Twain's condemnation of lynchers; and to stalemates, as in Pope's maligning of the self-canceling "successes" of Cibber's and Blackmore's careers. But the realm of mimesis can never, not even through Aeschylean combinations of ideology and justice or through Euripidean disasters, adequately demonstrate that the high *de-serves* to be reduced. Even Athena must resort to "Persuasion" in the *Eumenides* to rationalize Olympian superiority over the Furies—words explaining but not constituting the goddess's real power as it controls the mimesis, her "father's thunderbolts." Satire's reliance on reason and rhet-oric suggests, furthermore, that *irrational* "satire," whether nihilistic or affirmatively absurdist, is really not satire at all, but black comedy. Only when unreason is made to appear coincident with reason, for example, at the conclusion to the first part of *Don Quixote* or throughout Hašek's *The Good Soldier Švejk*, can the rational-rhetorical genre satire retain its identity while accommodating absurdity.

Except accidentally, thus contradictorily, justice is not possible in the historical world of entrenched institutional orders, caught as it is in the vise of interest and convention or buffeted by the winds of prejudice. Consequently, the satirist must sidestep the schematic of law; this is the reason why satire may slide into slander, *infamia*, desperate for at least the semblance of justice, or poetic justice. The simulation alone is available to the justice-seeking satirist since the law itself appears from a satiric per-spective to be still another device of injustice. Like the Senecan tragic mode, satire, in its historical origin as Roman *satura*, proceeds from a sense that the basis of social order, law, is eventually abandoned by that same order, leaving the expectant yet disillusioned citizen with hollowness at heart and rage in the brain. Moreover, it is not insignificant that the professions of law and medicine are customary butts. Representing man's overweeningly rationalist attempts to save health from disease and injury, order from lawlessness and vice, doctors and lawyers always fail to make the world either healthy or safe while they profit institutionally as holders-out of hope. Satire, like Euripidean tragedy of winner-loses-all in this respect, shows that nothing works as it should.

Because of this semblance-to-semblance relationship between satiric aim and reality, hypocrisy—which always *looks* just, poetically, like the satire it elicits—is the satirist's favorite target. This is the sin of officialness predictably attacked head-on by Juvenal in his "Second Satire" or Hašek in *The Good Soldier Švejk,* but also excoriated by Christ the satirist, in such litanies as "Scribes, pharisees, hypocrites." So satire's true lineage may be high indeed. Likewise, its operations are not only typically rough but complex and even subtle as well. Irony in particular, though not a special preserve of satire, lends the genre its intimacy of connection between speaking subject and the subjected, its openness to misunderstanding (Kuiper)—and, intriguingly, its artsiness, whether leavening an otherwise obvious Juvenalian bluntness with effects of tragic sensitivity or the obliquity of Cervantes with multiple moral, metaphysical, religious, and aesthetic ironies. For of all the decentering strategies of literature, satiric irony may be the most slippery, both thematically and linguistically: "Irony never shows itself as such, but dis-places the signs on which it works, and reminds language of its integral ability, 'to signify *something quite other than it says*'" (Lacan 155).

Yet however high or sophisticated, satire exudes a savor that remains richly crude. Verbally, satire is a richer genre than tragedy, epic, lyric, or nonsatiric comedy. All the vulgarities men are capable of saying or conceiving spring to life from satire's aggressive heat.[2] Formal satiric anger— "formal" because necessarily controlled, as literature, and not actual—the savage indignation of Juvenal, Swift, Céline, or Grass, ignites the satiric imagination, which delights in explosions of imprecations and dirty names and luxuriates in a vocabulary of heavy irony, odiousness, and irritation.

This naturalist bent of satire, though, is both a strength and a weakness. The genre's assumption of rational superiority represents no victory over either hypocrisy or vice and folly. The satiric stance is, rather, an admission of defeat. Despair is the formal source of satire's formal fury. And there can be no resolution to this despair within the moral, social, religious, or political confines of satiric attitudes. All by themselves, without either the transcendental immediacy of prophecy, the pressure of tradition, or the institutional backing of the law, morality, taste, doctrine, and factional ideology become the special resort of a kind of literature that lacks the political schematics of Athenian tragedy or the historical dynamics of the eighteenth- and nineteenth-century novel. It must be remembered that satire, although practiced earlier by Ennius, Lucilius, and Varro, came into its own just before, during, and shortly following the reign of Augustus, whose imperial policies after the civil wars may have perfected the administrative machinery of law and order, but only at the price of an intimidated, passive senate, a disemboweled popular morale, and a vitiated standard of public taste. By contrast, the ideological optimism and progress espoused by eighteenth- and nineteenth-century bourgeois culture eventually substituted earnestness for the complaisant morality of manners and wit reigning, with the help of such satirists as Pope and Voltaire, during the Enlightenment.

Satire, it would appear, thrives either when there is little credence in public standards of morality and taste, as in first-century Rome, or when morality and taste attenuate to superficial, arbitrarily strict codes of decorum, as in Augustan London. But the satiric impulse wilts when there is a domineering political consensus, as in the Athens of Pericles and Aeschylus, then expands in a climate of democracy verging on chaos, as during the subsequent era of Aristophanes. It also retires when there is an oppressive official sanguinity, as in Victorian England, but flourishes within a context of stultifying bureaucratism, as the case of Gogol and other czarist satirists shows. The consequence of satire's delicate poise between too much faith and none at all—between too successful politics and complete political collapse, and between overly conventionalized public standards and utter civic cynicism—is that the satiric genre is unstable. If political renewal has been the hope, satire characteristically veers off into tragedy, as in Juvenal and Ralph Ellison. If religious transcendence is looked for, satire slides into fantasy and romance, as in Cervantes and probably much of the apparently antireligious surreal Latin American fiction of today. If gradual historical amelioration is the panacea, satire subsides into other genres such as the realist novel, as in Twain, Thackeray, and feminist fiction starting with such cautiously satiric, noncomic works as Charlotte Brontë's *Villette.*

Tragedy, comedy, epic, and lyric with their Greek origins all escape reality rather handily, by becoming art. Poor satire, a genre first thrown together (as is betrayed by the etymology, *satura,* or farrago) *as* a genre by the crasser Romans, remains stuck in the mire of life as it insists on being in defiance of the rational shapes superimposed on it by satirists. Indeed, as the best satirists have often pointed out, life is its own satire and satire is hard put to outdo reality. The mirror is the appropriate figure not for the novel of Stendhal or the Aristotelian drama Hamlet recommends to the players, but for the satiric genre of Petronius. His nervily accepting irony, unlike the hysterical "tragedies" of his antagonist, Seneca, virtually reflects the excesses recorded by Suetonius and Tacitus—albeit within the margin of safety always enjoyed by satire yet not afforded to tragedy even when it is in the nonperformable Senecan "reading" mode.

Paradoxically, the ultimate source of satiric despair, human nature as a "no exit," also turns out to be the satirist's only secure standard: the "natural" opposed as corrective to the perverted. Furthermore, to grasp and not merely recognize this "natural," the audience of satire typically must already share the satirist's values as they serve to define human nature: "Satire may seem chaotic or nihilistic, but in reality it is more often traditional, if not conservative. Its positive values are so implicit, are offered with such elaborate obliquity of surprise and such sudden dénouement, that in order to communicate themselves they must be venerably familiar. (Postmodern underground satire proves the rule: it is addressed to true believers who already share the satirist's views.) A distinctive value of satire is its strangely secure candor—as if confident that truth exposed is better than truth colored or made bearable" (Fowler 66-67).

If, then, both satirist and audience agree that the target is targetable in the first place for violating the appropriately human, where is the despair? Surely the stability of the satiric standard, which is human nature, would entail at least the potentiality of redemption in the object of denunciation or irony, which is human nature again. Actually satirists love what they deplore; their despair is formal, rhetorical, gestural. As deconstructionists from Nietzsche to de Man and Derrida have amply demonstrated, *aporia* inserts itself between literature's desire to be constative and its linguistic praxis as gestural play. Nowhere is this *aporia* more evident than in satire, which negates what it advances as critique because of its despairing allegiance to human nature. When Don Quixote consoles Sancho, downcast from the blanketing he has suffered at the castle that is an inn, he explains, from a firmly Christian perspective, that those who have humiliated Sancho cannot be human, for they have behaved inhumanely: "What else can those be, who have so atrociously diverted themselves with you, but phantoms or beings from another world?" (117). But, of course, from Cervantes' satiric perspective they are perfectly human in having perpetrated such cruelty. And no wonder Brecht, during a different epoch, aspired in *The Measures Taken* to a theater of genuinely political action that would break free from the undialectical quagmire of human nature ironically represented in *Mother Courage*.

Thus satire is a semigenre only, a genre that stops itself from becoming a fully distinct alternative to other genres, and for two principal reasons. It is unstable as a genre in that it must detour around its perplexity about human nature by constantly seeking its resolutions outside itself, by subordinating itself to being a mode coloring or supplementing other, more dominant genres, especially tragedy and the novel, and, in return, acquiring color or determination from them. For in satire there are no built-in, absolute outcomes such as victory, loss, and stalemate in tragedy; no wondrous singularity of outcome as there is in comedy; and no sure teleology such as that prescribed by the novel, which as a form means development instead of stasis, open-endedness instead of closure, progressive ideology instead of eternal verities.

Satire is unstable in yet another sense owing to this suspension between attacking human nature and retreating to human nature. It is unstable as a linguistic maneuver, or set of moves, between a constative end—reduction of the already reduced or reducible—and a gesticulative modus operandi—irony. If on the one hand it wishes to correct the redeemable, as satirists from Horace to Ben Jonson and beyond have contended, satire curtails or at least hems in the irony inherent in its language structure. If on the other hand it wishes ludic freedom, as evinced, for example, in the stellation of Belinda's lock at the end of Pope's mock epic, it abandons generic impulses to reduce and substitutes opposite hankerings: perhaps to expand lyrically, as throughout *The Rape of the Lock*, perhaps to fantasize, as in Part Two of *Don Quixote*.

To catch satire as both a traditional genre and an unstable semigenre, it is necessary to start with the Romans, in whose culture it most nearly fulfills the criteria, described by Quintilian and others, for a bona fide genre. Juvenal's verse satires, although later than those of Horace, provide a sharper sense of both the general Roman prospect of satiric power and its historical antecedents back to Lucilius and including the less direct Horace. But we must next proceed to consider what even the Roman theorists and satirists themselves deemed a subgenre of satire, a distinct category that over time grew prolific in deviations from generic vectors: Menippean satire. Petronius's fragmentary *Satyricon* is already a case of satire allowed, by the tradition made Roman by Varro at the turn of the second and first centuries B.C., to slip into something half like picaresque novel, half like aggressive anti-epic or the softer mock heroic—with echoes of the Hellenistic Greek "novel" as well. Later, from the Renaissance on, a complex instance, thus one of the most fruitful for critical inquiry, of unstable Menippean satire is the Quixotic narrative. A selection of examples, from Cervantes' "novel" to Samuel Butler's burlesque poem, *Hudibras*, then on to Twain's early modern *A Connecticut Yankee* and Jaroslav Hašek's post-World War One *The Good Soldier Švejk*, should cover a sufficiently wide range, across many times and cultures, of developments in Menippean satire as a consistently unstable semigenre.

Juvenal: Satire to Tragedy

Roman satire from the first century A.D. is, of course, as varied a dish as the etymology would suggest: *satura*, a spicy mixture of foods, or farrago. All the generic registers, however, from suave Horatian to savage Juvenalian, as well as all the conventional forms, from verse parody of epic (Juvenal), verse epistle-essay (Horace), anti-Virgilian mock heroic (Sextus Propertius), to Menippean prose travel fiction cum verse interspersions (Petronius), are indelibly imprinted with Roman values and perplexities. These are both consistent in themselves and, as "neoclassicism," perennial, as shown by later variants of these satiric strains from Ben Jonson to Ezra Pound.

Juvenal's generic contribution extends well beyond the "Juvenalian" stance and pitch of *saeva indignatio*, which fuses brutish energy with painful moral sensibility. In a narrower sense of genre—for any genre can generate or assume savage indignation—Juvenal sets his kind of satire definitionally against epic. The programmatic "First Satire" is his preface to a kind of aesthetic composition that has its forebears, to be sure, particularly Lucilius and Horace, both of whom are explicitly mentioned. Yet Juvenal's own understanding of his generic status requires not only a sense of acknowledgment but also a distinctive prospect representing a break away from classical literary codes. The satirist, Juvenal contends, is neither an epic nor a tragic poet, but a truth teller. Accordingly, he spurns "boring" and "frivolous" myth with its characteristic values, which are no longer real or alive to a first-century Roman, and declares in favor of truth. But not because he *wishes* to become a truth teller: Juvenal's *persona* is compelled to write satire—"Difficile est saturam non scribere":

> When that spawn of the Nile, Curly the Cur of Canopus [or, in the
> original and most translations, "Crispinus," the actor and favorite of
> Domitian],
> Hitches his crimson cloak with a jerk of his idiot shoulder,
> Air-cools his summer ring, or tries to—his fingers are sweating—
> And is unable to stand the burden of one more carat,
> Then it is difficult NOT to write satire. [*Satires* 1.25-29]

So satire as literature first satirizes itself. It deliberately reduces itself to expose, lowers itself with artful display from high values of myth, epic, and tragedy to treat what the satirist claims he cannot avoid seeing although he would like to. Satire departs, of necessity, even from the "mother" genre of literature. Instead, Juvenal's genre will situate itself in Rome's streets; "everything human" (*Satires* 1.81) will sooner or later pass by, and the satirist need not await anything so lofty as a Muse: "How can you help but fill whole notebooks? Stand at the crossroads" (*Satires* 1.63). Moreover, since ancient genre, like medieval, is often defined primarily according to meter, Juvenalian satire becomes metrically anti-epic. Its dactylic hexameters, with their termination of lines in deadpan, forecast the famous technique in Pope's arsenal for the "art of sinking in poetry" *(Peri Bathous)*, which parodies contemporary derivatives of Homeric and Virgilian styles. This distorted echo of epic in Juvenalian satire is not sounded in homage. The trivializing, clackety measure is appropriate to Juvenal's ironically down-sized scale, which precisely negates epic scope just as the Imperial Rome of Claudius, Nero, and Domitian has itself exchanged the grand scale of the Roman world up to Virgil's Augustus for no scale, no stature, at all.

A genre decrying degeneracy, however, requires rhetorical equipoise. The Juvenalian attitude is tense, and the tension derives from a deep opposition that may assume multiple thematic insignia, most of them already commonplace yet all canted with a markedly Juvenalian style: past versus present, heterosexual fertility versus homosexual sterility, patrician warrior fathers versus prodigal sons, education versus fashion, respectable poverty versus dissolute wealth, native Roman versus foreigner (especially Egyptian and Greek, a bias supposedly reflecting Juvenal's probable exile to Hellenistic Egypt for a time), county versus city, sense versus Fortune, Epicurean (but not Epicurus himself) versus Stoic and Cynic, and production by independent but oppressed farmer versus consumption by haughty but slavish patrician.

Underlying all these oppositions is the generative paradox of "nature," which operates as both the positive force of "the natural," or the unperverted, and the defining limit enclosing man's "nature" within a range of moral possibilities, from evil and stupid to good and wise. As "the natural," this nature of Juvenal's functions in noble Roman style as stern yet beneficent patriarch: "Nature never dictates one thing and Wisdom another" (*Satires* 14.321). As "the essentially human," Juvenalian nature is a moral matter, yet it encompasses such a bewildering variety of behaviors that the satires cumulatively point to no clear moral path, at least doctrinally. Not exactly eclectic in moral philosophy, Juvenal endorses more Epicurean tendencies than Stoic, deploring both fatalism and optimism. Finally, this Juvenalian moral human nature is a leveled, almost neutral totality of good and bad, wise and banal: "This is the way things are, and all share a common nature" (*Satires* 13.166).

"The natural," then, is a discriminating concept that enables Juvenal to assume the stance of a morally superior denouncer in control of his genre. But the "common nature" of "the way things are" is an intrinsically expansive concept that pushes the satirist beyond moral grounds toward a paradox of tragic potential:

> My Muse is assuming, too grandly,
> Tragedy's buskin and mask . . .
> . . . and mouthing a theme, in Sophocles' manner,
> Foreign to Latin skies. [*Satires* 6.634-38]

These two tendencies of Juvenalian "nature," to restrict and to open out, are not fully contradictory, and in the reading they may even appear to be complementary. Yet they steer the satiric fervor in divergent directions, disabling satire from its relentless tracking of targets while accelerating it toward its announced destination. Juvenalian invective flails away at its targets yet never aims at their centers in the first place, but somewhere beyond. Juvenal is like Seneca the tragic moralist in this paradoxical breakdown of generic functioning. For Seneca, too, aims not at the core of horror in immorality, the sensationalist depiction of which is wrongly termed "the Senecan" in literary history, but beyond, at some void filled with an absence, with longing for a proto-Christian transcendence.

Perhaps the problematic of Juvenal's generic set of operations would come clearer if just one of his more important satiric butts is selected for analysis. The homosexual is one of the Juvenalian types particularly rich in possibilities created by the intersection of the satiric concept of "the natural" and the potentially tragic conception of "common nature," according to the options of loss and stalemate, if not victory. Like fourth-century Greeks (see Foucault, *Use*), Juvenal does not disapprove of homosexuality as a kind of sexuality that is in itself unnatural, perverted from a right course. Instead, he seems to concentrate on specific kinds of homosexuals, especially the young patrician, the hypocritical bisexual (both featured in the "Second Satire"), and the male prostitute (featured, not unkindly, in the "Ninth Satire")—and in that order, from worst to just unfortunate. Overt homosexuals who neither deny nor unduly celebrate nor exploit their proclivity, Juvenal "excuses":

I like Peribomius better; at least he's honest about it,
Shows what he is by his walk and his glances, so I can excuse him,
Him and his likes, whose urge is frank enough for forgiveness.
Worse, much worse, are the ones who denounce, with a Hercules' anger,
Vice, and waggle their tongues about Virtue, and waggle their rear ends.
. . . .
This is confusion confounded. [*Satires* 2.16-25]

Moreover, Juvenal sidesteps both adulation of woman and misogyny. Indeed, he resorts to female prostitutes as unhypocritical, relatively moral *satirists* gibing at aristocratic homosexuals in the "Second Satire": "Media doesn't lap girls, nor Flora go down on Catulla" (line 49). Conversely, he lambasts patrician women in the "Sixth Satire."

What disturbs Juvenal is not men's homosexuality, nor women's hypersexuality for that matter, as a deviant sexual mode, but its sterility: "Sterile they die" (*Satires* 2.141). To the traditional Roman sensibility of Juvenal, homosexuality perverts, turning men, especially young patricians, whose responsibility is the greatest, away from their quintessentially Roman function, which is to preserve and extend the gens, that basis of upper-class identity in both individual and society. Family as the object of cult worship among Republican nobles such as the Fabii and the Gracchi is desecrated when Roman matrons abort or kill their own children ("Pontia" in 6.639-40); and it is equally violated by young nobles' "marrying" other men:

Gracchus has given a dowry, substance and sum, twenty thousand
To a cornetist, or maybe a type who plays the white flute.
. . . .
The bride, almost in a swoon, reclines in the arms of her husband.
O ye nobles of Rome, is our need for a seer or a censor?
Would you be startled more, be more aghast at the portent
If a woman bore a calf, or a cow dropped a ewe lamb?
Here's an ancient house, long privileged, under tradition
To carry Mars' nodding shields along in the holy procession,
Sweating under their weight, the hands through the thongs on the leather,
Yet here's a son of that house, a Gracchus, given in marriage,
All tricked out in a veil, in a bridal train, and in flounces!
Romulus, father—whence came disgrace like this on your shepherds?
Whence, father Mars, such an itch to fasten itself on your grandsons?
Here is a man renowned for wealth, distinguished in breeding,
Being wed to a man, and you do nothing about it,
Not one shake of the helm, no spear point grounded in protest;
Never an outcry to Jove! To hell with you, father Gradivus—
Leave the neglected plains, the fields we used to call Martian. [*Satires*
    2.117-35]

Waste of substance in endowing a man-bride is Juvenal's moral focus at the start of this vignette depicting what has happened to the Gracchi, and to Rome. As a matter of economy, such waste is like the gambling away of what properly used to be expended on war: "Epic occasions, these, with a secretary disbursing / Funds for the war" (lines 91-92, from Juvenal's earlier outburst against the public dole in the "First Satire"). And it is immediately connected with the aspect of homosexuality singled out for Juvenal's condemnation: the young Gracchus is squandering his own seminal "substance and sum," that is, depleting his gens as basic unit of generation and regeneration, through fellatio with "a type who plays the white flute." In doing so Gracchus flouts not only the old Republican Rome of aristocratic dominance, but also his own Imperial Rome, which in Virgil's Augustan vision is "Law-giver to the world"; for the "marriage" is technically unlawful according to Imperial edict, as well as unnatural according to the Juvenalian satiric code.

Gradually, however, Juvenal's vignette departs from the moral emphasis of the opening, which concentrates on the shocking picture of the "wedding" itself. Satire shifts into another, larger frame of political identity in history stretching back to the foundation of Rome by Romulus, and even further back, into the mythic past of Mars. This is the world of tragedy with its firm outcomes of victory, loss, or stalemate. The moral realm is always contingent upon men's choices, that of the young Gracchus, for example. The tragic realm, however, devolves on forces such as time, which is indifferent to individual decisions for good and bad. And tragedy issues in hard, incontrovertible realities such as the dissolution of Roman integrity. Only in these tragic terms, it would appear, can Juvenal resolve his original and originating satiric paradox: that the moral decline of the Gracchi into an unnatural waste of shame is also a tragic instance of entropic "common nature," the winding down of the vigorous old Roman force and the wasting away of its Martian identity.

Rhetorically the vignette moves abruptly from the image of the young Gracchus reclining in the embrace of his "husband" to the institutions, the seer and the censor, of a hale and rigorous old Rome. As if mindful of Livy, Juvenal next conjures up the ominous imagery of Second Punic War times, when Hannibal's inexorable advance pushed the superstitious Romans into a frenzy of visions of such as a rain of stones, women bearing calves, and cows birthing lambs. Thus the meaningless unnaturalness of the young Gracchus's wasting of his substance is juxtaposed as ironic parallel to the portentous monstrosities attested to by the citizens and leaders of a youthful, simpler Rome, which first found its identity in resisting collapse before the African conqueror's onslaught.

Then Juvenal briefly narrows his retrospect to bring the power and solemnity of family history to his moral condemnation of the young Gracchus. He sees the "ancient house" of the Gracchi duly bearing its share of Republican Rome's martial tradition, "sweating under their [shields'] weight," only to return to the unnatural scion "in flounces!" The contrast is too sharp to allow the satire to remain corseted by moral rigor. Consequently, Juvenal retreats into his tragic backward glance, resuming his scrutiny of Rome's past in his desperate search for sense. Backtracking through Romulus the human father all the way to Mars the divine father, the satirist-become-Euripidean sardonically questions Rome's august progenitors, "Whence, father Mars, such an itch?" In his search for an explanation, of course, Juvenal finds no *moral* account of what has happened to the Gracchi.

What he does find, to his despair, is irreversible loss through the natural agency of time. So when Juvenal once again returns to the present, to his original target, one of those aristocratic "hypocritical queens" (so-called in Humphries' title for the "Second Satire") abounding in Imperial Rome, the question he has just raised, seeking explanation in the divine and legendary sources of Roman identity, turns into a curse. For the Roman past, as time in its natural course running from its divine source in Mars, can "do nothing about" the young Gracchus, who, though a descendant of a key Roman family and thus "long privileged," is himself nothing but time as decline. Being one of the Gracchi, the homosexual aristocrat attacked satirically at first by Juvenal now appears to his denouncer as no longer significant enough to merit moral upbraiding. Instead, Juvenal attacks Mars himself, taunts him with neglect, of the "ancient house," which is both noble and corroded from its ancientness, and of all Rome by extension: "To hell with you, father Gradivus— / Leave the neglected plains."

At this point Juvenal is fully into a negation of the very identity and integrity of his beloved ideal of Rome, in the splayed metonymy "fields we used to call Martian." In *On Old Age*, Cicero's Cato, hopeful of renewal in the midst of declining time, envisions this same collapse of nature and Roman *vis*, virtue as self-perpetuating power, when he summons up the serial equation head of grain = Roman fasces = phallic vigor = military spear = stalk = Roman culture rooted in agriculture = the cycle of nature (25-26). Juvenal violently sunders Cicero's unified symbol of Roman identity as a nature-based civilization with powers vital as the earth because his excursion through the past to find a vantage for moral criticism in the present has overwhelmed his Roman sense of morality as "the natural" with the discovery of Roman time as equally natural rot. "Ripeness is all," for Juvenal as for Lear, means, tragically, that man's loss is just a puny register of all nature's degenerescence, of universal loss of "substance and sum." Thus Mars, masculine source of Roman power fruitfully wedded to nature, Rhea Silvia, is no longer an appropriate divine mark of cultural identity for a Juvenalian Rome of young aristocratic fags unnaturally spilling their seed, for mere pleasure, where it will fall sterile. A Lear-like curse is the just desert, not morally but poetically, for both a nature gone sterile and its formerly favored *civis* gone homosexual: "To hell with you . . ."

A satirist following the moral trajectory of his genre in search of a rational basis for condemning a young patrician's unnaturalness, Juvenal ends as a tragedian cursing the very nature of nature and of Roman history perceived as a natural phenomenon: time as loss of *vis*, power spent, decline and fall. Human nature should be natural, but it is perverted by time, which wears down a civilization that draws its sustaining force from nature. There is no breaking out of this circle of natures, thus no ground for moral outrage, just despairing acquiescence. From a compositional point of view, Juvenal's savage indignation chokes his satiric persona. Criticism turns to curse. And this curse strikes at the root and branch of his own great standard of all value, the Martian identity of Rome. Thus Juvenal the satirist ends by bitterly negating his own identity, his own source of vitality and value. *Satura* commits rhetorical suicide, just as any self-respecting patrician would upon discovering his own family's disgrace.

Generically stated, *satura* becomes a tragic mode in Juvenal. The catalyst for this conversion is the satirist's appeal to history for grounds suitable to moral judgment, for morality does not *finally* explain. It is a futile resort, of course, because history then appears to the satirist as the very process, completely natural, whereby the evil of today has taken hold: the slide of time. And this historical past has "done nothing about" what it has itself produced. In seeking, through reference to his cultural origins, a firm sense of political identity, the satirist finds his genre turned into a tragic mode. Juvenal, as we have seen, admits as much, and he does so despairingly. For to wear "too grandly, . . . / Tragedy's buskin . . . / . . . mouthing a theme, in Sophocles' manner, / Foreign to Latin skies," is to relinquish one's properly Martian identity of progressive *vis*, which is heterosexual, natural, and moral, and assume, horror of all Roman horrors, a "Greek" identity of historical loser, which is homosexual, unnatural, and tragic. Rome equals victory; Greece (also Egypt) is a victim, capable at most of producing effete, overeducated slaves—a constant theme throughout the sixteen *Satires*. Consequently, the necessity of facing up to "Greek" tragedy when he turns in delusory hopefulness to his own Roman past of political victory and progress—this de-generation of *satura* into tragic mode—amounts to the satirist's experiencing a specifically political crisis of identity. The conservative Juvenal finds nothing in his turn to the past to conserve. The past loses its integrity, the Gracchi degenerate into the young Gracchus, a "Greek" Roman man "marries" another "Greek" Roman man. From this tragic modalism of Juvenalian *satura*, political chaos ensues. While Aeschylus's Agamemnon and Aeschylus the hoplite himself both smote the "long-haired Persian," thus creating the possibility of Aeschylean tragedy of victory in the triumph of time, Juvenal's young Gracchus has become, through the de-generative narcissism of homosexuality, the very Greek he has historically subjugated as a generically virile Roman. Indignant satire is transformed into a mode of the Euripidean tragedy of winner-loses-all in the debacle of time as degenerescence.

Petronius: Satire to Novel

Instability within Juvenalian satire discloses another prospect, the tragic, which stretches beyond the tight compositions required by the motive and goal, the telos, of moral critique. In the case of Petronius, this same generic instability may account for the premature birth of a brand new genre, the thoroughly parodic, *Ulysses*-like novel of aestheticized realism. Lacking Juvenal's *saeva indignatio,* Petronius still starts like any other satirist from definite marks, but in keeping with his Neronian courtier's reputation, they are social rather than moral. Undeniably a master of Roman *satura,* Petronius has always been a glaring exception to the common rule that satire must be moral. Formally, Menippean satire in Petronius's version, in its loose and indeed wide-open format of travel narrative with verse interspersions, is less efficient for focusing on moral purposes than the compact, diatribelike Juvenalian verse satire. However, the expansive *Satyricon* provides ample opportunities for satiric ascendancy over social attitudes, practices, and tastes ranging from inferior to condemnable: intellectuals' finickiness as well as the brutality of nouveaux riches, frigid hypocrisy as well as emotional melodramatics, snobbery as well as crassness, hypersensitivity as well as insensitivity.

Yet the drive to say things as they are *for their own sake,* the same drive that made the doomed intimate of Nero send his master a meticulous account of debaucheries participated in by both the Emperor and his *arbiter elegentiae,* overwhelms the satiric scheme of the *Satyricon*:

> Then why in heaven's name
> must every nagging prude
> of Cato's ilk cry shame,
> denounce my work as lewd,
> damning with a look
> my guileless, simple art,
> this simple, modern book?
> To prudes I now assert
> my purity of speech;
> such candor in my pen
> as will not stoop to teach.
> I write of living men,
> the things they say and do,

> of every human act
> admitted to be true. [151]

Granted, there is disingenuousness here, for Petronius is neither simple, aesthetically speaking, nor pure in a moralistic sense (the specific context of the verse is a defense of Encolpius, or "Crotch," addressing his laggard penis). Still, the poem serves as well as any other fragment of the *Satyricon* the function of authorial credo. However, Petronius's realism is not Juvenal's "Difficile est saturam non scribere." Juvenal's irony is morally activated, Petronius's, aesthetically.[3] For the effect of Petronian irony is to absorb, not galvanize, the reader (or auditor, if Arrowsmith, Introduction x = xi, is right about the recital occasion for the episodes constituting the *Satyricon*). Readers are immersed in the vividly rendered detail of lives completely lacking in either moral consciousness or moral point. Nietzsche (cited by Arrowsmith) and Arrowsmith ("Luxury") are both right in characterizing Petronius's effect as liberating: we are deliriously free of morality itself while following Encolpius and his male lovers scudding before the hot breath of female agents of the "Wrath of Priapus." But it is neither amorality, as Nietzsche claims, nor a vague sense of essentially Roman élan vital, as Arrowsmith has it, that liberates us. On the contrary, it is Petronius's camera-eye sensibility that aesthetically frees us to open up to the precise thing, situation, feeling, each stupidity or falsity *described*. The pleasures of the *Satyricon* are akin to those available through St. Simon, Pepys, or Boswell in the realm of obsessive journal-keeping, or to those extractable from Defoe, de Sade, Proust, Joyce in the "Circe" and "Ithaca" chapters of *Ulysses*, or Robbe-Grillet in the fictional realm of aesthetic realism. What commences as satire in Petronius ends as the traditional rhetorical mode of sheer description.

A good example of how satire is neutralized by aesthetic realism appears in the "Croton" episode finishing the extant fragments of the *Satyricon*. The temporarily impotent wastrel and now murderer, Encolpius, is desperately trying to get retooled for the sake of Circe; so he goes to the "humble house" of Oenothea, a witchlike crone who assures him her herbs and incantations will make him like new. Considered satirically, the ironies are pointed enough: a hypersexed antihero's difficulties with the only point of his otherwise pointless existence give us a satiric prospect of the futility of Roman *vis* under the Twelve Caesars that is as enjoyable as those in Suetonius's histories or the "Second Satire" of Juvenal. Yet we find that the real point of Encolpius's visit to Oenothea's is to give a surprisingly detailed description, which is gratuitous to the degree of aesthetic self-sufficiency, especially when Petronius has his narrator note the hag's careful reinsertion of a nail in the "blackened wall":

In the center of the altar she set a rickety table which she heaped with glowing coals. She then reached down a wine cup, badly cracked with age, patched it with hot pitch and replaced the nail which had come away from the blackened wall when she took the winecup down. Next, she put on a square apron, placed a large clay pot on the hearth, and with a long fork took down from the cupboard an old sack in which she kept her stock of beans—along with an old, battered head of pork, badly nicked and sliced all over. She undid the bag, poured a pile of beans on the table and ordered me to shell them as quickly as possible. I did as I was told, slowly and laboriously separating each bean from the dirty pods with my fingers. Scolding me for a slowpoke, she snatched up the beans and ripped the husks away with her teeth, spitting them out on the floor like so many dried-up flies.

I was amazed at the inventiveness of her poverty and the skill, the loving frugal care displayed in every detail of that humble house. [155]

This mimesis, which is more than Auerbachian in its significant facticity, occurs in the midst of what many scholars regard as an overconventional, thinly fantastic stretch of the *Satyricon* dealing mainly with the social absurdities of legacy hunting, which in the "Croton" episode leads to civic cannibalism in a way characteristic of Juvenal's "Fifteenth Satire," written a good half-century later. Certainly the detail is no more and no less symbolic or scene-setting than similar detail in Zola or Dreiser. Yet its vividness, which matches that of the painted mastiff at Trimalchio's entrance, outdoes even that of Dutch genre painting, and its meticulousness is as hypnotic as a typical mise-en-scène of Tolstoy's. Why ever did Petronius, the clear-eyed ironist capable of satirizing every aspect of Imperial Roman mores and vogues, lull his audience with these stretches of prose-poetry celebrating *l'objet*?

The aestheticism of the *Satyricon* is much like that of Roman portrait statuary, those unidealized heads of statesmen and men of affairs; it is even more like Hellenistic bronzes of satyrs. But this superreal quality neither explains nor quite escapes the ever-present satiric irony playing about each bit of realism granted us by Petronius, irony that does not adhere to the stony busts or semipornographic Hellenistic miniatures. For one thing, it is precisely this aestheticism that Petronius mocks in his characterization of Encolpius, the narrator. Encolpius's sentiments, like those of the Pre-Raphaelites and even more like those of Stephen Daedalus, reach their maximum fervor in moments of onanistic ecstasy before examples of the fine arts and in situations of sexual overappreciation, homo or hetero, after tiffs with his lover Giton and companion-rival Ascyltus, situations marked by self-savoring rhetorical declamations in the "tragic manner."

Aestheticism in Petronius's anti-Odysseus narrator and pederast Nestors is more objectionable than the incapacity for aesthetic response in those oafish yet vital businessmen-slobs like Trimalchio and his friends. All may be Petronian butts, the effete to the crass. Yet as a weirdly gifted realist, Petronius the Joycean "novelist" establishes a warmly tense kinship with the Trimalchios, but only half-shares a neurasthenic sense of irony with Encolpius and his Nestors, who lack the balls to be outright satirical yet arch their eyebrows if something does not suit their taste. Petronius Arbiter may have been the ultimate snob himself, but his documented animosity toward Seneca shows that his snobbism was directed as much against his peers in intellectual elegance as against his social inferiors. Instead of being contrasted with the supposedly narrow and blunt, totally unrefined Juvenal, Petronius the Menippean satirist with an aesthetic realist cast more often suggests a parallel to Juvenal the tragic denouncer. Oddly yet aptly similar to Petronius's taste-based animus against effete aestheticism and preference for the crude voracity of a Trimalchio is Juvenal's painstaking, morally motivated distinction between the silly young Gracchus, whose homosexuality is a betrayal of Roman identity, and the cynical yet dogged Naevolus, professional cocksman of the "Ninth Satire," whose homosexuality is a consciously chosen and even heroic career in the thoroughly Roman tradition of relentlessness.

Such shadings of social discernment in the aesthetic-realist satirist Petronius, like those in the only initially moralistic Juvenal, are the result of generic mixture, for which Menippean form furnishes maximum opportunity. For when morality, which at the core must be absolutist to sustain the force of judgment, is exchanged for meditative appreciation of subtly different tints of immorality, as it is in the *Satyricon*, categorical imperatives dissolve into aesthetic assays. Eliot noted the same exchange in James's late novels, which though full to repletion with moral self-analyses yet remain void of morality. Such shadings, however, are what novelistic perspectives provide if one's talent, like Petronius's, is essentially to describe; and such shadings are what the tragic prospect provides if one's tendency, like Juvenal's, is to seek the foundations, the explanations, of moral judgments in history. Both tendencies, as we have seen, distort *satura,* derail it from its straight and narrow critique.

If at least the beginnings of a typical Juvenalian satire are fully satiric, with the complexities of history ensuing later, it is almost impossible to extrapolate the properly satiric in the *Satyricon* from the aesthetically superreal or from the novelistic. Irony is the dissolving agent. The tragic is the ne plus ultra, end-of-exasperation cadence of Juvenalian satire: a kind of philosophical repose, still sardonic but lacking tension. The novelistic in Petronius, however, proceeds from the perpetuation of irony's tensions:

there are no resting places, no cadences to ease the reader/auditor of the *Satyricon,* for the aesthetic realism keeps a constant distance between socially estranged eye and strange object.

Petronian aesthetic realism, dependent on perpetuated irony, maintains an equilibrium similar yet not identical to that of comedy. For the *Satyricon* refuses to resolve its social issues into any kind of reasserted or ratified norm. Not only does the human richness of Trimalchio and his friends demolish with ironic backlash the snobbish irony of Encolpius, whose values we basically distrust although we rely on him pragmatically as narrator. It also undermines all possible moral, social, or religious norms, thus establishing the *Satyricon* as progressively novelistic rather than conservatively comic. Realistic complexity of characterization overrides the satiric critique and stimulates generic transformation within the work. This formal effect results from Petronius's technique of sustaining his irony with cool poise rather than applying it to deflate what has violated proportion: Trimalchio never "sinks." Nor does the technique extend to the bursting point what exceeds the social norm: Trimalchio himself never becomes monstrous, as his dinner does; indeed he grows only more and more ordinary in a positive, not a reductive, sense.

Indeed, we must turn to some modern concept of alienation for an adequate account of perpetuated Petronian irony, which produces effects more complex than those of the anti-Virgilian parodies by Sextus Propertius and more naturalistic than those wrought by Ovid's wry comic intelligence. How else explain the absence of moral condemnation and social superiority in the following portrayal of a nouveau riche father worrying about his bright son's future, a satiric portrayal definitely devoid of judgmental finality yet lacking definite values?[4]

[To Agamemnon, professor of rhetoric:] This crazy weather's knocked everything topsy-turvy, but we'll come up with something you like. Don't worry your head about it, there'll be loads to eat.

You remember that little shaver of mine? Well, he'll be your pupil one of these days. He's already doing division up to four, and if he comes through all right, he'll sit at your feet someday. Every spare minute he has, he buries himself in his books. He's smart all right, there's good stuff in him. His real trouble is his passion for birds. I killed three of his pet goldfinches the other day and told him the cat had got them. He found some other hobby soon enough. And, you know, he's mad about painting. And he's already started wading into Greek and he's keen on his Latin. But the tutor's a little stuck on himself and won't keep him in line. . . . He's had enough literature, I think. But if he doesn't stick it out in school, I'm going to have him taught a trade. Barbering or auctioneering, or at least a little law. The only thing that can take a man's trade away is death. [54-55]

This is a very enjoyable monologue. We like this speaker, the "ragseller Echion," much more than we like the haughtily silent narrator Encolpius, whose sharp eye Petronius pragmatically selects for the ironic perspective on which we depend throughout the banquet at Trimalchio's as well as most of the rest of *Satyricon*. Echion's chatter is uncalculated, and un-calculating—oddly enough, for he is certainly a man for the main chance—uncontrolled, like the "crazy weather" he refers to, indeed like most of us filling up our ignorance of why things are as they are with nervously silly references to what we cannot understand or manage at all, to what "it's doing outside." Moreover, his killing his brainy son's birds is not *really* cruel; he is certainly not like Huck Finn's Pap, who lashes out at the naturally intelligent son for his own lack of learning. This is not cruelty, but an ingenuous, unthinking, yet cunning brutality, which, Petronius somehow makes us conclude, is part of Echion's charm. The crass father's concern is, after all, for his son's welfare. He is tolerant enough of the "little shaver's" humanistic bent, even admiring, though puzzled by the boy's obsessiveness, which accompanies his precocity: he says not that "litera-ture" is trash but, tentatively, that "He's had enough . . . I think."

All these shadings, enhanced by the energetic disconnectedness of Echion's "deliberations," indicate as no other instances of classical realism do a kind of alienation. This is half tragic rootlessness deriving from Echion's and Trimalchio's belonging to an enterprising class mainly of foreigners on the rise in a profitably hedonistic age, and half comic screwiness: unrooted rather than rootless. Such alienation is strangely modern because it, as well as our attitude toward it as managed by a Petronius or a Joyce, reflects our own absolute insecurity, our own in-stability in a nontraditional society where perpetual change becomes a predictable facet of our identities. Echion's is neither a stable identity like those figures of nostalgia in Juvenal (Curius, for example, in the "Eleventh Satire") nor a despicably shape-shifting personality like Juvenal's Egyptian actor-schemer Crispinus ("Curly the Cur"). In fact, in all of the *Satyricon* there are no such things as stable identities or outright evil personalities, not even in the case of the scurvy murderer Encolpius, let alone a consistent direction of satire or constant genericity.

Such a state of affairs, however, is not so deplorable as we might believe from reading a satire *as* a satire, especially not when the matter is thor-oughly ironic aesthetic realism in a Menippean format. Petronian irony, like Beckett's Cartesian deadpan, adopts for its own this complete aliena-tion of an unstable yet appealingly live personality like Echion's. Irony in this case *is* literalism, accurately rendering the way Echion and Trimalchio *are*—and Encolpius and Eumolpus to boot. That is, life in the *Satyricon* is self-alienating, inherently insecure.

Particularly, the way Echion and Trimalchio *talk* proves that the life of self-alienation may be not only liberating but somehow moral in the total sum of things. They frantically respond to others' attitudes and rebound from their bemusement about their own lives. They jump from ordinary topic to extraordinary inference. They resent everyone: Echion, for example, is irritated by the snobbish intellectual Agamemnon. Yet they also admire in others what they themselves lack. They strike out from frustration—Echion at his son's birds, Trimalchio at his god-awful wife Fortunata—but equally from love. They tease their socially superior guests to get even yet also just to vent their natural high spirits: Trimalchio's constant practical jokes with the courses of the dinner. They consciously repel others with their vulgarity yet overwhelm them with their generosity. Trimalchio's feasts and Echion's invitations to dinner are not merely conspicuous consumption; starveling intellectuals and outlaws on the run can always get a good meal from these two. Finally, all this spontaneous talk is for its own sake, just as their life, however self-alienating, is for its own sake. Thus both, the talk and the life, transcend any directed satiric perspectives, which could not possibly contain then.

The value produced by the *Satyricon* is the ironic value created by Petronian irony: the value of valuelessness. Not that created by tragedy, where Juvenalian satire leads, for that indicates a definitely bitter loss to Juvenal. The perpetually tense Petronian irony can sustainedly acknowledge life's fifty-fifty mixture of sweet and bitter, then both deplore satirically and savor. Petronian value, which requires resistance to discrimination, is not the value created by Ovidian comedy, either, for that suggests a detached amusement like Encolpius's, which cuts us off from others as if they were inferiors. Ovidian comedy may be gentler than Petronian *satura*, but it is not so humane. Trimalchio, however, himself both an object of Petronian irony and an unwitting yet sometimes inspired spokesman for it, makes us brothers to the beasts and friends to ourselves. Hegel's metaphor for the dialectic may serve as gloss on both Trimalchio's "philosophy" and his "alimentary school of wisdom," the *Cena* itself: "For they [animals] do not stand stock still before things of sense as if these were things *per se*, with being in themselves: they despair of this reality altogether, and in complete assurance of the nothingness of things they fall-to without more ado and eat them up" (Hegel 61).

Yet this irony deriving from Petronius's aplomb at tossing together *satura* at its Menippean richest remains as distinct from satire ordinarily conceived as the tragic eventuations of Juvenal's turn to history for back-up to his moral condemnation. Both ironic aesthetic realism in Petronius and the sardonically "Greek" tragic modalism in Juvenal leave their origin, which is satire, far behind in their wakes. The definitive moral or social judgment generically fitting to ordinary satire, if it could be brought off in these two famous Roman satirists, would prove irrelevant, futile, short-sighted—because both Juvenal's tragic prospect of time's natural-unnatural decline and Petronius's ironic prospect of life's raging appetite for generic mixture of bitter and sweet reflect men as self-alienating creatures. Illimitable desire activates both satirist and target: Juvenal's desire to preserve Roman identity against time conflicting with the young Gracchus's itch for satisfaction, or Petronius's aspiration to complete realism encountering Romans who refuse to stay contained by their criminal, vulgarian, or plain no-good types. In tracking their targets each satirist inevitably transgresses the categories of judgment, whether moral or social, that make their hunts possible in the first place. By their own virtue as satirists, Juvenal and Petronius find their categories alien to the objects of their satire, while by their own vices as targets, the satiric objects are discovered to be alien to both the categories applied to them and to satiric barriers cutting them off from the full complexity of human reality enjoyed and suffered by the readers.

Tragedy, generically anchored in the civic spectacles of the Greeks, reflects not men's instability or inherent self-alienation but their alternative, one might say "objective," natures as potential winners, losers, or stalemated participants in a serious game. Tragedy is "objective" because it consists of imitations of actions, while satire remains "subjective" in that it depends on the ever-shifting perspectives of rhetoric and gesture. These satiric perspectives are produced not to depict men acting for clear-cut outcomes, as tragic prospects are, but to follow men attitudinalizing about themselves and others, whether in their behavior or their talk. And when we try, like Trimalchio or the interlocutor in the "Ninth Satire" by Juvenal, to settle matters in our minds, to discriminate between better and worse, to *talk* ourselves into correct judgments, we fare no better than either Petronius's butt or Juvenal's judge: we detect no clear-cut answers, but just fall into a muddle of cross-canceling values—generic mixture, in other words, of the bitter and the sweet. Therefore, Juvenal cannot follow through with his satire's condemnation of a male prostitute and satisfies himself, instead, with resignation, while Petronius cannot endorse his ironic narrator's narrowly judgmental scorn for a grand vulgarian and opts for a capaciously and sustainedly ironic perspective according to which Trimalchio fulfills his mission of "easing the philosophers out of their jobs" (63).

Why, though, does Petronian perpetuated irony more harmoniously blend with satire than Juvenalian tragic modalism? Resigning himself to the moral awfulness fated by history is all Juvenal can do. Since he turns to the Roman past to back up his moral judgments with incontrovertible tradition, his resignations are a rhetorical substitute for victory, loss, or stalemate, the active results of tragedy, its proper teleology. But Petronius's perpetuated ironies are not substituted for actions imitating history, which are irrelevant to what he sees as an aesthetic realist; his ironies are of the duplicitous stuff language itself is made of, with its "sliding signifiers." The words of a Trimalchio or Encolpius are extra slippery, sliding away even from what the speakers think they mean when they try, in speech after speech after speech, to evaluate who they are and what they do. Men are adrift for Petronius, as well as for the modern and postmodern novelist. They escape their natural homes, or the moral, social, and spiritual categories defining them; accordingly, they slip away from the words they have just uttered, by uttering still more words in the attempt to retrieve what might have been uttered. Nothing in Petronian *satura* is ever got right. This psychological self-alienation, then, is perfectly expressed by men's nature as users of language. Language extends this ambiguous nature to literature like the *Satyricon* that, long before Romanticism or Lacan, presented life *as* speech, the ceaseless, goal-less speech of unrooted man.[5]

No one in Petronius, as Arrowsmith wisely reminds us throughout the notes to his translation, is ever in step with what he is saying, so that Encolpius's fine statements are undercut by his turdiness and Trimalchio's materialistic ignorance of the right way of saying is countered by his truthfulness to men's actual situation. This truthfulness is inherent both in his language of absurdly symbolic yet always edible foods and in his own and his friends' tumbling, disjointed, and disjoining speechifying about everything and nothing. In a word, Petronian perpetuated irony achieves the aimless telos so easily available through episodic Menippean satiric form and so daringly realized through the self-cancelation of both self-alienated man and of self-contradictory satiric genre. Together these self-cancelations produce the harmonious discord of the following oxymoronic sally of the ignoramus Trimalchio, whose language lives with self-alienating possibilities, to a pederastic professor of rhetoric, whose language dies in the utterance because its Virgilian values no longer catch Trimalchian life: "If that's the case, there's no argument; if it isn't the case, then what does it matter?" (57)

Trimalchio *is* the *Satyricon*, but not because his fragment of the whole work, the *Cena*, is the only big complete one. Rather, Trimalchio is the perfect satiric butt, the perfect object of irony—and the perfectly unwitting *eiron* for Petronius, the perfect subject of irony, the indefatigable perpetuator of irony, and the encompassing symbol of a reality aesthetically intimated because satirically inapprehensible. And he is so largely because of Petronius's words, the origin and bane of a rhetorical, nonaction semigenre like satire.

Don Quixote: Satire to Fantasy to Romance to Novel

With Cervantes, Menippean satire really does become the novel. For most literary historians consider *Don Quixote* the first major instance of the dominant modern genre, whether it is the traditional realist or the modernist/postmodernist, self-conscious novel that is meant. Yet, as with Petronius, "novel" in this case *remains* Menippean satire; the dialectic of genres preserves or extends as much as it abandons or curtails. Cervantes, however, unlike Petronius, eventually in the course of *Don Quixote* departs altogether from satire in the ordinary sense of moral or social critique, although he maintains the Menippean scheme: discursive prose plus interspersed verse, journey-fantasy. This transition is not immediate. Before it becomes something other than satire yet not quite a novel, *Don Quixote* enters a threshold category of narrative I shall call "satire *against* the real." This is the initial aspect of a kind of fantasy that in Christian cultures, Catholic or Protestant, may then become something else in turn. In Part 2 of *Don Quixote*, this fantasy merges into a novelistic mode of romance; in Book 4 of *Gulliver's Travels*, the fantasy resolves into a novelistic mode of tragedy. The generic deviation here represents a divergence in the combined histories of Menippean satire and novel paralleling Juvenal's turn to "Greek" tragic resolutions of problems of satiric morality and Petronius's turn to novelistic aesthetic realism as *dis*-solution of problems encountered when social satire becomes irrelevant.

In its paradoxical mix of realism and fantasy, *Don Quixote* is the formal predecessor to certain Menippean-realist premodernist novels from the nineteenth century, such as Flaubert's *Bouvard et Pécuchet*, Melville's *The Confidence-Man*, and Twain's *A Connecticut Yankee*. Clearly, any such attempt to place *Don Quixote* in the history of the novel while attending to its fantasy elements can accomplish only so much in describing its dual nature as Menippean satire and novel.

Perhaps, then, it is foolish to treat *Don Quixote* generically, since the problems compound themselves so extravagantly. Yet it is precisely the sequence of generic intersections in Cervantes' big work that elicits both the distinct operations of each of its major constituent genres or modes and the overall control exerted by their totality: first Menippean satire, then, in order, satire against the real, fantasy, a mode of Christian tragedy, and romance (this latter compounded with picaresque, pastoral, realist novel)—not to mention subgeneric inset narratives (prose stories in pastoral contexts, "exemplary" novellas, anecdotes, jokes), epic, poems of several Renaissance kinds, chivalric romance, "history," captive narrative, and others. However onionlike this book may be, such genre-from-genre peeling is required if we wish to lay bare the variegated yet centerless structure of *Don Quixote*. As Cervantes himself remarks in his "Prologue to the Reader" of the "Second Part" (1615), where he parries the pseudo-sequel to the "First Part" written by Avellaneda: "Yet all in all, I am grateful to this gentleman, the author, for saying that my stories are more satirical than exemplary, but that they are good. They could not be that unless there was a little of everything in them" (415-16). To accept Cervantes' own sly acceptance of what was in his time in Spain the disreputable, even dangerous label "satirical," then to follow him in de-emphasizing if not altogether forswearing the reputable aim of moral instruction—all the while highlighting the generic import of "a little of everything"—is how I should like to conduct the following analysis of *Don Quixote* as Menippean satire-fantasy-romance-novel. Moreover, the generic crossings complicating and prolonging Cervantes's "satirical stories" show that something like a process of power exchanges is going on, which accounts for the way this first "novel" spins itself out of "a little of everything." *Don Quixote* as an unstable instance of semigenre furnishes an ideal opportunity for the genre theorist to scrutinize the microtraces of the historical-literary process that created a prototype of a major new genre out of a rich reservoir of old genres.

In *Don Quixote*, as in the *Satyricon*, the tensions of irony remain unresolved. The satire commences with what seems to be a clear-cut distinction between appearance and reality, as it does in both Juvenal and Petronius. But the moral criteria requiring exposure of the sordid reality behind the fraudulent appearance are irrelevant to the epistemological bearings of Cervantes's version of the appearance-reality bifurcation: madness-sanity. Equally inapplicable are the social criteria required for marking the offsetting limitations of con-man snob and candidly pretentious slob in Petronius's spectacle of the clash of apparent social good taste with apparent bad. Granted, the priest and Don Quixote's housekeeper judge the errant hidalgo's chivalric romances "immoral," but Cervantes is not satirizing the immoral effects of this fantastic popular literature, which at most deserves the purely aesthetic, light treatment of parody: the don as a character in search of the right book, a romance hero in a picaresque narrative. Nor is he satirizing the socially deviant, *ab*-errant behavior of the old gentleman who takes to the road in quest of adventures. Instead, the satiric technique of irony in this consummate Menippean novel origi-

nates in the perpetual tension inherent in Cervantes' definitions of quixotic madness and conventional sanity.

Don Quixote, like both Juvenalian and Petronian satire, does not
remain a satire, but undergoes metamorphosis into several other genres
over the course of the narrative. Of all literary works, Cervantes' Menippean satire, a Spanish epic and the world's first novel, offers the most
comprehensive demonstration that satire is an inherently unstable genre,
never providing its own resolution to its ironies and needing other genres
to structure the extension and conclusion of the narrative. An especially
dramatic manifestation of the first of Cervantes' generic shifts frames Part
1: the Andrés episode. Its initial phase comprises Don Quixote's maiden
adventure after his dubbing, which takes place during his pre-Sancho
sortie. In the second phase, just preceding the return to the inn-castle, the
knight-errant is nearly deterred from any further adventures, for at the end
of the phase Don Quixote is reduced to profound melancholy by the
reappearance of Andrés, who curses his deliverer instead of thanking him.
The shift is from ordinary satire with its three targets of hypocrisy (social
impropriety), materialism (moral impropriety), and theological-meta-
physical impropriety to a transitional genre of Cervantes' invention, what I
term "satire against the real." This transition allows us to pass over into
three new generic worlds: that of fantasy, which bridges Parts 1 and 2, that
of Christian tragedy, which supplements the fantasy of Part 2, and that of
romance, which through allegory of art transcends the Christian tragedy of
Part 2 and extends its fantasy to a higher level. All these genres together
serve to organize the final sally of Don Quixote and Sancho.

In the Andrés sequence (39-41) Cervantes targets the conscious mis-
direction of faith by a Christian who would live his faith while knowing it
cannot and should not be lived. The youth Andrés has been flogged by his
master for allegedly neglecting the flock. Don Quixote angrily intervenes
because whatever the justice or injustice of the case, the master is taking
advantage of the boy's powerlessness, assailing one who cannot defend
himself. The knight-errant's faith, as such, is not satirized here, rather his
assumption that his faith will be matched by a kind of man he remembers,
once Andrés clarifies his master's social and moral status as a peasant, to be
incapable of responding in good faith. For Don Quixote will not punish the
master beyond requiring his word to pay the boy any wages withheld. The
don is thus shown to be a perfectly good Christian, as well as an intelligent
Renaissance Catholic gentleman who knows that even though the master is
no knight he is nonetheless accountable for his excessive and cruel punishment of the boy: the peasant stands correctible by any witness, a fortiori by
a knight actively seeking out injustices to undo. But Don Quixote's purity
in living his faith as though this world were not the vale of tears his very

calling as a knight presupposes blinds him to the entirely human nature of the offense and offender *and* himself as a believer in transcendence.

Thus the origin of all ironies in *Don Quixote*, the effective, that is consciously recognized yet unavoided conflation of appearance and reality, is carefully treated by Cervantes the satirist as a liability, but one intrinsic to proper Christian faith. For to see in Don Quixote's situation vis-à-vis Andrés and the peasant master an epitome of the Christian's situation is, after all, to allow satiric irony to touch the very essence of faith. An up-and-down world of power and powerlessness simply does not allow Christian faith to fulfill its very function as the only bridge to the other, changeless world of perfect trust and charity. This irony of ironies implicit in an intricately skewed theological rationality is the final madness exposed to satiric scrutiny in the first genuine adventure of knight-errantry in Part 1.

Andrés reappears in the penultimate section of Part 1. Then the full party of Don Quixote, Sancho, priest, and barber, plus the thrown-over lovers disguised as rustics who have wandered maddened by their sorrows through the Sierra Morena, all reconverge on the ill-fated inn-castle where Sancho was blanketed. The servant boy's curse on Don Quixote for having intervened between him and his brutal master has usually been cited as the most reductive of Cervantes' satiric critiques of the knight-errant's idealism, which just makes things worse in their un-ideal world: "For the love of God, sir knight-errant, if you ever meet me again, though you may see them cutting me to pieces, give me no aid, but leave me to my misfortune. It will not be so great that a greater will not come to me by being helped by your worship, on whom and all the knights-errant that have ever been born God send his curse" (244). The effect of this curse is to send Don Quixote into one of his deepest episodes of melancholy in the entire narrative; his near-comatose state when the party reaches the inn shortly after Andrés's reappearance matches the depression he experiences in prelude to his death, when Sansón Carrasco finally vanquishes him on the Barcelona beach. Indeed, Andrés in a sense does kill Don Quixote as active adventurer in Part 1. The knight's subsequent deeds he performs mainly as an agent of restraint, as careful peacemaker, for example, in the dispute over the packsaddle trappings in the inn courtyard.

Since Cervantes has already applied his irony to the Andrés intervention at the time it occurred, there is no further ordinary satiric point to be made. Don Quixote has been satirized for social and metaphysical-religious lapses, all of them caused, yet also preventable, by his faith, which is correctly Christian and not aberrant. There is no need, then, to have Andrés smash the don's idealism, for that has never been the object of Cervantes's satire. So why does Cervantes bring Andrés and his savior back together? This second phase of the Andrés adventure marks a generic departure, which devolves upon the selection of a new target. The effect, one of the most stunning in all literature, is to change ordinary satire into "satire against the real" itself, to deflect its aim from social, moral, and religious categories to the very nature of reality. For all his value as devastating corrector of Don Quixote's misplaced faith, for all his value as sign of the absolute status of human pain and injustice, the victimized boy denouncing his deliverer in savage indignation remains in the wrong. And given the altered perspective of satire in this second phase of the Andrés question, Don Quixote is right in his immediate response to the curse: "Don Quixote was getting up to chastise him, but Andrés took to his heels at such a pace that no one attempted to follow him" (244).

Now it seems that the mad knight-errant is vindicated and that the boy, doubly victimized by both oppressor and savior, is being criticized for his curse. The reason for this inversion of the earlier, ordinary satirizing of misapplied good that causes evil is that Andrés has allowed his sufferings to gut his faith in the possibility of justice. That is the sin Don Quixote means to chastise, for Andrés' good as much as in his own defense. To curse with the finality of the curse thrown by Andrés is not just to decry the misapplication of faith, but to despair, to fling away the good, which is after all faith. In contrast to Andrés, Sancho, also victimized for the sake of his master's faith, has earlier, in chapter 28 of Part 1, refused to let the deeply felt and unforgotten humiliation of the blanketing fester into despair. Sancho escapes the plight of Andrés by heeding, however skeptically, what Don Quixote says when the knight-errant tries to reassure his blanketed squire: "'Fear not, Sancho' said Don Quixote. 'Heaven will deal better by you'" (118). Not that Sancho himself believes this; but he believes his master believes, and that will have to suffice.

Andrés, however, has no intercessor, for the merely arbitrating, unavenging angel in his case has been a purely Christian knight-errant misdirecting his faith toward the peasant master, the devil incarnate to the boy. If not the knight, then the squire might serve as proper intercessor for Andrés. But the boy's lashing has bitten too deeply: "I have been until now in a hospital getting cured" (242). He simply cannot accept Sancho's wise and compassionate offer; Andrés rejects the eucharistic promise of the squire's humble feast of despair:

Sancho took a piece of bread and another of cheese from his store and gave them to the lad. "Here, take this, brother Andrés," he said, "for we have all of us a share in your misfortune."

"Why, what share have you got?"

"This share of bread and cheese I am giving you," answered Sancho. "God knows whether I'll ever need it myself or not, for I would have you know, friend, that we squires to knights-errant have to bear a great deal of hunger and hard luck, and even other things more easily felt than told." [243]

With his covert allusion to his own suffering and shame in the blanketing misadventure, Sancho recalls the humpbacked Magdalen Maritornes, who brought him wine to revive him, and offers to the boy the same communion of pain. But Andrés seizes the food, spurning its promissory substance for its merely material value as sustenance.

What has happened to ordinary satire during the course of this second phase of the Andrés episode is that Cervantes has turned its aim away from the problems of faith and directed it against a reality ruthless in its indifference to the pain caused by the way the materialism of the iron age can twist well-intentioned intercession into grotesquely ironic torture. The distortion results from the way faith is misapplied when Don Quixote, determined by the purity of his faith, shines its beacon on reality, or its appearances, rather than toward the true life beyond. But once Andrés delivers his curse, the don's misapplied faith assumes a profounder significance, one that bursts the frame of satire as it has been understood to this point. Don Quixote's dejection and Andrés' despair are both aspects of the mistake of Judas when he refuses to accept that the poor will always be with us but Christ for only a short while. Loss of faith, temporary in the don's case, permanent in the servant boy's, is the inevitable consequence of insisting, with Judas, on its effectuality in the here and now. In contrast, the twisted effectuality of insubstantial chivalric fictions mistakenly mixed up with the hard materiality of power is realized so searingly by Cervantes in this episode that the satire bends away from the errors of the faithful back toward reality—not just its social, moral, and spiritual aspects, but reality as such.

Things are so bad, we learn from the ultimate perspective of Andrés' despair and Don Quixote's abortive attempt to chastise it, that an exceptionally good knight's best capacity, the power of belief, when directed at the reality of intersecting power and powerlessness, perversely augments the advantage of the unjust, sending the intended "saved" into the pit of hell. Therefore, Cervantes abandons his ironic perspective on faith and its natural propensity to despair. Instead, he begins to satirize the world itself. To satirize reality, the book's satiric perspective must now become Don Quixote's own overlapping foci of appearance-reality and no longer depends on ordinary satire's gauges of morality, social norms, and religion.

The irony of satire against the real is total irony, stopping these gauges of ordinary satire. They are replaced by one sole distinction, that between our experience as it is bounded by space and time, and our certainty that the true nature of man must lie beyond our immediate comprehension of his atrociousness. Fallen man is not man at all. His general tragedy is a mere dream. Calderón retains his Christian bearings to allow recognition of the undeniability of suffering however illusory it is. But Cervantes, as satirist grown hostile to the real itself (like late Twain), generally moves not toward the Christian tragedy of winning losers, though he sometimes approaches it in Part 2, but toward fantasy. Things are so bad they are funny, preposterous, absurd. The miserable Andrés himself glimpses this new perspective afforded by satire against the real when he explains, "If it hadn't been for the pain I was suffering, I would have laughed at the things he said" (242).

Looking backward from this point in the narrative, we see Cervantes begin his plot by elaborating his paradigmatic irony toward Don Quixote's madness, an irony attaching to parallel self-contradictory definitions of appearance and reality. Then, once he ventures forth, Don Quixote enters the picaresque world open to both sane and mad. The generic dimensions are set by ordinary satire from the first phase of the Andrés episode to the second. The heretofore exuberant, if physically pummeled, knight-errant then falls into despondency, a change marking the generic shift to satire against the real. So when he rejoins the priest and barber and the whole caravan of soon-to-be-rejoined lovers and homecomers, Don Quixote takes to his bed. "To sleep: perchance to dream"—that is what he does as, for the second time, he enters the inn-castle, which is no longer a castle to him yet is still subject to enchantments. First he wields his sword in his dream, slaying Dorotea–Princess Micomicona's giant, to the detriment of the inn's wine supply. The night having been whiled away by the other guests' debate about the reality of chivalric romances, the next day Maritornes the once merciful, abetted by the formerly innocent-minded inn-keeper's daughter, plays a painful practical joke on Don Quixote, taking advantage of what has become his prolonged state of enchantment. Increasingly, multiple enchantments accompany Cervantes' next generic shift, away from satire against reality to full-fledged fantasy.

But the transition to dream, whereby we uncritically merge our reading perspective with Don Quixote's own hermeneutics, also marks his and our departure for a new realm of adventure, one that extends through the end of Part 1 and a good deal of Part 2. This is the realm of words, inaugurated by dream then fortified against reality by playfully self-refer-ential language with cross-interpretations, as in the knight's literal under-standing of Maritornes's language of common swearing (352). Her purpose is to exaggerate in order to wake a dreamer up, but the purpose is subverted by fantasy's potential to expand exaggerations infinitely. Satiric irony no longer serves as critical limit. Indeed, it vanishes once fantasy deploys irony in the perfect ludic freedom *created by* the hero's imagination.

Tragedy imitates and thus indicates action, Don Quixote's version of Sancho's blanketing as a "sad tragedy" included (117). Tragedy's words are strictly subordinated to its plot, in this case to the shoulders of the humiliated squire. Satire, in distinction, consists in words directed attitudinally at actions demanding evaluation; satire covers the range of such evaluations as Don Quixote's erroneous faith, as well as Andrés's despair. But when the actions require evaluations that are self-canceling, for example when faith leads to despair instead of hope, satire against the real supplants ordinary satire. When satire against the real shows Don Quixote recoiling first into despondency and then into dream, fantasy supplants it—for satire against the real leaves nothing but absurdism to motivate the narrative.[6] Words now target words, the cessation of directed irony paralleling the don's cessation as active seeker of adventures in the world, the beginning of ludic irony luxuriating in dreamlike sliding signifiers. Cervantes knew by 1605, when Part 1 was published, where Part 2 would take up again in 1615, with its doppelgänger pseudoknight and squire foisted upon the public by Avellaneda, with its longer sections of involuted repartee conducted largely at leisure and often in comfort, and with its minimal instances of physically audacious chivalry and its abundance of visions, games, and elaborate masquerades.

Yet we must not forget that the fantasy bridging Parts 1 and 2, like the fantasy in Rabelais and Swift, *originates* not in the ludic impulse, as it does in post–*Finnegans Wake* experimental fiction and Nabokovian formalism, but in pain, the pain enlivening both ordinary satire and satire against the real. When reality is undeniable yet unacceptable, we follow the don to a life of word adventures. Power in Part 2 is no longer figured in shapes discernible and judgable according to social, moral, and metaphysical-religious categories. Instead, power evaporates into the self-propounding and conflicting phantoms of aestheticism. In the end, after satire, there is nothing but the Word. Menippean satire in Part 1, words originally outward-bound yet pulled down and dragged away by experience, becomes meta-Menippean fantasy in Part 2, words inward-bound and fleeing from experience to transfiguration by means of still other genres. First, there is a Christian mode of tragedy, marked by Don Quixote's outburst at the Ebro, just before his visit to the duke and duchess: "God help us; this world is all machinations and schemes at cross purposes one with the other. I can do no more" (590). Next comes romance, composed of frequent pastoral and religious references, especially in the statues-of-the-saints episode in chapter 58 and the actual as well as planned pastoral activities toward the conclusion. Finally, the novel obtrudes, to fulfill the demands of Cervantes' critique of chivalric romance, in which the hero lives forever through sequel after sequel. In *Don Quixote* as the first realist chivalric romance, or novel, the hero must die in his bed.

But what can control the play of signifiers if there is nothing left but the Word? Desire, if we are to believe René Girard (1-18, 44-52). But desire in Part 2 is not a value of the psyche, neither the characters' nor Cervantes' nor the reader's. Rather, given the diachronic movement of *Don Quixote* in its entirety, from its beginnings in ordinary satire through satire against the real to fantasy, then on to romance and the novel, desire represents the force of revulsion against that very reality that is supposedly one of the positive achievements of this antichivalric romance. Fantasy is the first plateau reached by the narrative as it reels away from the iron age exposed by the satire in Part 1. What the narrative is reaching toward is the fulfillment of desire, generically construed, in the possibilities of transcendence offered by romance. Romance offers the final answer of literature, or the Word made Art, to the nonliterary drift of satire with its dubious attraction to the worldly world of signifieds. Desire in Part 2, then, is itself to be construed generically, as the longing of satire to be literature.

Shifts in genre allow a given satire to detour or override impasses of meaning. In Part 1 of *Don Quixote*, errors of faith targeted by religious satire require the narrative to turn toward fantasy, which opens into the looking-glass world of Part 2, where the don is no longer the object of satire but a medium for nonsatiric free play. In the *Satyricon*, Roman lapses of taste and instances of social if not moral hypocrisy lose their satiric spin when Petronius begins to luxuriate in novelistic aesthetic realism. Juvenal, searching for an explanation of the moral corruption of his Imperial Rome, delves into the past, only to release the antisatiric potency latent in the tragic conception of time as loss. Even Swift, accomplishing through a language of transparent irony a purely rational critique of European behavior, still requires the Christian tragic conception of Original Sin to explain the futility of reason in the yahoo nature of mankind and to suggest the hope of redemption. All these recipes for satire contain their own proportions of moral and social ingredients, while *Don Quixote* and *Gulliver's Travels*, Book 4, add the critiques of faith and reason, respectively, to the classical mix of *satura*.

Yet in satire that is proportionally more political in its subject matter—as during the late seventeenth, the eighteenth, and the late nineteenth centuries—than it is social or moral or religious, generic instability is more complex in its effects on meaning. This instability is sometimes the result of the employment of antithetical techniques in the same work, sometimes the consequence of political thematics. It will be remembered that political power as symbolically incursive action drives its imitations in tragedies on straight tracks leading to victory, loss, or dead end. However, satire, as a genre of rhetorical attitudinalizing, channels power toward clearly visible ends only if it remains concentrated on rational critique, whether applied to moral, social, or religious experience; and we have already seen how even such highly visible targets can fade, so that new, nonsatiric perspectives are disclosed as a work unfolds.

If "political" in the context of generic differentiation characterizes something special in satire, the reason must lie in what makes politics itself distinct from history in general and from particular moral, social, and religious attitudes. "Politics" I take, then, to apply to the traces, more pronounced in certain satires than others, of programmatic action and ideology. Of course, most satire has political implications, from the *saturae* of Romans fearful for their lives to the satires of the blithe English Augustans and the deadly direct Swift. But when the satiric voice identifies itself with parties and affiliated ideologies bearing time-bound labels, such as Swift's "Tory" or Twain's "Single Tax," the resulting topicality may be either an aesthetic affliction causing brilliant works to be ignored by later readers, as Seneca's anti-Claudian *Apocolocyntosis* and many of Defoe's tracts have been, or a source of possible confusion, technically in the work itself as well as psychologically.

Still other difficulties may arise in interpreting and evaluating predominantly political satires if we apply the somewhat less topical yet always shifting categories "conservative" and "liberal." Radical leftist satire, like reactionary rightist, tends to spill over the aesthetic limits of irony into polemic, which addresses itself to believers or the already converted; or it becomes propaganda against the swayable, not-yet-believing enemy. The centrist-tending conservative and liberal kinds of political satire, however, often adopt the Jonsonian purpose of correction, or at least persuasive enlightenment of others sharing some of the satirist's values. Persuasion is still a part of conservative and liberal rhetoric, while the mobilizing or teaching aims of propaganda and outright reconstruction ("brainwashing"), directed at those who do not share the satirist's values— or the ritual purpose of celebration, directed at total believers—are substituted in polemic for persuasion. Because of this commitment to persuasion, requiring flexibility in strategy, satires demonstrating conservative and liberal politics are a particularly fertile ground for the study of the complex effects of generic shifts.

Butler: Conservative Satire to Mock Epic

Samuel Butler's *Hudibras*[7] and Twain's *A Connecticut Yankee in King Arthur's Court* offer a fruitful comparison of conservative with liberal political satire. Butler's is a very topical verse satire against the Puritans and other dissenting losers from the historical vantage of the early Restoration. Twain's Menippean novel is a parody of Malory and a satiric burlesque of feudal civilization in the sixth century, as well as during the nineteenth century as it appears from the vantage of the 1880s, when American progressivism was flexing its rapidly developing industrial muscles. Yet both satires represent easily demonstrated alignments with broad political programs and ideologies: Politically, Butler champions the Restoration as against the preceding Commonwealth, and ideologically promotes Stuart monarchism guided by an Anglican Establishment and a still-strengthening bourgeoisie. Twain sides with Henry George–style reformism politically, and ideologically favors democratic egalitarianism directed by the Constitutional tradition of separated church and state, checked and balanced interests, and optimism. So while religion unequivocally rears its head in both satires, it is in the specific contexts of politics that the source of satiric directionality must be located: for Butler the context is the resolution of the recent civil war through the final dissolution of the Puritan victors' hegemony; for Twain it is the conflict of a modern Yankee spirit with the consolidation of the Catholic Church and the British monarchy in the primitive stage of the Middle Ages.

In its ambivalence toward the eventual historical victory of its own "side," *Hudibras* as political satire deploying the stratagems of burlesque and mock epic is like the *Eumenides* as tragedy: Athena-Athens "the victor city" resorts to "Persuasion" of the Furies, but only after it-she displays the "Father's lightning bolts." Aeschylus's work, however, which is revolutionary, not conservative, directly tackles the problem of how progress can ensue after horror while retaining the best of the enemy force, "the mind of the past." The *Eumenides*, that is, after managing a victory in a power game, aesthetically imposes a "fantasy of hope" that is to be believed in whatever history may indicate to the contrary. Butler's satiric denigration of the quixotic Puritan knight guilty of both serious hubris and ridiculous "brassiness," on the other hand, evades its problem of how order can successfully be restored following an interruption caused by dissenters. *Hudibras* has no proper rule to impose at all, aesthetic or political. For instead of the tragic dialectics of game, Butler's conservative satire possesses only gestures—the rhetorical techniques of burlesque and mock epic—declaiming the will to restore what has always been; the work is therefore natural, sane, and human, like the Restoration it promotes, as opposed to what is deviant, crazy, and grotesque, namely, Puritan "Reform" and "Revolution."

The satiric will is not so potent as the tragic game because it remains gestural: no clear set of outcomes is inevitable, just the possibilities offered by ceaseless attitudinalizing. As Robert Elliott has suggested in his anthropology of satire, the satiric impulse, as realized for example in certain Eskimo rituals of community abuse, stops short with name-calling, with bad-mouthing, with reiterative imprecation. Tragedy, on the other hand, casts sticks and stones, with some hitting true, some falling to the side, and others blocked; the words of tragedy are always directed by plot, which traces history-like actions all the way to their ends in victory, loss, and stalemate. If tragedy's primary means to its definitive outcomes is the imitation of action, conservative satire's basic method of sounding superior to the historically overpowered yet not annulled butt (for Puritanism remains a powerful political and cultural influence through the Restoration and long after) is a function of its own generic instability: shifting between the techniques of burlesque, mock epic, and parody, whichever seems more effective at the moment.

But these options are all merely verbal, rhetorical, attitudinal, gestural—lacking the entirely figural yet comparatively solid imitativeness of tragic action. Thus the various techniques employed can play at cross-purposes, as Butler's burlesque and mock epic do when directed against the outmoded Puritan "Quixote," Hudibras. For what burlesque reduces, with its high-content-to-low-form directionality, mock epic, with its low-content-to-high-form directionality, automatically reelevates by virtue of the contrast alone.

The iron tracks of tragedy may also consist in nothing but words. However, they are words making figures that are powered toward certain destinations. Words that depend on their aim alone, however, tend to slip away from definitive results: their signifiers slide beneath their signifieds. A conservative, thus centrist, satire such as *Hudibras*, which derives its impetus from subjective will, not from objective-seeming dialectic, and which employs words as gestures rather than as imitative actions, ends up having expended its power in abusive name-calling disguised as "correction," for the sake of advertising social and moral ascendancy. This is automatically the winner's advertisement because a conservative never can lose; he wishes only to restore the order that prevails in nature, long after short-term losses. This externality of the conservative position, in turn, explains why satire has historically been a genre favored by conservatives: Juvenal, Horace, Dryden, the Augustan Tories, contemporary American right-center journalistic satirists. A conservative ideology does not pin its hopes on hope, which the conservative equates with fantasy, delusion, temporary disturbance; there is nothing winsome about political conservatism. Thus the conservative's ideology is intrinsically rhetorical. It ventures no program to build because it has *yet to be* built, resting content, instead, with reiterating, restating, forever verbalizing and never proposing fantasies of imitative action, forever criticizing disorder from the conviction of a natural order that has merely to be renewed. This purely verbal nature of the victory of conservative satire enunciated by automatic winners comes, however, at the price of sacrificing what would appear to be the original object of political satire—hitting the bull's-eye. Instead, conservative satire preens itself, striking poses of social and moral ascendancy. It is always open to the charge of snobbishness.

What, then, would be the case of liberal political satire? Could the Puritans have hurled a *Hudibras* at the Cavaliers from the heights of the Protectorate? Milton casts his eye at the divine horizons of history in his epic and tragic poetry. But he largely ignores satiric possibilities. His political prose is earnest and value-proposing, as in the *Areopagitica* or in his arguments for liberal divorce laws. Marvell wrote poetic satire of great ironic subtlety, but not exactly against the Restoration's conservatism in itself. Instead, in "The Last Instructions to a Painter" (1667), he aims at Restoration men's and women's venality and the disasters of particular politicians and cabinet policies, especially naval. In the British context of sixty years later, the thoroughly political Swift remained a pragmatic Whig even after becoming a Tory, just as he had always been an Anglican religious conservative even when a Whig. Yet the power of liberal political satire in Book 4 of *Gulliver*, as in *A Tale of a Tub* and "A Modest Proposal," is less than the power possessed by a deeply conservative theology, which underlies and in some ways contradicts Swift's humanitarian liberalism. The "Drapier" and "Bickerstaff" satires employ irony practically, for specific political ends, but not ideologically. In comparison, *Hudibras*-style satire is thoroughly political in aim, that is, both theoretical and practical, but not in execution. Generally speaking, though, conservative satire is mostly theoretical, even theological in its sweep: "Economic reform is foolish because greed is natural to man." And liberal satire, from Marvell to more modern instances, seems to concentrate on practical issues, leaving ideology to "serious" discourse (Voltaire would be the exception in the eighteenth century, Diderot and Rousseau the rule).

Twain: Liberal Burlesque to Novel

To jump ahead to the nineteenth century and the American political scene, Twain's *A Connecticut Yankee in King Arthur's Court* is an obvious instance of liberal satire, and it possesses Menippean and quixotic features making it both comparable and contrastive to Butler's conservative satire. The ideological essence of liberalism is the malleability of man: he can be changed, even for the better, as liberalism typically stresses. We have already discussed the ideology of progress as "the fantasy of hope," applying to Aeschylean tragedy but not to Butler's conservative satire, which in fact rejects the hopefulness of reformism. In *A Connecticut Yankee* this hope is articulated in a pragmatic, Yankee-style statement wryly downplaying its Rousseauistic aspiration: "Training—training is everything; training is all there is *to* a person. We speak of nature; it is folly; there is no such thing as nature" (208).

The particular occasion for this liberal remark of Hank Morgan's, however, is his visit with that most lethal of femmes fatales, Morgan le Fay. Her marvelous penchant for evil he concludes to be an inevitable consequence of backward medieval ways: a bad habit, nonetheless a habit, instilled by "training." So at the heart of Twain's liberalism lies a paradox: the dreadful Morgan le Fay is *innocent*, as Hank is forced to admit, much to his uneasiness. For eternal-seeming medieval religious and social practices—practices inspiring, for example, her hilariously perverse rationale for torturing a serf, who was proved innocent by dying without confessing—are the only reason she does such things with complete artlessness. When she "slips" a dagger into a stumbling page as if it entailed nothing more than another domestic task for her servants, who have to wipe up the blood, she is demonstrating the same force of training that the liberal Hank believes is the key to progress, the basis for breaking away from feudal traditionalism. Men, even Arthurians of all classes, can be made useful, responsible, self-respecting citizens of an America-like "republic" with the right kind of training. However, the bad are bad only because they have had the wrong training.

No wonder Hank is profoundly bothered by Morgan. The twentieth century will discover the same paradox in the same notion of malleable men's becoming both Fifth-Columnist tyrants and Loyalist martyrs, both Nazi automatons and dutiful Soviet heroes, both torturers and tortured throughout the postwar world. Only the vocabulary is new: "programmed," "reborn," "cured," "reintegrated," "growing," "revolutionized"—but not entirely new: we still have "retrained." Hank Morgan and Twain's liberal fantasy of hope is the promise of chaos realized with straightforward logic at the novel's conclusion, "The Battle of the Sand-Belt": in an eerie holocaust, melted flesh corrupts in the sun, slowly killing the well-trained, innocent technocrat heroes responsible for saving the "republic" with their electrified fencing.[8]

Aesthetic incoherence in *A Connecticut Yankee* is the result of the inherently necessary conversion of liberal satire into progressive novel. The satire requires the progressive conception of novelistic, developmental character, according to which "training is everything," to override the impasse created when the liberal ideologue Hank despairs at encountering no "bottom" to people, just abstract traits ingrained by bad training. Yet when Hank finds a basis for hope in the surprisingly progressive manhood of Arthur and in the potential decency of the charcoal burner, and when the rationalist male in Hank responds progressively to the conservative yet semiprogressive womanliness of Sandy—then political hope is shown to bring personal hopelessness. For Sandy's life of the heart is trapped in the irrational medieval past, while her Yankee husband must awaken from his dream of time travel to find himself cut off from his wife by the very progressiveness of history that he espouses. Therefore, the aesthetically, logically, and dialectically inevitable destruction of both technocratic civilization and medieval precivilization in the conclusion, "The Battle of the Sand-Belt," appears from the reasonable perspective of liberalism to contradict the human needs for personal communion and stability it would be only reasonable to satisfy *by means of* historical progress.

The instability of satiric semigenre in *A Connecticut Yankee* becomes the particular failure of liberal satire to realize either its political or more generally its human ends even when it turns to a novelistic conception of character to salvage them. Juvenal, Petronius, and Cervantes all take advantage of satire's instability to make their works richer by means of generic transformation. When, however, it is a question of conducting a consistent political critique, whether conservative as in Butler's case or liberal as in Twain's, within a coherent aesthetic structure, generic shifting results not in complexity but in a quagmire of aesthetic, political, and just plain human contradictions.

Yet satire has been the genre most often resorted to for political critique in the history of literature: not only persuasion-oriented, humanist, liberal satiric utopias like More's, but also abusive, Tory, conservative factional pamphlets and poems by Restoration and Augustan satirists; not only radical burlesques by such as Mayakovsky and liberal satires by such as Byron or Twain, but also conservative satires by Evelyn Waugh, anti-totalitarian satires of all kinds (Orwell to Cortázar), even fascist satires by Pound. All of these political satires are both ideologically and formally unstable. Perhaps it is the very reasonableness, or the pretense to reason, of satire representing all stripes of the political spectrum that frustrates political satire, which typically ends in thematic futility and technical incoherence. At the same time this devotion to reason may be temporarily useful in impelling nonpolitical satire forward into such new realms as fantasy (Cervantes, Borges) and the novel (Petronius, Raymond Queneau) or back into such old dominions as tragedy (the Sophoclean/Euripidean Juvenal, the Euripidean Jacobeans).

Finally, the essence of politics, which *is* reason, may be hostile to the illusory non-essence of art. This is the central problem, in yet another sense, of the whole satiric genre, which derives its authority equally from the stubborn signifieds of nonfiction and the playful signifiers of ironic language rhetorically guided and misguided. If the essence of politics were not reason, not even reasonableness, but unreason, could political satire then completely demolish its targets and avoid dissipating its energies in ambiguities and ambivalences? A handful of satires, most of them from the twentieth century and nearly all post-World War I, tantalizingly suggests a political prospect of power for satiric genre, no longer for tragedy alone: Jarry's *Ubu Roi* (1896), the Marx brothers' *Duck Soup* (1933), Ionesco's *La Leçon* (1950) and *Rhinoceros* (1958), and Hašek's *The Good Soldier Švejk* (1921-22) provide an erratically produced and widespread sampling of possible satires of unreason in a variety of forms, dramatic, cinematic, and Menippean. Brecht, of course, comes to mind, especially *The Caucasian Chalk Circle* with its Sancho-like peasant governor-for-a-day, Azdak; this play is disqualified, however, by its solidly communist conclusion as a tragedy of victory.

Hašek: Menippean Satire to Anarchism

Politically speaking, it would seem at least upon first glance that only *anarchist* politics can avoid the contradictions of conservative or liberal satire and the conversion of satire into novel or tragedy. For with the possible exception of syndicalism, most varieties of anarchism despair of any program for transition to a just order, preferring instead an irrational explosion of the old order into the new orderlessness, the cleanest of slates. Neither Butler's conservative anxieties about an unallayed, resurgent Puritan reformism nor Twain's liberal paradoxes of emotionally empty and socially suicidal progressivism play any part in an anarchist politics of definitive rupture between rotten past and brand-new future. We cannot trust the actual politics of satiric authors as a guide to the specific political directionality of their works, especially given the slipperiness of unreason. Hašek was a Communist, indeed a strict Bolshevik commissar in Russia during the civil war and a frustrated Communist revolutionary in the newly formed postwar Republic of Czechoslovakia. But his single great work is not communist at all, it is anarchist through and through.

This big, unfinished work, *The Good Soldier Švejk*, with its affinities in quixotism to Butler's verse and Twain's prose narratives, affords the best estimate of the relative powers of satires cut along different political biases. Formally, stylistically, and ideologically, Hašek's ironic deconstruction of the Austro-Hungarian empire at the outset of World War I is perfectly consistent and always clear, even in translation. In fact, *Švejk* is the only satire considered so far that is purely Menippean. Unlike the *Satyricon* it never drifts into novelistically realist social detail; unlike *Don Quixote* it does not telescope into higher genres of allegorical import such as fantasy and romance; and unlike *Hudibras* and *A Connecticut Yankee* it evades both problems of incoherence and outright generic transformation. *Švejk*, therefore, stands in exception to the rule that satire is an unstable genre. From beginning to the kind of end it can claim as an unfinished work, it remains a prose travel narrative of fortuitous episodes in a world conceived as absurd, while the army songs Švejk resorts to when alone serve as more than adequate substitute for the requisite interspersions of verse in classical Menippean *satura*.

Most important, there is no development of either plot or character in *Švejk*. The World War—traced up to but just shy of the Battle of Sokal (1915) near the southeastern front at the River Bug by the time Hašek died[9]—seems in the course of the narrative *not* to be happening, at least as a planned deployment of military power. Unlike all other fictional war narratives, *Švejk* makes the politically telling, specifically satiric point that a nation-state in name only, such as the patchwork Dual Monarchy, cannot exactly move its cogs so as to make war in the first place. The casualties in Švejk's army actually fall by pure accident, unlike the existential "accidence" experienced by individuals in *A Farewell to Arms* or in Stendhal and Tolstoy. Moreover, the Czech soldiers know from the start that it is stupid to aim at victory against their Russian brothers for a German or Hungarian Austria-Hungary: "A monarchy as idiotic as this ought not to exist at all" (208). Interestingly, few of Hašek's soldiers or civilians die at all; *Švejk* ends after 700-odd pages with the orderly Švejk and Lieutenant Lukáš just arriving, after much digression and outright retrograde motion (particularly in the "Švejk's Anabasis" sections), *behind* the front. Prague and the troop trains to Galicia are the sites of Švejk's "nonaction," and meandering deferral rather than organized advance typifies his army's "maneuvers."

If there is no development of plot, parodically—since there is no development of an offensive on the southeastern front, just massive armies roaming back and forth across a woebegone Galicia—so Švejk himself, his master Lukáš, and assorted soldiers and officers never change. They have no characters; they *are* characters. This is a difficult distinction to persuade *Švejk*'s readers of if they think the work is a novel and not a Menippean satire. All the characters in *Švejk* stay who they are when we first encounter them: Lukáš remains an intelligent, gentle officer frustrated by an imbecilic and sadistic cadre; the senior officers remain caricatures; Vaněk the quartermaster sergeant tenaciously plies his survivor's life of cunning apathy; Baloun's personal reality is gorged by his trait of gluttony; and Švejk abides as the mysterious yet transparent Švejk. No one learns anything, no one grows, no one declines; all are antipathetic to the heroes and antiheroes of the eighteenth-, nineteenth-, and twentieth-century novel.

The *Good Soldier Švejk* is a successful political Menippean satire. Hašek's work has been downgraded for its loose structure, but the narrative continuity is measurable not according to the organicist criteria appropriate to the novel, but according to the rhetorical standards proper to satire. The disjointed plot is suitable to maintaining political consistency, which depends on didactic direction rather than aesthetic seamlessness. Each episode is a microcosm rendering the same absurd macrocosm, yet to find the same anarchist critique at the end of each episode is to *learn* something. Thus Hašek avoids the quandary of both liberal and conservative satire that ensnares *A Connecticut Yankee* and *Hudibras*: Twain's and Butler's inability to teach because of their multiplicity of attitudes, often paradoxical, toward the political views they espouse, an inability responsible for political satire's turning either self-contradictory, as it does for Butler, or undidactically aesthetic-novelistic, as for Twain. Episodic repetitiveness is a political virtue in *Švejk*, and it both reflects the clarity of Hašek's anarchist critique and explains the unique effectiveness of literalist satiric technique and style. For literalism, in taking the words of the "sane" and simply showing the insanity or inanity of actions, makes reason perfectly coincide with unreason. Thus the character of Švejk is translucent. Since he takes words with complete literalness, the "imbecilic" hero's lunatic misadventures are shown to be the logical consequence of rationality. And that rational world becomes the chaos it really is when Švejk strictly obeys its words.

That the anarchist brand of politics is itself apolitical may indicate the greatest irony of all: that reason, the soul of politics defined as the conscious effort to control life for the collective and individual good, is the villain, while unreason, the soul of anarchy as the human power to subvert all alienated orders, is the heroic power capable of liberating both individual and commune. Or, if we do not wish to take literary evidence seriously when it comes to thinking about politics but, instead, keep literature separated from history except as murky reflection—then perhaps all we can come up with is a literary rule: that, except in a truly anarchic world, satire is not after all a genre particularly suitable to politics, which more properly establishes the paradigms and directs the syntagms of tragedy, whether those of Aeschylus or of contemporary Third World revolutionary mimetic schemes, and of the novel in the tragic mode, such as feminist novels concentrating on novelistic developmentalism.

CHAPTER FIVE

Satiric Semigenre

Satire considered theoretically presents problems different from those posed by tragedy. To many, usage dictates a fairly clear distinction between "tragedy" and "tragic mode," while the term "satire" applies indiscriminately to both the genre and its varieties of mixture with other genres. Moreover, to say a novel is satiric usually suggests something more superficial, technically and thematically, than to say it is tragic. My own explanation for this discrepancy in attitude toward two independent genres with classical origins, of course, is that although this remains only vaguely sensed in most critical treatments of specific works, satire is an unstable genre that, in seeking resolutions to problems it both assumes and refines, transforms itself into other genres, particularly tragedy and the novel. *Satura*, in the beginning and throughout its history, equals mixture.

Yet there is also a kind of reasonableness in an alternative explanation: that what is satiric depends on criteria many of which are subjective, or perceptual, while tragedy and "the tragic" are more or less objective categories. This can be the case, however, only in discussions of the units of any given satire, in arguments about whether or not a particular allusion or intonation is satiric, especially when the work is from a strange past and is unusually topical, like Marvell's "The Last Instructions to a Painter." For when discussing satire as a kind, it is not so much specific references or tones that matter as the structural, epistemological, and rhetorical categories. Consequently, in this chapter I shall deal with these larger categories alone, but in the traditional descriptive vocabulary of "subject," "theme," "form," "technique," "language," and, last but not least, "genre."

Certain tendencies of transformation in Menippean satire seem to be associated with different subjects and themes. If the subject is social yet not moral, as in the *Satyricon*, satire shifts toward the novel defined as aesthetic-realist prose fiction. If the subject is ultimately religious, as in *Don Quixote* and Book 4 of *Gulliver's Travels*, satire dissolves into fantasy and romance combined with a Christian mode of tragedy (the Catholic Cervantes) or into fantasy and Christian tragedy without the romance (the

Protestant Swift). If the subject and themes are mainly political, as in *Hudibras* and *A Connecticut Yankee*, things get complex. Conservative satire such as Butler's falls apart into contradictory subgenres—mock epic, burlesque, and diatribe, for example—while liberal satire such as Twain's encounters a *crise de conscience* forcing a shift toward the psychological novel of developing characters. Evelyn Waugh's and Aldous Huxley's Menippean novels demonstrate these same generic and subgeneric splits along conservative and liberal axes during this century. Surprisingly, the anarchist Menippean satire *The Good Soldier Švejk* avoids the paralyzing paradoxes of conservative and liberal satire while also skirting polemic and propaganda, which are the bane of both fascist satire and Marxist social realist fiction in the satiric mode. Hašek's form remains pure Menippean satire in that no genre shifts are required to resolve any problems of political treatment. Perhaps, too, anarchist "nonideological" ideology is the perfect match in content to the technique of irony, which keeps Hašek's literary self as satirist separate in function from his Bolshevik historical identity.

Of the non-Menippean satirists who have written in verse, I have considered only Juvenal in detail, whose subject category would be moral. This concentration on morality requires Juvenal to seek out some level of explanation that is both more fundamental and higher than morals, and in his case the search leads to what he himself calls "Greek" tragedy. Horace, whose subject category would be social rather than moral, becomes, like his descendant in British satire, Pope, a verse essayist (*sermones* and epistles) instead of a tragedian.

Such patterns in subject and theme are hardly generalizations, but they remain significant for two reasons. They amply demonstrate the instability of satire as a genre. And they suggest that, excepting "pure" anarchist Menippean satire, generic transformation and mixture can either solve compositional problems (as in *Don Quixote* and Book 4 of *Gulliver's Travels*), enrich otherwise single-dimension works (as in Petronius and Juvenal), or involve thematic directionalities in paradoxes that finally annul the satire altogether (as in Butler and Twain). In conclusion, then, subject matter and theme not only can influence form from within, as we see in Petronius, Cervantes, and Twain, but can activate genericity as well, even to the point of new creation, for example, the creation of the aesthetic-realist novel out of Menippean satire in Petronius and Cervantes.

If form rather than subject and theme is the chief concern, one is tempted to emulate Boileau and adduce certain prescriptive rules of decorum. For instance, as a comparison of verse satire with Menippean satire shows, the latter excels in sustaining complex ironies and is thus more suited to criticizing social, religious, and political values—values, not actions—while verse satire excels in moral denunciation, a forte of verse satire from Juvenal to Ezra Pound. The proliferation of short forms of verse satire with moral content (or immoral—but not amoral), such as the epigram and limerick, would seem to underscore the specialization principle.

Irony, arch or innocent, is the central technique in satire. Extension to absurdity, if controlled by its antithesis, deflation, so that it avoids the nonsatiric dimensions of the surreal and the comic, is the next most potent technique. Irony is an attitudinal maneuver in satire, closely coordinated with the higher-level, strategic deployment of power according to the ends of moral, social, religious, and, though more problematically, political ascendancy. Unlike dramatic, or "tragic," irony, which is neutrally descriptive, tracking discrepancies between what men and women believe to be their situation and what it is (Clytaemnestra, Heracles, Lear), satiric irony is evaluative, suggesting discrepancies between what they see their situation to be and what they believe it should be according to various moral imperatives, articles of religious faith, social norms, or concrete political ideologies. Irony in satire is subjective; in tragedy, as in epic and comedy, objective.

Religious faith, particularly Catholicism, occasions the most elaborate satiric ironies, as in *Don Quixote*, probably because the breach between the understanding of the ways of the world and faith in the way the world should be is virtually complete, although allegorically bridgeable. Thus fantasy is often the upshot of pursuing ironies from a religious perspective. There are also deep affinities between Catholic irony and anarchist irony, both of which are total and equally beyond morality: there are many parallels in theme, tone, and character between *Don Quixote* and *The Good Soldier Švejk*. Moral ironies generally apply to instances of hypocrisy, so long as the satire is simply abusive, directed with no thought of analysis. But when Juvenal, for example, tries to explain the reason for moral ironies, the satire fades under the shadow of tragedy. When Swift, the most Juvenalian of later moral satirists, notes moral ironies, whether in "A Modest Proposal" or the Menippean *Gulliver*, he must also resort to tragedy, though in a specifically Christian mode. Social ironies affect the shape of satire in a unique way: unless reined in firmly by reductive devices such as litotes, social ironies lacking moral sting can turn a Menippean satire into comedy, as they do in Rabelais, or a verse satire into an exercise in gentlemanly good humor, as in Horace. If perpetuated, as in Petronius, these social ironies can float free, recoiling against the ironist (Encolpius), against the author's own refinement, and against the reader's expectation of negative critique. Irony becomes then the very structure of the work, keeping it on an even keel although eliminating predictabilities. However, satire is converted in the process into novelistic realism, which avoids comedy by sustaining a value-free amorality instead of building a solid moral scaffolding. Political ironies, unless of the totalizing anarchist variety, can result in the confusion of satiric directionalities, as in Butler, or they can develop into full-fledged paradoxes destroying satiric confidence, as in Twain. All in all, the most consistent and coherent instances of specifically satiric irony seem to proceed from Christian, both Catholic and Protestant, rather than classical assumptions—and from anarchist strategies. In these instances symbolic incursions into this world of historical contingency are launched from an entirely secure faith that things should be a certain way—the way they *never* will be until the end of the world for the Christian, or the way they simply *will* be, absurdly, via no transitions, for the anarchist.

Extension to absurdity controlled by satiric reduction amounts to more than hyperbole, the natural effect of which is comic, rich in savor but lacking in critique. And unlike satiric irony, however it may be deployed tactically to serve whatever strategic end, absurdity widens the gap between what seems to be and what should be into an abyss. Satiric irony takes measurements—of the precise distance between, for example, Don Quixote's madness and the priest's sanity, or between Gulliver and the yahoos and Gulliver and the Houyhnhnms—while extension beyond irony abandons all measure once the point is reached at which total inversion occurs. Inversion takes place when, for example, Don Quixote in Part 2 himself becomes the norm according to which we judge the deficiencies of sanity. That is, when we the readers insist on remaining skeptical of the value of faith, because of our having been conditioned by ordinary satire's critique of the don's error of faith in Part 1, we become the butts of Cervantes: we have failed to note that faith in Part 2 has very reasonably come to supplant reason, for the madman here succeeds for the same reasons he failed in Part 1. Cervantes' religious fantasy, with its antecedent "satire against the real," satirizes moral and social satire: thus it constitutes an extension to absurdity. Similarly, when Gulliver is forced to depart from the Houyhnhnms by means of the canoe made of stitched yahoo hides, we are suddenly forced, emotionally even more than rationally, to recognize not only the talking horses' ethical superiority over our human nature but the working-class "sorrel nag's" superior capacity for love, as expressed in his farewell: "Take care of thyself, gentle yahoo" (228). The lowest Houyhnhnm, with no soul yet with unerring moral instinct, is higher than the Christian yahoo, who, however degenerate, is supposed to transcend the most perfect utilitarian in wisdom. Therefore, we are forced to admit, the otherwise barbaric detail, dropped offhandedly, of the juvenile yahoo hides represents the progress, not the regression, of the "teach-able yahoo," Gulliver. Satire, as Cervantes's playful artifice and Swift's earnest yet delicately delivered absurdity equally demonstrate, is sheer rhetoric. We should not apply the criteria of tragedy or the realist novel to such rhetoric: the clarity of the imitative actions of winning, losing, or stalemating in tragedy, the verisimilitude of representation in the realist novel. And of all the techniques peculiar to satire, extension to absurdity is the most rhetorical.

The voice addressing the reader directly, as in verse satire, or indi-rectly, through characters in Menippean narrative, makes talk the core of satiric style. Satire preserves the sense of orality, indeed enhances it by making it ordinary instead of epic, and by liberating it from the comic stage, where it must always serve the action and fit the comic characters. The Juvenalian persona and his interlocutors such as Naevolus, like the Menippean characters Trimalchio and Švejk, spill over the edges of the satire with its moral, social, religious, or political purposiveness. Satire is not just satiric. The style of talk, whether the satirist's, the butt's, or the narrator's, is responsible for this extrageneric dimension of satire, which seems to want *not* to be just generic. Style, in fact, plays a large part in satire's instability: satiric talk's peculiar orality is boundless. For the loose, talky flow of satire, especially the Menippean kind, makes it more recep-tive than any other genre except the essay to the undetermined, the marginal, even the trivial. These are important literary concerns, es-pecially at those times when the criterion of unity—whether the arbitrary unity of Renaissance neoclassicism or the organic unity of Romanticism and post-Romanticism—tyrannizes both creativity and taste. Satiric style provides a safe haven for all those aesthetic uselessnesses that in resisting art maintain both writers' and readers' freedom. The genre's reputation as "low" owes much to this strength of satiric style.

Only the eighteenth-century novel and the essay approximate this looseness of style in satire. By "looseness" I mean the generous allowance in satire for leisurely attention, for the periodic relaxation that is a part of the reader's experience even when caught up by the vehemence of a Juvenalian spokesman. This spaciousness characterizes Menippean satire in particular: the *Satyricon, Don Quixote,* and *The Good Soldier Švejk* all have plots, yet in their episodic structure they at the same time oppose the action-based inexorability of tragedy and the developmental inexorability of the novel. The madman and his squire are always stopping to rest in the shade of a cork tree; Trimalchio artfully arranges pauses in his feast; Švejk will stop anywhere anytime to expatiate on why something has gone awry. As we have seen, satire is generically unstable in comparison to the novel in part because satiric characters do not develop, and when the characters

resist subordination to rhetoric by taking on roles beyond satiric func-
tionalism, the satire changes into other genres. The characters may then,
without themselves changing, be *seen* differently, as sane rather than mad
in Part 2 of *Don Quixote*, for example; or they may be forced into developing individualities more suitable to the novel than to satire, as do Hank and
Arthur in *A Connecticut Yankee*. Yet whatever may happen when satiric
instability results in generic changes in plot or character, the satiric style of
ceaseless ordinary talk maintains the extrasatiric dimensionality that
seems as intrinsic to satire as satiric directionality itself.

The *Satyricon*, *Don Quixote*, and *Švejk* could go on forever. The
fragmentary state of Petronius's satire and the unfinished state of Hašek's
one big book are also fortunate, however, because the talk of Trimalchio or
Encolpius, of Švejk or "Hašek" the intruding narrator, is antisystematic.
Petronius, like Juvenal later, hated Virgilian tidiness, and Hašek, like
Cervantes and Rabelais, is ready to deliver worlds more of the talk he has
heard on the streets of Prague. Yet Trimalchio's eruptive non sequiturs, his
innovative incoherencies, are never irrelevant to Petronius's satiric indict-
ments of pretentiousness, nor do Švejk's oblique and even tangential
anecdotes ever fail to corroborate Hašek's depictions of Europe's absurdly
methodical descent to barbarism; moreover, the two characters' positive
idiocies represent perspicacity about all sorts of matters. At the same time
they are more than just relevant to their satires' strategies. Indeed, speeches
such as the following illustrate a certain "necessary irrelevance" in satiric
style. The first is by Hašek as narrator speaking from his own real-life
experience as a dognapper, the second is by Švejk:

> But the dog, especially if it is a thoroughbred, must feel instinctively that
> one fine day it will be purloined from its master. It lives in continual fear
> that it will and must be stolen. For instance, when a dog is out for a walk it
> goes away from its master for a moment. At first it's happy and skittish. It
> plays with other dogs and climbs on their backs for immoral purposes and
> they climb on his. It smells the kerbstones, lifts its leg at every corner and
> even over the greengrocer woman's basket of potatoes: in short it has such
> *joie de vivre* and the world seems just as wonderful to it as it does to a
> young man when he has passed his school-leaving examination.
>
> But suddenly you notice that its gaiety vanishes and it feels that it's
> got lost. And now it is assailed for the first time by real despair. It runs
> in a panic about the streets, sniffs, whines and drags its tail between its
> legs in utter hopelessness. It puts its ears back and rushes along in the
> middle of the street no one knows where.
>
> If it could speak it would cry: "Jesus Mary, someone's going to steal
> me!" [190]

"Upon my honour, sir," said Švejk with the expression of a martyr, "I don't know any German writer personally. I only once knew a Czech writer personally, a certain Ladislav Hájek from Domažlice. He was the editor of *The Animal World*, and I once sold him a mongrel as a thoroughbred pom. He was a very cheery and nice man. He used to go to a pub and always read his stories there, which were so sad that everybody roared with laughter at them. Afterwards he wept and paid for everybody in the pub and we had to sing for him: 'The Domažlice gate's in a beautiful state. It's thanks to the art of the amorous heart of a painter I knew who the girls did pursue, and who can't now be found, as he's under the ground.'" [472]

These speeches, which possess the fortuitously common yet rare quality of found things, preserve a sense of contingency essential to the satires they occur in. They establish a norm of indispensable stupidity against which we are able to judge the satire's efficacy as it takes aim at its targets of dispensable stupidities. Pope captures a similar sense in verse satire as he itemizes Belinda's vanities. Both the speeches from *Švejk* are about being lost, dog or Czech editor. They are both ironic, and in a satiric, not comic, way because they posit hard-edge disharmony and alienation instead of reestablishing harmony and amity: the haunted insecurity of the dog in an incomprehensible yet somehow threatening world, the derision in the pub at the writer's sad stories. Yet the style of satiric talk that chattily attempts to get the thing, however marginal, told exactly the way it is even if it means putting the brake on either satiric momentum or narrative sequentiality is a way whereby the auditor-reader can break free from genre itself, from satire *as* satire, to a new perspective from which satire is *for* the dog, *for* the editor of *The Animal World*. The penchant of satiric talk for the contingent, like its scorn for formal unity, is the equivalent of the Petrarchan sonnet's extremely formal linguistic self-elaboration: although opposites, they both immortalize the mortal by means of words cast out to retrieve the pitiable perishables constituting our experience.

At this point a comparison of the distinct languages of satire and tragedy may be helpful. One of the reasons satiric talk can "save the contingent" is that language in satire is pure rhetoric, words aimed at. . . . Tragic language occupies Aristotle's bottom layer of tragedy in his formalist subordination of its components: the order moves from diction (language) to thought (*dianoia*) to character to plot (the arrangement of imitated action into episodes) to tragedy (conceived as imitation of historical or legendary action). This drastic subordination of language can apply only to tragedy as a genre. Yet tragedy is at the same time preeminently verbal, because expression as distinct from imitated action devolves solely on the actors' speeches: the genre lacks the narrator of prose narrative and any medium between audience and action such as is offered by a book of poems or even a film-dream. Still, the language of tragedy merely mediates between the imitated action and the auditors, while the form of the action constitutes the plot. Actors speaking elaborate the how and why, but the process of victory, loss, or stalemate *is* the action—and the imitation, and the form of the imitation. However, despite this emphasis on plot in Aristotle, the subordination of the human, or of people speaking from their characters, to the historical, or what is happening to them as they act, actually means tragic language is not supplementary or ornamental at all, but just the opposite. For since language in tragedy so *strictly* correlates with action, it can be considered functionally, if not logically, *constitutive* of the action—this is the reason, after all, why we can read tragedies and why action is not historical until "historicized" by language.

Nevertheless, however constituted by language both tragedy and satire may be, there is a significant difference in the ways signifiers relate to signifieds in each genre. In tragedy language always refers to action producing victory, loss, or stalemate. Satire, on the other hand, "imitates" no action whatsoever, no clear outcome. Instead, satire gesticulates, verbally, at the motives and values of actions, whether they are moral, social, religious, or political. Tragedy can imitate the actions reflecting moral choices, social attitudes, religious principles, and political plans. All satire can "do," however, is decry and commend, analyze and affirm, criticize and espouse. The language of tragedy, like tragic irony, is objective; the language of satire, like satiric irony, is subjective. This discrepancy in generic language systems is why high tragedy always remains beyond good and evil while low satire remains stuck in their midst. Satiric language must do the dirty work of evaluation, thus its tendency to be foul, to become topical, even journalistic. Tragedy as imitative language speaks oracularly, even from the seeming heart of violence and violation, in a language of objective presentation, of "art."

Furthermore, satire's rhetorical composition, lacking the tragic dimension of direct mimesis and depending as it does on verbal gestures, manifests the genre's tendency toward instability in typically subverting its own telos of moral, social, religious, or political ascendancy. Rhetoric subverts satire by adducing larger and larger conceptual frameworks to explain immorality, social decline, religious error, or political inadequacy. The explicative dynamics of satirical rhetoric cannot be satisfied with presentations of the consequences of action, for example, the total loss experienced by Euripides' winners Medea and Heracles. Tragedy remains aloof from good and evil because *performative* language is aesthetic, while evaluative language is rational. Satire *as* rhetoric is necessarily rational in its means, however irrational the motive to satirize may be. For what else is rhetoric but rational selection of language to show, to prove, to explain, to evaluate? But in its rational pursuit of its victims, satirical rhetoric heeds its own signifying process more than the telos of critique, and lets the victims off. Like the law it fulminates against, rational satire subverts itself: those charged and even poetically sentenced go free—on "parole."

Juvenal condemns the young Gracchus, tries to explain how he could be so bad when his family was so good from the earliest times, and discovers that the tragedy of time automatically means decline and fall: the young Gracchus is not to blame, after all. Trimalchio is a vulgarian, so when Petronius puts speeches in his mouth to explain this vulgarity, the vulgarity triumphs over the narrator Encolpius's socially ironic perspective on his host—who is a great guy indeed. Don Quixote is a madman. But when Cervantes explains the don's error of faith in the Andrés episodes and has the don reassert his faith against Andrés's despair, the satire can no longer be aimed *at* the don, whose internal and external adventures now serve as positive evaluations of the madman's faith in contrast to the skepticism of the world and the reader. So Don Quixote is no longer mad for being mad; we are, for being sane. Gulliver must serve as a conduit of Europe's absurdity; consequently, Swiftian irony renders the absurdity transparent. But the reader's corrected reason cannot redeem the fallen state of mankind. Therefore, Swiftian rational satire of yahoo man, corrupted by his degenerate reason itself, must finally resort to Original Sin and Grace to suggest hope after reason shows grounds for nothing but despair.

Tragedy deploys power straight, as outcome, not evaluation, as imitated action, not words that remain tied to the action signified. Satire, however, must deploy power by aiming words at targets within the hearing of those it wishes to affect. An imitation, tragedy exerts the force of a game, with three possible ends. An argument conducted by reason and colored by emotion, satire exerts the potential force of persuasion or rejection. As direct mimesis, tragedy simply performs itself over and over again as nonjudgmental art; it is very Greek. As evaluation, satire is like thought itself: it needs another base or bases besides itself on which to ground its judgments—a very Roman quality indeed, and as capable of being transfused into Christian dualism as the Roman ideal of civilization was adaptable to medieval Christianity. Both genres are figural deployments of power. But tragedy's figures play out their games. Satire's figural status, however, is qualified by rhetoric and the liberated play of irony; it is not only figural but also, by its nature as verbal gesticulation rather than performance, figurative. The words of tragedy's figures, of its actions configured in characters, are actual; those of satire's figures as they adapt to this, that, or another directionality are potential. Tragedy celebrates; it *is* emotion. Satire cerebrates; it causes emotions.

Perhaps now it is clearer why tragedy is the figural deployment of power in *political* configurations. It is dedicated to executing plans: "plot" is a term that alters little in significance whether applied to politics or mimesis. Reason, of course, is a tool in politics, serving power as inter-est—but only a tool. As Hamlet, the satirist as tragic hero, knows only too well as he meditates on Fortinbras, reason must not interfere with victory and can do nothing to palliate loss. Victory, loss, and stalemate themselves are not rational phenomena though reason may be brought in to justify each, in both real politics and imitative.

In satire, by contrast, reason may dwell on politics for the sake of clarifying *values,* just as it may consider society, morality, and faith as fields of value. For reason to do so, however, it must be cut off from the possibility of itself enacting political or social or moral or religious schemes for realizing these values. Satires have frequently been written to aid political causes, as we have seen in the cases of Butler and Twain. But insofar as these satires are reasonings for causes, they cannot *be* those causes, which are designed to win, lose, or dangle. Aeschylus's tragedies, whether the *Persians* or the *Oresteia,* could actually be their cause of Athenian victory, at least as far as any celebrative imitation can. Twain's satire, on the other hand, can throw out great formulations on the political table in the name of progress and common sense; but *A Connecticut Yankee,* because it is reason-bound, refuses to play the game of liberal politics, by demonstrating holocaust to be the result of progress and common sense.

Since they *are* their politics in a way fundamentally impossible for reasoning satire, tragedies are by and large no longer written by rationalist postindustrial societies. Whether they can be written is another question; probably they would be very different in effect from those written by the Greeks, Shakespeare, or even Kleist. Yet Aeschylean tragedies of victory *could* be written by and for revolutionary movements both within ra-tionalist postindustrial societies and throughout the developing post-colonial countries. And the tragic mode, particularly of the novel, in either the Sophoclean or Euripidean register, can efficiently represent contem-porary currents of feminism and black culture.

In the twentieth century irrational black humor has supplanted gen-uinely satiric irony, with the exception of *The Good Soldier Švejk,* which lurked unfulfilled as a literary model at the threshold of modernism. Hašek hit on the secret of making pure Menippean satire out of the absurdity of Central European politics: to throw over reason for the nonideology of anarchism, to write satire of unreason. History, however, especially the history of Austria-Hungary, anticipated Hašek when World War I went about unreasonably engulfing Europe's most rational nation-states. Later, Kafka had the opposite misfortune, when history copied his semisatiric allegories of irrationality. Few satirists in the postmodernist period, however, would be willing to adopt, even hypothetically, a thoroughgoing anarchism. In America, for example, Heller, Roth, Barth, and Irving may toy with the prospect of social, cultural, and moral anarchy but lack the nerve for anarchism, while Vonnegut and Barthelme have backed away from absurdist satire toward black comedy. In nonliterary American popular culture anarchic if not anarchist satire is generically potent in the guise of stand-up comedy, both black and white, but an earlier tradition of anarchic film satire—the Marx brothers' *Duck Soup,* W.C. Fields, Chaplin's *Modern Times*—oddly remains without heirs. Eastern Europe, Russia, and South America, all of which possess continuing literary and film traditions with the potential for tragedy, may also be the best hope of anarchist satire.

While tempting to speculation, though, such updatings do not enlighten us about how a genre such as satire really does mediate between history and culture. As rational critique in the discursive formation of rhetoric, satiric power can reveal much, and in greater detail than tragedies, about historical personages and their images, factions, and individual satirists. It can, that is, provide glosses for the historian. However, satire's rhetorical language system and its gesticulative bids for moral, social, religious, or political ascendancy show that the genre's true strength as a dialectical tool lies in its status as archive of reason's ever-losing struggle with moral, social, religious, and political interests. Nothing changes in response to "corrective" satire. Unstable satire changes, though, when it cannot find a rational explanation for what it satirizes.

CHAPTER SIX

On and of the Essay as Nongenre

Before pursuing the generic implications of the essay as a kind of discourse from Cicero to the late nineteenth century, it is necessary both to retrieve my theoretical beginnings and to forecast my destination, which is a theory of genre as such. If genre can be formulated, as either method itself or hypothesis, without exactly defining it—my hope expressed at the end of chapter 1—then it is differential power. Deployable according to an indefinite number of sets of operations, or presentations, genre I have so far considered in its pure guise as tragedy and in its self-contradictory incompletion as satire, which I call "semigenre."

Tragedy demonstrates power deployed for outcome; thus its action is political. It is a game with three possible resolutions: victory, loss, or stalemate. Satire deploys power rationally, not for outcome but for display of moral, social, religious, and factional superiority over its targets. Since it is attitudinal, gestural, rhetorical, satire must, unlike goal-bound tragedy, resort in its structural unfolding to other genres to resolve the problems called up for attack.

Formally, tragedy's mimesis subordinates language to plot. Thus any possible conflict or contradiction at whatever level, personal or national, always becomes in tragedy a political struggle framed by win, loss, or draw. Following Scaliger, I hold that tragedy is the inverse of history: if in history emotions are aroused to achieve ends, tragedy deploys its power to achieve the three emotions of exultation, despair, and prolonged tension; these characterize Aeschylean, Euripidean, and Sophoclean tragedy respectively. Self-declaring ideologies such as anticolonialism, Marxism, dissident liberation philosophies, Nietzschean will to power, French Revolutionary bourgeois nationalism, sixteenth- and seventeenth-century European imperialism, and mid-fifth-century Athenian nationalism are some of the specific political correlates of genuinely tragic actions.

The only ideological match entirely suitable to the verbalism of satire is anarchism, the ideology of fiat "Dullness" that concludes the coronation in *The Dunciad* or commences the World War in *The Good Soldier Švejk*. If satiric evaluations begin to spill over into the programmatically political realm of radical-reactionary, liberal-conservative resolutions, they negate themselves by revealing the targets of critique as necessary to the ongoing life of the critique itself. The formal result is the generic switch, whereby critique can transform itself into the developmental hope of the realist novel, the religious or aesthetic salvation of Quixotic fantasy or Petronian realism, or the tragic modalism of Juvenalian retrospective and Swiftian Christianity. This formal, albeit not only formal, instability of satire makes it, in comparison with tragedy's efficient deployment of power toward outcome, a semigenre, forever at odds with its own scheme of evaluative utterance.

At the extreme opposite of tragedy in the range of genres, and in its own way as far removed from satire's instability, is the essay. This kind I shall consider as nongenre. Neither a deterministic game nor a set of verbal gestures, an essay deploys power freely. It is discourse as discourse, discursivity as such, textuality untrammeled by generic boundedness. Its objective is unintended, while a satire is nothing but intention, and undestined, while a tragedy *is* outcome. An essay's unprogrammatic identity is freedom to sport negations, to disorient, to play, to abnegate the self by constructing a voice out of ceaseless discourse the very drift of which is to disclose what becomes as its contradictions and diversities destroy what seems to be. The art of the essay is liberationist artifice, as Montaigne expressed in the injunction "Among the liberal arts, let us begin with the art that liberates us" (*Essays* 1.26 C, p. 117).[1] The essayist chooses not to choose, wills not to will, shirks stable identity, directs himself or herself not to find but to be surprised: "Power keeps quite another road than the turnpikes of choice and will, namely, the subterranean and invisible tunnels and channels of life. It is ridiculous that we are diplomatists, and doctors, and considerate people: there are no dupes like these. Life is a series of surprises" (Emerson, *Essays* 482-83).

The "politics" of the essay aims at total victory by installing the eternally changeable Reich of the Word. This politics is really a religion, one in which the essayistic voice nonchalantly blasphemes, "I am that am," yet never fails in its duty to its own discursivity: "All writing comes by the grace of God" (Emerson, *Essays* 483). One of the topoi of the essay genre, friendship, underscores this liberationist aesthetic, as if the solitary voice, the monologue delivered from exile or retreat or retirement, moved through nothing but textuality itself toward reconnection with the world: Cato the Elder looking back to earlier Scipios as he expatiates before the latest Scipio, Montaigne struggling with the death of La Boétie, Machiavelli writing in defeat, Bacon writing in mental retreat from his career in public service, Rousseau and Nietzsche in premodern and modern estrangement, Emerson in abdication from the pulpit.

Instead of tragedy's firm harnessing of language to action or satire's rhetoric of intention-contradiction, the language of the essay mimes nothing but itself and aims at no superiority of value over its endless plain of discourse. Its language is, simply, writing, a transparent "graphesis" of the mind Montesquieu first noted in appreciation: "Dans le plupart des auteurs, je vois l'homme qui écrit; dans Montaigne, l'homme qui pense [In most authors I see the man who writes; in Montaigne, the man who thinks]."[2] Montaigne's own grasp of the essay's distinctive way of powerless power is sure: "If my mind could gain a firm footing, I would not make essays, I would make decisions" (*Essays* 3.2 B, p. 611). The essay, then, is the genre of absence, the perpetual dislocation of "footing"—nongenre. "The way of life is wonderful: it is by abandonment," Emerson claims essayistically, in "Circles" (*Essays* 412). This is the life registered by the essay, not for the nonsensical sake of pursuing such a life, or even understanding it, but in the process of living it by writing it: "The first remark brings on the second" (Montaigne, *Essays* 1.40 B, p. 186).

For all its freedom from the strictures of tragedy and the ideological-formal problems of satire, as nongeneric genre the essay is remarkably distinctive, as unmistakably shaped and immediately recognizable as tragedy and as markedly intoned as satire. Essays are, as it were, generically amorphous. Consequently, they stand glaringly aberrant, to many theorists not even qualifying as instances of a definite, single kind when genre study is conceived as an exercise in classification. Traditional literary historians like Rosalie Colie can recognize the generic markings of the essay in terms of its affiliation with such Renaissance forms as the Machiavellian discourse, the adage of Erasmus, the philosophical treatise, and the anatomy. But the essay, while completely historical like all other genres, bears an identifying mark that seems to have little relevance to such determinations as Athenian politics in tragedy or Roman crises of *imperium* in satire. That mark is somewhat ineffable, too, for all its distinctiveness. The essay possesses *voice*. One can be even more precise: the essay possesses the voice of the old man. Since it lacks any prescribed subject matter, the essay is definable neither by what it says nor, since a genre-specific style is lacking, by how it says what it says.

Instead, what is crucial is *that* the essay says: utterance for the sake of utterance—"voicing." The old man's audacity is to talk freely, at large, ceaselessly, as if he were listening to himself, despairing of an attentive audience, yet not as a diarist talks to himself. The old man's audacity is to talk to himself, usually about himself, publicly if not "in public." This self--

sustaining talk indicates words in place of action, the opposite of the quintessentially public genre, tragedy. Moreover, these are words guided, or given rein, not by self-contradictory reason as in satire, but by self-renewing desire. Jean Starobinski rightly notes that this desire, as Montaigne would have it in "On some verses of Virgil," becomes the verbal "incarnation" of ardors long past realizing: "The power of *incarnation* and sexualization that language has is indistinguishable from the *excess* of meaning that surrounds each word like an aura and thus bridges the gap that Montaigne believes generally separates the word (mere 'wind' that it is) from the thing" (192). In what amounts to the same desire-become-word-become-thing, Machiavelli defers to the future plans defeated in the present by the reliving of past Roman victories read in Livy; likewise Rousseau revives a totally estranged self by substituting verbal prolongations and narratives for primal sincerity; Emerson sermonizes nature's text of creativity into realized faith; and Nietzsche, the essayist philosopher as "free spirit," perpetually revaluates values.

Thus the essay considered as a genre realizes the arch-Romantic aspiration to transcend the bounds of genre. Lacking centeredness, the essay is desire continuing "for as long as there is ink and paper in the world" (Montaigne, *Essays* 3.9 B, p. 721). A prospect of power, like tragedy and satire, the essay deploys power neither toward ends nor toward critique. It simply deploys itself. That is, the essay is pure prospect—groundless, wide open, empty, like the Platonic *matrix*. Frameless, it frames itself. If an essay were to achieve an end, its prospect would have no vantage, no beginning; for the essay commences from itself ex nihilo, lapses into voids, starts anew. The Emersonian "series" is the larger, nonorganizational organization imposed, "inorganically," on instances of this genre. Even the topic of an essay—old age, friendship, experience, reveries, good and evil—is nothing else than the self's, the textual voice's, topicality, sheer pretext for prospective text. "Keep writing" is the essayist's credo: "For what Montaigne describes so lavishly, by stages, is the way in which intentional action, directed inward, becomes aware of the tension and rhythm that drives it forward. . . . What stands out, then, is not a map or portrait of the 'deeper' self, finally deciphered, but rather the tireless subject who, knowing nothing, is engaged in a never-ending investigation of himself. However far the ego's self-investigation proceeds, it never acquires anything other than a muscular awareness of its own progress" (Starobinski 226-27). And the reader of essays? Unlike the spectator at tragedies (even if reading, one is a spectator) or the coconspiratorial reader of satires, the reader of Cicero, Montaigne, Bacon, Rousseau, Emerson, and Nietzsche, even of scientists such as Sir Thomas Browne and Darwin, reads not for information, not for wisdom, not for emotion, not for critique, never for goal. One reads as a pure reader: "keep reading."

How, then, does the essay as nongenre contribute to my argument that genres are deployments of power? First, like satire, which is a representative semigenre, the essay shows that genre cannot be only one kind or even one degree of power. The concept of genre must be flexible enough to accommodate the essay's self-referential textuality as well as tragedy's political and satire's rational deployments. This textual genre's distinctiveness in the kind of relation it displays between language and action demonstrates in an even stronger way than the other kinds that literary genres are characterized by differences in discursive formation.

For example, tragedy is mimetic, its language honed to the political presentation of the edges of power: win, loss, or stalemate. Satire is rhetorical, its gestural language aspiring to yet never affording the definitiveness of tragedy's game configuration, or even the developmental prospect of the novel. To resolve its contradictions as a semigenre, satire typically becomes a mode of other genres with clearer, relatively unobstructed prospects. The essay as nongenre is sheer textuality, offering itself as *vox in deserto*: language becomes constative action, rhetoric transmuted into a peculiar kind of inner—thus, strictly, nonmimetic—mimesis. What exactly is mimed? The essayistic voice mimes itself.

Thus the essay as nongenre connects with history by cutting all ties with it, even the illusory tie maintained by tragedy's mimesis of action and the tie of intentionality binding satire to its targets. The essay declares for the Word *instead of* history. Yet in doing so it reconnects. Hermetically sealed off as the Word desirous only of itself, the essay can still be a historical act, the inherently critical act of registering itself "sexually," as its own history. The dialectic of the essay is truly *negative*, not in Adorno's sense but in the sense conveyed by Cicero's and Montaigne's retreat, Rousseau's "retraite absolue," and Nietzsche's "beyond good and evil."

Retreat: Cicero and Montaigne

Cicero's *Cato Major,* or *De senectute (On Old Age),* has been called an "essay" consistently, though loosely, throughout this century.[3] Alternative generic tags have ranged from "tractate" to "treatise." The work is prefaced with a dedicatory "letter" to Atticus, in which Cicero mentions his piece as "something on this theme" ("de senectute vellem aliquid scribere") and as a "book" ("hunc librum");[4] "book" for the Romans, however, indicated a manuscript of almost any size. And *On Old Age* has been formally pinned both as a "dialogue" (or "little dialogue" in the Platonic manner) and as primarily a "monologue," that is, a dialogue according to "the method of Aristotle" (Falconer 6) or "the method . . . of the New Academy" (Petersson 572).

The essay begins with a half-framing, half-chronology-setting exchange between Cato the Elder, who was eighty-four in 150 B.C., the fictive date of Cato's speech, and two representatives of the generation of his grandchildren, Scipio (thirty-five) and Laelius (thirty-six). Probably completed between 45 and 44 B.C., *On Old Age* was referred to by Cicero himself: once, in his letters *Ad Atticus*, as "O Tite, si quid" (from the first words); once, in *De divinatione*, as *De senectute;* and *twice*, in both the *Laelius (On Friendship)* and *Ad Atticus*, as *Cato Major* (Falconer 4). When set in the context of Cicero's philosophic program represented by the eight works beginning with the *Academica* and ending with *De officiis*, not only *On Old Age* but also *On Friendship* and *On Glory* (lost) are acknowledged by many as "words of philosophic sentiment not essential to the development of his argument" (Hunt 1): "They could have been included in the *Tusculans . . .* but, written as they were, they became less technical, more directly founded on ordinary experience" (Petersson 572).

From the spokesman Cato's monologic prominence, as well as from Cicero's recognition in *On Old Age* of this consummate Roman's historical primacy, reinforced by the citations in *On Friendship* and *Ad Atticus*, it would seem reasonable to think of the work in the following way: Cato's is really the voice of Cicero in an essay that articulates the "last Republican's" half-cautious, half-emphatic summation of all the virtues that once were Rome's. They are no longer; Cato the Elder, eighty-four in 150 B.C., signifies the culture that Caesar's victory has terminated. And Cicero, Caesar's old friend, ally, then antagonist, can adopt in 44 B.C. the superannuated retrospective of Cato the Elder's on the time of Rome's and his own coming-of-age: the Second Punic War through the absorption of Greece during the period 220-150.

What is the result, generically speaking? Cicero's *Cato Major* is a personal statement, but one that can find no more personal voice than Cato's. Cicero lies low at his country homes because first Caesar's rise then his sudden fall make the pro-Pompey friend of Brutus's both suspect and potentially dangerous. Old, bereaving the death of his daughter, burdened by debt, canceled as an active politician, Cicero writes. He writes "philosophy." But accompanying his desire to console himself by resuming his youthful studies of Greek thought is Cicero's determination to announce, as simply as possible to those who will understand (like his significantly cognomened friend Atticus), what Rome once did mean, could have continued to mean, but, like Cato at eighty-four, had no chance, perhaps no will, to prolong.

This "Rome" for Cicero is the meaning of "nature" to Cato: Roman force (*vis*, virtue), ineluctably self-renewing, like the tilled earth, the soil itself, which Cato lyricizes in a digression that is really the centerpiece of the entire essay (*De senectute*, sec. 15). Yet grafted onto this celebration of Roman *vis* is the need of the old Republican, Cato-Cicero, to bridge the gap between dutifulness, defined as "Roman," and learning, identified as "Greek." Cato the Elder taught himself Greek when he achieved his autumn. Correspondingly, Cicero, sere with grief personal and public, wishes to retire, as actively as Cato, though in a new sense imposed by necessity. His final mission he identifies: to synopsize Greek philosophy for himself and other Romans who still retain their sense of continuity with the past—to enlighten the dark age fallen upon Rome with the civil wars, the triumph and fall of Caesar, and the new civil wars that will usher in the empire.

Is this "essay" of Cicero's on the innocuous topic of old age a work of mere "philosophic sentiment" (Hunt 1), one that, together with *On Friendship*, "stand[s] outside of his philosophical series" (Petersson 572)? Or is one of his most personal works of amateur popularization really one of Cicero's most original articulations of Roman culture as both distinct from and continuous with the best of the fast-receding ancient world? The essay genre properly begins with *Cato Major de senectute* because it indicates something different from philosophy but not inferior, "less technical" (Petersson 572) but not lighter; something flush with the author as self voicing itself rather than dialogue, whether Platonic or Aristotelian. Philosophy dedicates itself to the timelessness of idea, but there is always something old that sounds through Cato's wandering garrulity, something valedictory, retired, in retreat.

Not only the formal aspects of this initiating instance of the essay but also the essayist himself, Cicero the former consul and provincial governor, the patrician leader in action and by repute, seems to determine the genericity of *On Old Age*. Cicero cannot be said to have invented the genre the way Aeschylus, for example, can be said to have established tragedy out of his own experience as an Athenian aristocrat turning back the Persians. It is Cicero's historical situation, as it will be later in varying degrees for Montaigne, Machiavelli, Bacon, and Rousseau, that becomes suggestive in itself and not simply as it affects the individual. A man in and of history, Cicero the essayist is out of history, by necessity and by choice. Old Roman politicians like Cato, however, may still guide their polis through "influence" (secs. 6 and 17): "And what shall I say of Paulus, and of

Africanus, and of Maximus, of whom I have spoken before? These men had power [*auctoritas*], not only in their speech, but in their very nod. Surely old age, when crowned with public honours, enjoys an influence which is of more account than all the sensual pleasures of youth" (sec. 17, pp. 72-75).

Yet Cicero's *auctoritas*, unlike Cato's, lacks the "public honours" requisite for one seriously espousing Republican values; even after Caesar's assassination the world will not, despite Brutus, reverse itself. Catonian power as "authority" befitting the *senes* of the old ruling class is a mere dream for Cicero, more significant than nostalgia yet nothing but a dream. The bitterness of the powerless old man of power eventually breaks through Cato's defense of his own kind of autumnal glory when Cicero's tough-minded alter ego reiterates at the very end of his monologue his ongoing analogy between old age and the final act (*peractio*) of "life's drama": "Moreover, old age is the final scene, as it were, in life's drama, from which we ought to escape when it grows wearisome and, certainly, when we have had our fill [*satietate*]" (sec. 23, pp. 98-99). Fulfillment, or nature's "ripeness" as Cato has it according to another of his favorite analogies, suddenly turns into ironic disgust heroically tinged with the proper Stoic casualness. Catonian political influence has changed into mere Ciceronian repute, the shadow of deactivated political manhood. This is the historical situation of the essay's generation: retreat.

Yet political futility can mean personal freedom. Power in *On Old Age* is displaced from the public honor of glory to the private reverberations of words. The liberationist genre is the genre of words as substitutive actions—the vacuous politics of textuality. This same verbal order that sustains Cicero during the interim between civil wars keeps Machiavelli's brain alive after his body is exhausted by torture, lends Montaigne his sense of individual wholeness once he has bowed out of the religious wars going on all around his country retreat, provides the busy magistrate Bacon with an alternate and more secure fame, resurrects the mind-blown pariah Rousseau, creates a second career for the former minister Emerson, and makes possible the sense of audience denied Nietzsche by his intellectual isolation.

Lacking the old Roman *auctoritas* of deeds and influence, Cicero does what Montaigne, Rousseau, and Nietzsche will do later, Montaigne with Plutarch and Seneca, Rousseau with Montaigne, Nietzsche with Kant. He fabricates a network of authorities of the Word. In *On Old Age*, Cicero, speaking through Cato, tries to make it appear that the Old Roman who taught himself Greek in retirement can serve as a link in a sequence of oral transmissions that convey to Rome the "great thoughts" of the Greeks, especially Pythagoras, Plato, and Epicurus: Cato hears his "Tarentine host" Nearchus recount "the tradition" of Plato's visit (sec. 12, p. 51); Cato learns from his "elders" of Epicurus, "a man at Athens who professed himself 'wise' and used to say that everything we do should be judged by the standard of pleasure" (sec. 13, p. 53); and Cato "Romanizes" the great "Pythagoras and his disciples—who were almost fellow-countrymen of ours, inasmuch as they were formerly called 'Italian philosophers'" (sec. 21, p. 89).

The reason this linkage of Cato-Cicero's Roman identities with even the oldest aspects of Greek learning is so important to the genericity of the essay, whether the incipient genre practiced by Cicero or the *essai* as conceived by Montaigne, is that it invents a kind of history able to supplant the history that is no longer possible, the history that Cato is readying himself to leave behind fulfilled and that Cicero is retreating from unfulfilled. The reign of deeds and influence is over; the rule of learning commences. Philosophy is Cicero's only available history, the history of words that forms the same tradition that Montaigne will later substitute for a history of religious conflict and the void left by the death of the best and the brightest, of his friend La Boétie. Textuality has by default inherited power from history, which has expelled one of its makers. Therefore it must establish its own *auctoritas* of Western traditions of learning.

The essay genre thereby gains its proper identity, declares its own world. The benefit accruing to the essayist is immense: the power afforded a Cicero or Montaigne to range at will over a new terrain consisting of nothing else but verbality. This is the power to shed historical selfhood—whether history has abandoned the self or the self, history—to free oneself by means of the new politics of the word, to find one's new identity in "the book": "I have no more made my book than my book has made me" (Montaigne, *Essays* 2.18 C, p. 504). For Cato, as for Cicero and all those following his precedent, the Word opens up a new arena for action and influence within the bounds of the essay, which is a frame unbounded by history yet a formation entirely determined by the historical situation of retreat. Nonetheless, the prospect is one of power, the power of self-fabrication out of the materials of learning: "I would rather fashion my mind than furnish it" (Montaigne, *Essays* 3.3 C, p. 622). And the requisite science for wielding this new shield, the essay, is not passive but aggressive: "Any defense bears the aspect of war" (*Essays* 2.15 C, p. 467).

No wonder, then, that Cato the Elder voices Cicero's new life of the essay with the kind of rejuvenation appropriate to the power of words. For the voice of Cato is Cicero's means of revitalizing the Rome whose death throes he himself is suffering. Nature is the reference in *On Old Age* that controls this impossible textual reversal of time, just as it is the source of all recuperations. That is why section 15, which is often appraised as a charming digression on the part of Cato, is really the off-center center of the essay, and one of Cicero's definitive as well as thoroughly Roman statements of what Rome signifies. The adventure of freedom from history offered by the essay genre, which is permitted to build whatever gene- alogy of learning it may find necessary to shore itself up, also empowers the essayist to be original. In *On Old Age*, Cicero is no longer subservient to Greek learning, but master of what he selects from that past as he proceeds to construct his new Republic of textuality.

The turn from the close of section 14 to the beginning of section 15 proves Cato's paean to Nature's *vis* is no digression, technically, for Cato is moving from preset point, "the pleasures of the mind," to preset point, "the pleasures of agriculture." Still, the cleverness with which Cicero warms up the torpid sensuality of his ancient Roman is proof of a calculated *effect* of digression to a new plane of discourse and sensibility. As he speaks, Cato's own words incite him beyond sensual delight—"incredibil- iter delector"—to a luxuriating transport of roused sexuality, whereby he regains a sense of youth: "et elicit . . . erecta geniculato vaginis iam quasi pubescens" (secs. 14-15, pp. 62-63).

Montaigne might have been similarly aroused by the Latin of Cato's speech, as he attests to being by the labials and assonance and imagery of Virgil and Lucretius, in "On some verses of Vergil." *On Old Age* is, in fact, Montaigne's late essay in miniature. Cicero sets the whole genre of essay in this passage. The rebirth of the self expelled from or abandoning history can be accomplished by concocting out of the very materials of language itself a genealogy of learning, which then serves as the "action" of an old man's deedlessness. But it can also be accomplished by turning to the eroticism of the Word, whether the "essay made flesh and bone" in Montaigne or Cicero's essay dug out of Cato's delectation of "the soil itself, its nature and its power." The Word, that is, is both the way to rejuvenation and the very stuff of youth.

In the process, of course, Cicero the essayist resurrects his dead Rome. Once he starts there is no stopping Cato's words. They warm him with the moist heat of the earth, and "the first remark brings on the second" (Montaigne, *Essays*, 1.40 B, p. 186). This process of essayism carries Cato-Cicero to the full re-creation of the political world that in history has come to naught and thus must be "re-*stated*." The associations of metonymy work from beginning to end through pure verbal reflexivity: from the "pleasures of agriculture," which are sensually pleasurable to the point of "incredible delight," to Nature's abundant return on the farmer's account of both principal and interest, then to "the soil itself" ("ipsius terrae"). From that follows the entire sexual process of seed, heat, growth, youth, phallic maturity in the emergence of "the ear" of wheat itself from the "foreskin" sheathing it ("erecta geniculato vaginis"), proud, erect, naked, and, finally, the "grain in *ordered* rows and protected by a *palisade of spikes* against . . . attacks" (secs. 14-15, pp. 62-63, my italics).

The product of this natural-sexual-verbal metonymy is allegory: "ear of grain"/Nature associated with "palisade of spikes"/State. Emblem of Rome, especially the Republic, is the *fasces*, borne by lictors escorting the consuls and indicating strength through unity, the sticks bound by the aggressive martial force (*vis*) specified by the single ax blade emerging from the top. The earth's maternal warmth germinates the male seed of grain, the form of which with its "ordered rows" and *spici* emblematizes the Mars-conceived state *e pluribus unum*. This Rome possesses, Cicero implies, the vigor (*vis*) of Nature itself as matrix phallicized by agriculture. An old Roman like Cato, then, must be reborn through Cicero's words by means of a simulated sexual reproduction, which is the same for man or Nature. Rome is Nature.

This is more than ideological naturalization of the status quo. Cicero's essay genre, with its clear metonymic closure exerting firm allegorical control yet never allowing the mystical-metaphorical expansion of earth-seed-immortality in the cycle of nature, moves well beyond the inherent naturalizing procedure of literature. The essay genre launched by *On Old Age* is the unbounded nongenre of self-liberation. It is the genre of political regeneration, through the voluntary or involuntary situation of retreat, of the self purged of history. This self, Cicero-Cato's voice, reproduces itself through the artifice of its own genealogy of learning and through the sexualization of language.[5] The essay is self-reflexive discursivity, the proper function of which is to declare a private politics of liberation from history by generating a verbal state, the state of verbality—this extreme nongenre is the extreme opposite of the purest genre *of* the state, public tragedy.[6]

Montaigne's language in "On some verses of Virgil" (*Essays* 3.5), as noted earlier (Starobinski 192), becomes sexualized, like the language of Cicero's Roman epitome. Are the operations of Montaigne's *essai*, however, the same as those of Cicero's genre? Although Montaigne voluntarily retired in his prime from public service, with intermissions later, while the really aged Cicero involuntarily withdrew from politics, the similarities in their historical situations override this surface difference. Montaigne's turn away from action to learning at a point in his life he regarded as already past mid-life matches Cicero's: it was a deliberate retreat, to which the Latin inscription on his study wall adjoining the tower library at his country estate, attests: ". . . retired to the bosom of the learned virgins, where in calm and freedom from all cares he will spend what little remains of his life, now more than half run out" (qtd. in Frame ix). Both extrication and liberty in the positive sense of freedom to pursue new goals are self-declared objects for Montaigne, as for Cicero-Cato: "If the fates permit, he will complete this abode, this sweet ancestral retreat: and he has consecrated it to his freedom [à sa liberté], tranquility, and leisure."[7] Of course, the parallel of civil wars—between rival factions for Cicero, between Catholics and Protestants for Montaigne—is striking, especially when the closeness of each to these conflicts is considered: both men had friends, Montaigne even had family, on both sides, and both were geographically close to the fighting, Cicero never far from Rome and Montaigne in the section east of Bordeaux where the Protestant revolts were longest-lived and strongest.

More important, generically, Montaigne's essai, especially at its maturity in Books 2 and 3, reprises the liberationist movement of On Old Age: the retreat from action, to liberty "in the bosom of the learned virgins," to self-re-creation through the sensualizing and propagating capacities of language itself.[8] However, Montaigne enriches and extends this Ciceronian process. "On some verses of Virgil" provides the closest possible correlate to On Old Age, in its similarity of subject and robust treatment of old age; but this late essai from Book 3 is also the most complete instance of the movement typical of all Montaigne, however compacted or truncated this same movement may be in the rest of the Essais. The central object of "Virgil," which is to resurrect a life grown sluggish with advancing age by overturning the orthodox soul-body hierarchy and elevating the bodily over the mental, is clear from the outset: "It is my body's turn to guide my mind toward reform [de guider l'esprit vers la reformation]" (Essays 3.5 B, p. 638; Essais, p. 262).[9] Soon after declaring this Catonian kind of pagan reanimation through identification with the material rather than the spiritual, albeit in a post-Cicero style of anti-Christian irony, Montaigne baldly reiterates one of Cato's points, which had become a commonplace: "I would rather be old less long than be old before I am old" (Essays 3.5 B, p. 639; Essais, p. 264).

Then about halfway through the essay—Cicero's similar passage on the ear of wheat is likewise halfway through On Old Age—Montaigne engages with the particularly rejuvenating erotic effects of Lucretius (Essays 3.5 B and C, pp. 664-65; Essais, pp. 299-301). At this point the movement that defines essai in Montaigne properly begins. Language, and in particular Latin—the language his father required him to speak as a child and a language Montaigne believed to possess unique inherent qualities—becomes "flesh and bone":

Plutarch says that he saw the Latin language through things. It is the same here: the sense [le sens] illuminates and brings out [produict][10] the words, which are no longer wind, but flesh and bone. The words mean more than they say. Even the weak-minded feel some notion of this; for when I was in Italy I said whatever I pleased in ordinary talk, but for serious discourse I would not have dared trust myself to an idiom that I could neither bend nor turn out of its ordinary course. I want to be able to do something of my own with it. [*Essays* 3.5 B and C, p. 665; *Essais*, p. 301]

Thus in Montaigne language all by itself is like language conjoined with Nature in Cicero. The material and intellectual *sens* in Montaigne's French conveys "sensory" and "sensual" in addition to the "signified." For Plutarch and the Latin-speaking Montaigne words really are physical, not merely representational. They "can do" (Frame's "I want to be able to do"); they are "power to . . . " ("J'y veux pouvoir quelque chose du mien," *Essais*, p. 301). This materiality of language is not that of an inanimate tool. In the following passage directed at language in itself, the essayistic voice of "Virgil" grows beyond sensuality to a knowing carnality that would equate language with a woman: "Handling and use by able minds gives value to a language, not so much by innovating as by filling it out [*comme la remplissant*] with more vigorous and varied services, by stretching and bending it [*divers services, l'estirant et ployant*] . . . they teach the language unaccustomed movements [*luy aprenent des mouvements inac-coustumés*]" (*Essays* 3.5 B, p. 665; *Essais*, p. 301).

Clearly by now in this old man's *essai* to regain a sense of vitality, the sexuality of language proffers the appropriate elixir: a concoction half-natural, based on the ingredients of Latin, Montaigne's psychologically significant childhood tongue, and half-synthetic, consisting of erotically coached "unaccustomed movements." His responsiveness to Latin, how-ever, suggests to Montaigne the contrast offered by his responses to the language he is now writing, French: "In our language I find plenty of stuff but a little lack of fashioning [*faute de façon*]" (*Essays* 3.5 B, p. 665; *Essais*, p. 301). But the language of the *Essais* must be this French, Montaigne's adult language, which "essays" to retrieve the youthfulness of his Latin yet also yearns to give the essayistic voice an identity. This identity arrives. For the next movement to be generated by this parthenogenetic *essai* genre is from *sens* and sexualized language to self-realization. Better yet, since it is not Montaigne the person who fashions this self, but instead the languages of Latin and French—the self of the essayistic voice—the movement could be described as "self-ization," the automatic construction of self out of textuality: "For this purpose of mine [*Pour ce mien dessein:* 'plan' as 'design'] it is also appropriate for me to write at home, in a backward region [*en pays sauvage*: hyperbole], where no one helps me or corrects me, where I usually have no contact with any man who understands the Latin

162

of his Paternoster and who does not know even less French [. . . *et de françois un peu moins*]. I would have done it better elsewhere, but the work would have been less my own; and its principal end and perfection is to be precisely my own" (*Essays* 3.5 B, pp. 666-67; *Essais*, pp. 302-3). Finally, in a mocking (the temptation is to say "Whitmanesque") coming out of the closet, Montaigne's *essai* declares itself, interestingly enough in quotes, to be an independent voice: "'Isn't this the way I speak everywhere? Don't I represent myself to the life? Enough, then [*suffit!*]. I have done what I wanted. Everyone recognizes me in my book, and my book in me' [*J'ay faict ce que j'ay voulu: tout le monde me reconnoit en mon livre, et mon livre en moy*]" (*Essays* 3.5 B, p. 667; *Essais*, p. 303).

"Who reads this touches a man," the passage says in effect. This declaration of its own independence uttered by the essayistic voice needs to be followed up by a constitution. Cicero's Cato constitutes himself as old Roman *redivivus* by identifying the language of ongoing textuality with "the soil itself," with its *vis*, which is capable of re-creating Republican Rome, the ear of wheat. Montaigne's *essai* enriches this Ciceronian procedure, making it fully self-conscious. This accounts for the signal effect of Montaigne on his readers, from Pascal to Emerson: "One of the mysteries of the *Essays* is how the portrait of Michel de Montaigne seems to become that of every man and thus of the reader. No one has explained this" (Frame vi). No explanation is required. For the genre *essai* as textuality—the voice of the *essai*—constitutes itself in the process of being read. Voice is sexually produced: the fertile stuff of language, having stimulated the almost impotent roué-writer by its inherent eroticism (that of the Latin of his youth), is inseminated by his fashioning (in his adult French). The reader of the *essai* is himself or herself fashioned from the writing in a direct way not possible in any other genre because of extralinguistic features—for example, tragedy's mimesis toward outcome and satire's involvement in rhetorical designs and values. Discourse, as Montaigne practices it, is genericity itself, the fertility of all topics and their identity: "Any topic is equally fertile for me [*Tout argument m'est egallement fertille*]. A fly will serve my purpose; and God grant that this topic I have in hand [*en main*] now was not taken up at the command of so flighty a will! Let me begin with whatever subject I please, for all subjects [*les matieres*][11] are linked with one another" (*Essays* 3.5 B, p. 668; *Essais*, p. 304).

This is the uncentered nonnature of the kind of literary discourse called the essay. Language, both inherently erotic and sexualized by the essay's old-man voice, is its own father and its own mother: the onanism of the Prime Mover taking *en main* the phallus-matrix of language as both Christian logos and Roman *vis*. Earlier in "Virgil," Montaigne has wavered between two attitudes toward sexuality. On the one hand, he acknowledges the inexorability of sexual urges, as when he decries virginity because it represents absence of positive movement, thus of life: "There is no action more thorny, or more active, than this action" (*Essays* 3.5 B, p. 655). On the other hand, he gives in to comic despair (not Juvenalian) at the reductionism sexuality induces in our appraisal of a world in which man's reason is only secondary: "The whole movement of the world resolves itself into and leads to this coupling. It is a matter infused throughout, it is a center to which all things look" (652). And shortly after he defines the *essai,* or rather, has it constitute itself, Montaigne, "leaving books aside and speaking more materially and simply" (668), concludes that sexuality itself, as distinct from language, shows "it was in mockery that nature left us the most confused of our actions to be the most common, in order thereby to make us all equal and to put on the same level the fools and the wise, and us and the beasts" (668-69). If sexuality itself eradicates all distinction, all hierarchy, then language sexualized of course similarly abolishes all distinction.

Therefore, by a neat conflation of nature and language, "any topic is equally fertile" and "all subjects [*matieres*] are linked with one another." Sexuality is "a matter infused throughout" both language and nature, a circumstance making both linguistic and historical distinctions impossible. *And* therefore the *essai* as self-propagating language, especially an old man's voicing of this language when real sexual opportunities grow scarce, is the genre of complete liberation, actually libertinism. The essayist writing, the essay reader reading, are merged; that distinction, too, must fade before the onslaughts of libertine language. Montaigne's *essai* genre indeed goes beyond Cicero's attempt to reconstitute Rome through an old man's sexualized digressing. It is already on the way to Whitman's or Baudelaire's or Yeats's expansion of the Word's "absent presence" to sexualized communion with a reader actively fashioned into a compliant partner. Ironically the very genericity of the *essai* originates in the nothingness of both language, which is "wind" *until* sexualized ("the words, which are no longer wind, but flesh and bone"), and sex, which is the movement across the gap between desire and completion. Montaigne needs no Freud, for he admits to the despair at the source of all the hope in sexuality soon after he arouses his *essai* genre to open self-declaration: "As soon as the ladies are ours, we are no longer theirs" (*Essays* 3.5 B, p. 672).

Not limited to these explicit sexualizing possibilities, the self-propagating *essai* possesses implications that are inexhaustible. Once liberated by its own libertinism, the *essai* can proceed to reproduce itself as its own kind of politics, morality, and aesthetics.

The politics of the Ciceronian essay is a function of metonymy: Cato's language re-creates Republican Rome through associations connecting desire with Nature, with fruit and process. Metonymy in Cicero is productive. For a Christian like Montaigne, more drastic measures are needed to reforge the ruptured links between retreating essayist and the world of affairs and discord left behind. Montaigne's essayistic voice, liberated not only from history but also from dependency on nature, can make itself, or "sound" itself, *politic*. If "any topic is equally fertile for me," as this voice declares, and all "subjects" are leveled to uniform *matieres*, then both sides of any issue broached by that voice may be adopted simultaneously.

This politics of paradox begins to operate openly immediately after the passage in which Montaigne points out nature's mockery in reducing all to the same level, "us and the beasts": "Those who will not allow serious ideas [*opinions*][12] in the midst of games [*parmi les jeux*] act, as someone says, like a man who is afraid to worship the statue of a saint if it is undraped" (*Essays* 3.5 C, p. 669; *Essais*, p. 306). On one side of this paradox lie "serious opinions," the wording alone undercutting the seriousness, even the substantiality, of reason. This is the Montaigne of "diversity." Experience, institutions, customs, moralities, religions, politics, selves—all are so *divers* that reason itself is nothing but a mere game: we are all of us, always, "parmi les jeux"; it is our situation. Reductive laughter is the only response, as the quote from Horace immediately preceding this passage dramatizes: "Against truth said in laughing / Is there a law?" (*Essays* 3.5 C, p. 669).

On the other side of the paradox lies the stark fact of sexuality, the only constant, "a center to which all things look" as Montaigne has said earlier (*Essays* 3.5 B, p. 652), and not a self-evidently good constant at that. Moreover, sex is a constant that is reliable only for the young and stout, not for himself, as Montaigne sardonically notes parenthetically in a late (C) addition to the essay: "B Perhaps we are right to blame ourselves for making such a stupid production as man, to call the action shameful, and shameful the parts that are used for it. C At present mine are truly shameful and pitiful [*peneuses*]" (*Essays* 3.5, p. 669; *Essais*, p. 306).[13] There is, of course, no way out of this trap, and Montaigne seeks no exit. Diversity, however, or the uniformity of all distinctions made apparent by self-productive language as well as by sexuality, affords an opportunity for Montaigne to produce a nonevasive, humane politics of equipoise: "Are we not brutes to call brutish the operation that makes us?" (*Essays* 3.5 C, p. 669; *Essais*, p. 306). Here Montaigne's *essai* voice, by means of a politics of paradox, enables his historical self to continue to stand apart, alone in his tower library surrounded by warring Catholics and Huguenots, precisely suspended between the Catholic fideism so pronounced in "Sebond" and the Calvinist depravity of man espoused militantly by many of his friends and even some of his family.

The sexualization of language and the parthenogenesis of the *essai* as the leveling genre of diversity inevitably suggest a morality peculiar to "essayism." The founding insight of Montaigne's moral critique throughout the *Essais* is that the human animal is both natural and self-referential, artificial, arbitrary. In a diverse world only the panoramic view of the essayist, or the diversity reportage sounded endlessly by the voice of the *essai*, can be true to both halves of man: the "partial and fanciful [*partisanes et fantastiques*]" (*Essays* 3.5 B, pp. 670-71; *Essais*, p. 308) creature of his own diverse social existence ("experience" in Montaigne) making up one half, the creature of nature-sex-God, or of "the universal and indubitable laws," making up the other (*Essays* 3.5 B, p. 670). If we are ashamed of our own sexuality, we are permitting our social, partial selves, indeed our very reason as the source of this partiality, to tyrannize over our God-given natures: "ᴮ We are ingenious only in maltreating ourselves: that is the true quarry of the power of our mind—ᶜa dangerous tool when out of control. . . . Alas, poor man! You have enough necessary ills without increasing them by your invention, and you are miserable enough by nature [*de condition*]¹⁴ without being so by art. You have real and essential deformities enough without forging imaginary ones" (*Essays* 3.5, p. 670; *Essais*, p. 308.

Essayistic morality, then, serves as corrective when the balance between man's *condition* and his "invention" is upset: "The positive rules of your own invention possess and bind you, and the rules of your parish; those of God and the world leave you untouched" (*Essays* 3.5 C, p. 671). Thus not only the long "Sebond" of Book 2 but all of the *Essais* provide their own corrective. For the genre, as we have seen, is the "invention" of itself as language, which makes man essayist rather than brute or god. The *essai* performs this moral function as a kind of self-policing, always remarking on the relativity of values entailed by diversity, always declaring candor according to reason ruled by nature—the only formula for balance in such a chaos. Toleration is Montaigne's virtue long before it becomes Voltaire's. And it is a virtue built into the *essai* genre as Montaigne extends it beyond the Ciceronian dimensions; it is not derived from a philosophy of enlightenment, but from the self-creativity of the discourse of diversity. Even Montaigne's method of composition proceeds from the complete complex of generic operations, not from a pregeneric moral decision or philosophic "thought." Montaigne's morality is self-manifested: it is not "expressed" as either *pensée* or Voltairean aphorism, but is instead the at-length process of diverse appraisal and critique.

In short, the *essai* also produces its own aesthetics. While his "politics" departs somewhat from the Ciceronian position, Montaigne's aesthetics, in line with Cicero's, is a matter of metonymy and allegory. However, metonymy is more than a figure for Montaigne. It becomes an intellectual schema, one I shall term "mental metonymy," a method that avoids the opposite extremes of organic unity and automatic writing, and that accommodates the B- and C-level encrustations that make Montaigne's book a history-archaeology of his opinions, whether they shift or deepen.

Again, in "Virgil," Montaigne's ongoing deliberation on sexuality serves as an epitome, this time of his aesthetics of prose discourse: "He who has no enjoyment except in enjoyment, who must win all or nothing, who loves the chase only in the capture, has no business mixing with our school. The more steps and degrees there are, the more height and honor there is in the topmost seat. We should take pleasure in being led there, as is done in magnificent palaces, by divers porticoes and passages, long and pleasant galleries, and many windings [*et plusieurs destours*]" (*Essays* 3.5 B, p. 671; *Essais*, pp. 309-10). Detour has always been a characteristic delight for readers of Montaigne. But *destours* are not exactly the same as digressions, not at all the same as running off on a tangent. A detour is a side route along a given thoroughfare, a reconnecting loop, not a disconnection. The *essai*, unlike tragedy, has no destination, no gamelike set of outcomes that is predetermined. This is not to say, however, that the *essai* follows no routes. Lacking destinations, Montaigne's essays follow routes of association that trace with microprecision the processes of his thinking and sensibility, as Montesquieu noted. The detours are really the windings *of* these routes, not off them. Moreover, in the sexual sense of this passage, the windings *are* the route, just as they are the activity of sexual pursuit. And a little further past this passage, if one thinks sexual pursuit, unlike the *essai*, after all does have a destination—"As soon as the ladies are ours, we are no longer theirs" (*Essays* 3.5 B, p. 672). Sex turns out to be not just analogous to the *essai* but entirely metonymous with the genre. For they are both processes, or operations, and each inheres in the paradoxical void of desire/satisfaction, love/indifference, libido/death wish, presence/absence—here one moment, gone the next: "And Thrasonides, a young Greek, was so much in love with his love that having won his mistress' heart he refused to enjoy her, so as not to deaden, satiate, and weaken by enjoyment that restless ardor on which he prided and fed himself" (*Essays* 3.5 C, p. 672).

Although more than an analogy, sex is not quite a metaphor for the *essai*, not even for "Virgil" specifically, however closely the sexual here and throughout the *Essais* may approach identification with the discursive. Diversity is the heart and soul of writing in Montaigne, with every topic suggesting every other conceivable topic—yet writing and sex may be associated but never merged. The aesthetic point of Montaigne's essayism is to note every particular, follow every association, so as to make them all appear uniform in significance while avoiding reducing them to amorphousness (such is, once more, the moral point about the brute-human ambiguity of sex in "Virgil"). This aesthetic method is not empirical; in Montaigne reason is always granted autonomy and superiority, though so immensely qualified by "experience" that it shies away from Cartesian rigor in its exercise. Nor is it nominalist; diversity allows everything its own peculiar value, yet it is always a value relative to that of everything else.

"Mental metonymy," or the more general "prolongation," therefore, is probably as close a description of the aesthetic method of the *essai* as can be applied without undue distortion. Certainly it adheres to the actual unfolding of an instance like "Virgil." For example, one may start anywhere in the text of this one essay, as from this passage four-fifths of the way through "Virgil," a passage making a moralistic parental point in a comically bluff manner: "Our fathers trained their daughters' faces to bashfulness and timidity (hearts [*courages*] and desires were the same); we, to self-assurance: we don't know what we're doing [*nous n'y entendons rien*]"[15] (*Essays* 3.5 B, p. 674; *Essais*, p. 313). Isolated, this passage may sound like an aphorism, a quotable quote. But the difference between aphorism and any particular statement in the genre *essai* is profound. Aphorisms are expressive, *post*-thought: items in nutshells, "gems." This statement of Montaigne's essayistic voice, on the other hand, *is* thinking as process, *essai* as self-conceiving and self-prolonging *genre*. It is not isolable. For it is precisely its status as one particular amidst a metonymy of diversities that produces textual life, the discursivity of discourse.

Most of the delight generated by Montaigne's sweeping conclusion that modern fathers have gone over to the opposite extreme in encouraging their daughters' liberty comes from our own textual recall. As readers of the essay "Virgil," we recollect that several pages earlier[16] this same essayistic voice has expatiated, in the flagrant act of delectating its own linguistic sexuality, upon the deadening effect of too sudden surrender—"Without hope and without desire we no longer go at any worth-while gait"—and of too bold and too frequent surrender—"Dearness gives relish to the meat [*donne goust à la viande*]" (*Essays* 3.5 B, p. 672; *Essais*, p. 310).[17] Thus the comedy: the father deplores the daughter's liberty, though admiring the occasional benefit in her resulting self-assurance, because he knows, and savors, his own libertinism. Or, to express the point in terms of mental metonymy, the reason the *essai* grows dubious of too much liberty granted to daughters is that it has earlier dwelt on the way in which true eroticism, luxuriated in by men of sense and sensibility, depends on a nice balance between enticement and postponement. The *association* of the two kinds of liberty is what makes for a metonymy instead of a one-liner, an *essai* statement instead of an aphorism—the one kind of liberty for the female and the other for the male, the one a danger and the other a treat, the one a possible conditioning for virtuous self-confidence and the other a flavorful seasoning of a potentially disappointing sexual meal, the one a virtue in the moral sense and the other a virtuous vice in the erotic game. One might put it even more extremely: the essayist says what he says about liberty for daughters *because* (logically, not chronologically) he has said, and continues to ponder, what he has said about liberty for men and their quarry.

But this leads only a little way along the track of this instance of mental metonymy in "Virgil." Even earlier than the passages warning of the fragile relationship between time and ardor (*Essays* 3.5 B, p. 672) occurs the key passage constituting the *essai* genre: "Let me begin with whatever subject I please, for all subjects are linked with one another" (668). This genericity statement already defines the liberty Montaigne later discloses to be the core of sexuality itself, which is, in turn, a metonymy (or reverse metonymy) for the vagaries of Venus—the on-again, off-again theme of "Virgil." Venus is "that goddess [*cette Déesse*] to whom are attributed so many changes and lovers. Yet the truth is that it is contrary to the nature of love if it is not violent, and contrary to the nature of violence if it is constant" (*Essays* 3.5 B, p. 675; *Essais*, p. 315). Thus from genericity the passage moves to sexual liberty—then immediately forward to the morality of toleration: "And those who are astonished at this and exclaim against it and seek out the causes of this malady in women as if it were unnatural and incredible, why don't they see how often they accept it in themselves without being appalled and calling it a miracle? It would perhaps be more strange to see any stability in it. It is not simply a bodily passion" (*Essays* 3.5 B, p. 675). The inconstancy of Venus is a metonymy for still another version of inconstancy, the old man's pulse, which Montaigne's *essai* voice aspires to reawaken through the eroticism of the Word. First acknowledging the "impudence" of old men's feeble genitality ("foiblesses en lieu où nous desirons plaire," *Essays* 3.5 B, p. 676; *Essais*, p. 316), this voice merges with its erotic message to cure this *foiblesse* by substituting the firmness of the Word for infirmity: "I like modesty, and it is not by judgment that I have chosen this scandalous way of speaking; it is nature that has chosen it for me. . . . Let's get on [*Suivons*]" (*Essays* 3.5 C, p. 678: *Essais*, p. 319).[18] This intrepidity of voice then unleashes the *essai*'s full strength as discourse of ardor to overcome the curb of "modesty," so that this blend of decorum, humility (the old man's before nature's meagreness), and remaining natural force will not perform solely as the virtue of candor, but become, as well, the activator of sexual vitality for the declining essayist. However, before directing this reinvigorated sexual liberty as a mode of both essayist's license and old man's licentiousness, Montaigne's mental metonymy pulls up briefly with his reiterated moral lesson of toleration: the sexual transactions of men and women are a "true compact [*une convention libre*]"[19] (*Essays* 3.5 B, p. 678; *Essais*, p. 319).

Now the *essai* is truly free, having deferred or paid lip service to decorum, to the humble sexual potential of old age, and to the mutuality of sexual consent. It is free to be "impertinently genital": "Never was a man more impertinently genital in his approaches [*Jamais homme n'eust ses approches plus impertinemment genitales*]" (*Essays* 3.5 B, p. 679; *Essais*, p. 320). Yet because of the mental-metonymy approach to composition in the *essai* genre, it is immediately apparent that the phallus is phallic discourse, the erotic power of language, whether inherent or sexualized through the sexual action of discursivity: "It is time now to speak of it openly" (*Essays* 3.5 B, p. 679). Language and sex, each a particularity amidst diversity, run together in a dialectic made possible by metonymy, which associates ceaselessly without collapsing words into deeds. Otherwise Montaigne's *essai* could not accomplish its desire as self-generation. This desire triumphs and, given the sexual-linguistic arc, appropriately subsides in the remaining pages of "Virgil."

For after declaring open speech, the *essai* can generate the heat vital to the old man's talking—essaying—sex:

> Love is a sprightly, lively, and gay agitation [*une agitation eveillée*]; I was neither troubled nor afflicted by it, but I was heated and moreover made thirsty by it. A man should stop there; it is hurtful only to fools. . . . I would prescribe it [*comme medecin, l'ordonnerois*] to a man of my temperament and condition as readily as any other recipe to rouse him [*l'esveiller*] and keep him in vigor till he is well on in years, and to keep him from the clutches of old age. While we are only in its outskirts and the pulse still beats . . . we need to be stimulated and tickled by some biting agitation such as this. [*Essays* 3.5 B, p. 680; *Essais*, pp. 321-22]

To awaken the still-beating pulse is the proper service of both *essai* discourse and Venus. Writing is the instrument of the soul ("*l'âme*," referred to by feminine pronouns in both Montaigne and the translation) for the care of the body, and this is not an ignoble charge: "It is . . . for her to hatch them [bodily pleasures, *plaisirs corporels*] and foment them, to offer and invite herself to them, since the authority of ruling belongs to her

[*la charge de regir luy appartenant*]" (*Essays* 3.5 C, p. 681; *Essais*, p. 323).
The discursivity peculiar to the *essai*, writing as sexual process and writing
as liberty—to say what it will because *it* is in "charge"—is what makes
possible such an inversion as the soul's noblesse oblige to the body in
Montaigne. Like sex, this genericity of language in the *essai* revives the
writer. This is not discourse *on* sex, or on any subject whatsoever. The
writing is the subject, the subject sexualized, itself made discursive; and
when the subject is sex as it is in "Virgil," the function of reawakening the
senses belongs to the word made flesh and bone. Once revived, the
essayistic voice resurrecting itself by verbal fiat can rest.

This rest, the subsidence of the *essai* as erotic effort, is signaled by the
resolution of metonymy into allegory, a recapitulation of the method of
Cicero. Appropriately Montaigne's allegories are positioned at the ends of his
"chapters," or rather *in* them, since there are no ends in the sense of final
goals in the *Essais*. For once the pulsing discursivity of sexualized language attains satisfaction in fashioning its own revival, there remain these
alternatives: to start up again or arbitrarily finish. Montaigne does both.
He writes individual *essais* as chapters of one grand *Essai*; significantly,
each *essai* in each of the three books was originally set as a lengthy single
paragraph, indicating there is no end till death—thus all the C passages,
those inserted after 1588. Yet he also rests at the close of each sex-discourse
"essai." This is the reason Montaigne's contradictions are not, finally,
contradictions. "Virgil" ends by returning Venus to her proper caretakers,
who are—surprisingly, given all the rest of the *essai*—not old men after all
but beardless boys. Virgil's Venus is exchanged for Cupid in the following
allegory. But there is no contradiction here, since the discourse of ardor
has simply subsided; detumescence is the new "topic": "The shorter the
possession we give Love [*luy*, "him," simply] over our life, the better we
are. Look at his bearing: he is a beardless boy [*c'est un menton puer-
ile*]. . . . See how he goes reeling, tripping, and wantonly playing; you put
him in the stocks when you guide him by art and wisdom, and you
constrain his divine freedom [*sa divine liberté*] when you subject him to
those hairy and callous hands" (*Essays* 3.5 B, p. 684; *Essais*, p. 327).

Once again declining into an old man's *foiblesse*, the essayistic voice is
not merely true to the moment but faithful to the nonnature of the
sexualized language it essays to keep uttering. Montaigne does not claim
sex is important for the elderly. Rather, the *essai*'s voice *makes* the old man
satisfied. Once revived, then let down, the old man must return Love's
flame to torchbearing youth. The language of the *essais is* action, but the
action of textuality, not of mimesis. Thus contradiction is modulated into
discursive rhythm. The freedom of textuality is positive liberty to create
itself; and it can and will do so, with ineluctable sexuality, because it is free

from referents. With the words of "Virgil" acting out their own drama, there is no old age, no sex, no youth, no impotence. No realities apart from the text, thus no contradictions.

Even the nonsequitur "moral"—of toleration again—in the closing section consisting of mixed B and C passages is possible only through the liberty of language in the liberal genre of *essai*. In the world of real sex, men and women will never achieve such neutrality, for it would negate the violence that Montaigne has earlier acknowledged to be the essence of desire, and that he maintains throughout "Virgil" to be the source of all vitality. But in the world of words, this very diversity of male and female can smooth itself out into self-awareness of difference. Exhausted from their tension and burnt out by their fires—the way the old voice of the *essai* is finally burnt out—men and women can admit the folly of accusing one sex only to excuse the other: "I say that males and females are cast in the same mold. . . . It is much easier to accuse one sex than to excuse the other. It is the old saying: The pot calls the kettle black [*le fourgon se moque de la poele*]" (*Essays* 3.5 B, p. 685; *Essais*, p. 329).[20]

"On some verses of Virgil" proves the *essai* of Montaigne to be an extended and enriched variation of the genre already entirely self-conceived out of the discourse of Cato in Cicero's *On Old Age*. Throughout all three books of the *Essais*, the voice of man in retreat—of the old man specifically, now forty to fifty-nine years old instead of eighty-four—turns both essayist and reader away from the action of deeds to the activation of learning, extracted from books and experience, by means of the sexualization of language. Language revitalizes this voice in the process of utterance. In "Virgil" the language generates its own genre. It can start with any topic and move by means of mental metonymy to all others. Diversity is maintained though the generic discourse reduces, or elevates, every particular to the uniformity of grist for its mill. Sexuality as metonymy deploys the nothingness of desire and satisfaction and the disparateness of male and female to rouse the feeble pulse of the essayist. So too does the *essai* itself stand, finally, after much self-stimulating discourse of ardor, a potent kind of genitally impertinent, perpetually rising and subsiding discursivity.

In its metonymic fertility and resultant freedom in and of discursivity as well as from the determinism of history expressed as the tyranny of "serious opinions," the essay genre conceived in Cicero and fulfilled in Montaigne still stands as a prospect open to maximum liberationist drives. Among the genres the essay never has dominated; its literary-historical occasion is always the retreat it represented to the retiring Montaigne. Yet it can accommodate as the other genres cannot, including the poetic, those deepest rhythms of the kind of personal transformation that is also completely political. Thus twentieth-centuy women authors who follow the generic tracks of their time, whether Woolf the self-conscious novel or Adrienne Rich the lyric, often detour to the essay for their freest correlations of the personal and the political. The discursive libertinism identifying the essay is an activation of the transformative "selfization" potential of language as such. Feminism may even have its genre in the Montaignesque *essai*. For it remains the generic prospect that is specifically powered by language sexualized. However, it has been the French feminist *essai*, from de Beauvoir to Luce Irigaray and Hélène Cixous (also, perhaps, Derrida and late Barthes) that has most completely adopted this prospect as its own. British and American feminist essayism remains hindered by the aspiration to the perfection of stasis—the aphoristic "moment" of Woolf's impressionism, the sharply definitive insight in Rich—represented by the English-language tradition launched by Bacon's formal essay. How this Baconian closure operates in the essay genre in a way that shuts down the wide-openness of Montaigne I shall try to explain in the next section.

Lover of Fortuna and Enemy: Machiavelli and Bacon

Any history of the essay genre must treat Machiavelli and Bacon. Yet the first is hardly ever considered an essayist, at least in English-speaking cultures. The "English Machiavel," as Bacon (along with Hobbes and others) was sometimes called during the seventeenth century, is often credited with inventing the formal, or nonpersonal, essay, among his other achievements as statesman, philosopher, scientist, and spokesman for scientific method. Machiavelli wrote in a form like the tract, or treatise, yet the stamp of his personality and experience is as vivid as that of Montaigne in the *Essais*. His own term for his most comprehensive work is "discourses," as in the *Discorsi*. And while as distinct a writer as Bacon from both Cicero and Montaigne, Machiavelli nevertheless fashioned a form so relevant to what I think are the central elements of the essay—liberty in thought and language and self-referential discursivity—that his discourses are important instances of the genre.

Besides, Machiavelli is indispensable to a study of certain transformations largely wrought by Bacon in the genre of Cicero and Montaigne. Here one must examine not only his influence on Bacon's political pragmatism—a somewhat distortive influence, for Machiavelli is not usually what Bacon and most other late Renaissance Englishmen made him out to be—but also his similarities to and differences from Bacon as a discourser. Not until Rousseau and the Romantics, especially Emerson, did the essay genre burst the strait jacket fabricated by Bacon and return to the un-bounded genericity of Montaigne. Indeed, even after Emerson, up through the present, many see in the Baconian "essaye" the quintessential form.

Machiavelli did not write either *The Prince* or the *Discorsi* until the republican government and faction he participated in were defeated by the Medici (1512), after which event he suffered imprisonment and torture. To write was his goal in retreating to his farm, and he was permitted to do so unbadgered by his foes. This was a situation virtually identical to Cicero's, except Machiavelli eventually returned to active civil life, two years before his death in 1527. Bacon, in contrast, fell from high place and power long after he had commenced writing essays, two editions of which were published well before his sentencing by the House of Lords in 1621 for accepting bribes: *Essayes* was first published in 1597, and a second edition, with new essays added and earlier ones revised, appeared in 1612. Later, in 1625, a third edition was published (*The Essayes or Counsels, Civill and Morall*), one year before his death.

Both Bacon and Machiavelli, however, held steady attitudes toward the possibility of collapse in political life. Remarkably lacking in bitterness, the *Discorsi* reflect a firmness in Machiavelli's approach to *Fortuna* that had developed over years full of political successes and failures alike. As we know from a famous passage in *The Prince*, Machiavelli continued to love *Fortuna*, "a fickle whore" but "always, woman-like, a lover of young men" (Crick 20). Even following her rebuffs of his suits, Machiavelli maintains a disposition toward fortune that is cautious but positive: given one's youth, she might grant favors, and it is certainly worthwhile to keep accosting her.

The disposition of Bacon, as a young man already enjoying big successes, long before his fall, is to judge *Fortuna* more coldly. He puts it succinctly in one of his aphorisms from the masque for Elizabeth (*Gesta Grayorum*): "The monuments of wit survive the monuments of power" (qtd. in Warhaft 20). Such a difference in their appraisals of *Fortuna* is more than a difference of personality, more than a difference between one who was primarily a politician, becoming a scholar only after losing most of his matches, and one who succeeded as an essayist-theoretician both while winning new appointments and honors and then again after losing it all. Bacon, even as a young man of prospects, concluded that political power is lesser in the scheme of things than learning ("wit"). Machiavelli, even as a defeated politician forced to become an essayist, continued to commit himself to time as change; writing is action continued for the Florentine, and he is incapable of hating the lady who has treated him so shabbily. In a letter to his friend Vettori, in prose as lively and present as anything in *The*

Prince or the *Discorsi*, Machiavelli cleverly recounts an ordinary day of his exile near his farm, a day spent playing trictrac at the tavern and "fighting over a penny"—but afterwards, toward evening, *writing*. This is an exercise he loves so much that he still has the mockingly kind eye of a complaining lover for "unkind" *Fortuna*: "And so, surrounded by these lice, I blow the cobwebs out of my brain and relieve the unkindness of my fate, content that she trample on me in this way to see if she is not ashamed to treat me thus" (qtd. in Ridolfi, 151-52).

What a contrast with Bacon, who, whatever his prospects, made up his mind early on that *only* writing ("wit") would furnish him with the proper "monument." Bacon looks not for continuity of action *in* writing, but for suspension from time altogether, from politics or time as power, through recourse to a supposedly timeless discourse *about* things political.

This is not a distinction between Bacon the literary artist and Machiavelli the political theorist; Machiavelli is as fine a stylist as Bacon, perhaps even a finer one. Nor is it that Bacon alone aims at a high level of abstraction while Machiavelli remains immersed in historical particulars; both try to extract generalizations from experience while deliberately avoiding universals. Rather, each resolves the Renaissance problem of time his own way, each thus producing his own distinctive kind of essay. The Machiavellian is the formulative, in and of history, politics, and ethics. The Baconian is the aphoristic, suitable for "monuments" outside and opposed to the dimension of history, politics, and ethics. Each kind, it should be emphasized, is thoroughly essayistic, that is, devoted to liberty in substance and manner and to self-reflexive textuality.

In his effort to situate his writing with respect to time, Machiavelli acknowledges that his *discorsi* are an extension from the present back to the past via the writing of Livy, then to the future. Bacon, on the other hand, sees his essays as experience shaped into provocative nuggets that both immortalize themselves as wit and serve as aids to either outright careerist advancement or enrichment of the general fund of worldly wisdom. A comparison of two key passages on time itself as it bears on discourse shows the deep difference between Machiavellian and Baconian essayism. The first is the peroration of the "Preface" to Book 2 of the *Discorsi*:

> Furthermore, human appetites are insatiable, for by nature we are so constituted that there is nothing we cannot long for, but by fortune we are such that of these things we can attain but few. The result is that the human mind is perpetually discontented, and of its possessions is apt to grow weary [*ed un fastidio delle cose che si posseggono*].[21] This makes it find fault with the present, praise the past, and long for the

future; though for its doing so no rational cause can be assigned. Hence I am not sure but that I deserve to be reckoned among those who thus deceive themselves if in these my discourses I have praised too much the days of the ancient Romans and have found fault with our own. Indeed, if the virtue which then prevailed [*se la virtù che allora regnava*][22] and the vices which are prevalent today were not so clear as the sun, I should be more reserved in my statements lest I should fall into the very fault for which I am blaming others. But as the facts are there for any one to see, I shall make so bold as to declare plainly what I think of those days and of our own, so that the minds of young men [*gli animi de' giovani*][23] who read what I have written may turn from the one and prepare to imitate the other whenever fortune provides them with occasion for so doing. For it is the duty of a good man [*offizio di uomo buono*][24] to point out to others what is well done, even though the malignity of the times or of fortune has not permitted you to do it for yourself, to the end that, of the many who have the capacity, some one, more beloved of heaven [*alcuno di quelli, più amato dal Cielo*], may be able to do it.[25]

The Bacon passage is from "Of Innovations" (number 24 in *The Essayes or Counsels 1625*):

As the births of living creatures at first are ill-shapen, so are all Innovations, which are the births of time. . . . the first precedent (if it be good) is seldom attained by imitation. For Ill, to man's nature as it stands perverted, hath a natural motion, strongest in continuance, but Good, as a forced motion, strongest at first. . . . time is the greatest innovator, and if time of course alter things to the worse, and wisdom and counsel shall not alter them to the better, what shall be the end? It is true that what is settled by custom, though it be not good, yet at least it is fit; and those things which have long gone together are as it were confederate within themselves; whereas new things piece not so well, but though they help by their utility, yet they trouble by their inconformity. Besides, they are like strangers, more admired and less favoured. All this is true, if time stood still, which contrariwise moveth so round that a froward retention of custom is as turbulent a thing as an innovation; and they that reverence too much old times are but a scorn to the new. It were good therefore that men in their innovations would follow the example of time itself, which indeed innovateth greatly, but quietly and by degrees scarce to be perceived. For otherwise, whatsoever is new is unlooked for, and ever it mends some, and pairs others; and he that is holpen takes it for a fortune, and thanks the time;

and he that is hurt, for a wrong, and imputeth it to the author. [Bacon 108-9]

Set against "Of Innovations," Machiavelli's "Preface" appears not to be "politique" at all in its effects—surprisingly, since ingratiating one's readers is a standard function of a preface. Machiavelli simply announces that, allowing for his own susceptibility to the common bias in favor of the past, his discourses will aspire to objectivity. And although he will use time to inspire young men to do what he has been unable to do in deed, his larger discursive aim is to *serve* time, a genuinely humble, not unctuous expression of his *offizio*. This is the Machiavellian writer's own kind of *virtù*, a writer's technical excellence backed by knowledge and experience, all put in the service of the chance for a republican future. Accordingly, Machiavelli's style is expeditious yet relaxed, roundly shaped by clear antitheses, sparing in analogy, carefully worded. Always formulative, whether the matter is psychology or history or politics, even in a prefatory setting, the Machiavellian way with *discorsi* is shown by this extract: to instill a mental discipline of time through prose that *obeys* the rhythms of change and continuity. This discipline is to be the long-term result of discourses on liberty not only offered as the lesson of the Roman Republic, a lesson to be extracted from the past and conveyed to the future, but also assumed to be the mode of civilized and civilizing history. Discourse itself then becomes a current of the power still charging the past. Failing to make liberty the lasting rule of a republican Florence, Machiavelli's *virtù*, that combination of Renaissance prowess and Greco-Roman *arete*, shifts to a new role. Now it will consist of writing for a future that will redeem the present through a past that is itself discourse, Livy's Augustan history of the Republic, serving Machiavelli first as model, then as mediation.[26]

In contrast, instead of obeying time, Bacon's prose *harnesses* time. His primary technique is the aphorism. Instead of leading the young from the present to the past and toward the future, instead of merging with time's current, which is the way of Machiavelli's prose of continuity, Bacon's aphoristic discourse infers lessons from experiential knowledge, or prudence. These aphorisms become a linguistic mold that is supposed to stabilize time. Since time denies perfection, even undercutting perfectibility ("Good" is "a forced motion"), Bacon derives hope not from fickle *Fortuna* herself but from his ability to construct monuments of language. Power thus transformed by the power play of language loses its current. This is the opposite of not only Machiavelli's but also Montaigne's and Cicero's liberation of language by charging it with temporality.

Baconian discourse aspires to overcome the problem of time by fusing language with time via the aphorism. The result is self-contained tactical movements the sum of which make a kind of hermetic essay, emblematic of time but lacking temporal nerve. Thus the syntax that stops after "strongest in continuance" in imitation of the artificiality, the dependence on will, of the "forced motion" that is the "Good" strikes us with its aphoristic completeness of form and content. But this very Good loses its motion altogether to the goodness of the aesthetically perverting imitation. The prose masters its subject, innovations, so completely that only further language can lend it significance; only the rest of the essay can liberate the good from its discursive harness.

In his "essayes" of 1597, as well as those of 1612, Bacon devoted himself to the practice of what he designated the "Initiative method"; another method, "the Magistral," supposedly came to dominate the essays of 1625, both originals and revisions (Warhaft 4, 7): "The magistral method teaches; the initiative intimates. The magistral requires that what is told should be believed: the initiative that it should be examined" (qtd. from *De Augmentis Scientiarum* in Warhaft 4). The magistral method was to adopt a style that would be copious, concrete, well illustrated, and tightly organized (Warhaft 7). The initiative method was supposed to result in a style that would be fragmentary, provocative, not arranged in significant order—in short, aphoristic (Warhaft 5).

Yet the stylistic effects of these two methods are the opposite of what Bacon believed. The magistral style would not sacrifice point for smoothness; thus it would also tend to encapsulate what is supposed to flow. And the very fragmentariness of the initiative, aphoristic style, its substitution of syntactical and lexical self-containment for a temporalized language that "courses," would result in hyperorganized essays that, however concretized and figured, "stop" time. The quotable quote is inimical to the libertinism of essayistic language. It aids the memory not by stimulating further thought but by fixing what cannot be fixed, what resists monumentalization—the discursivity of discourse.

To return to "Of Innovations" and to the point that only the rest of a Baconian essay can rescue what is subdued early on by aphorisms: Bacon's means of liberating what he captures is a two-step procedure. The first is to resort to antithesis for the effect, at least, of textual movement; difference is equated with motion. The second step is to forge a highly artificial union of the Word and time. Neither ploy achieves genuine liberation from the aphorism, and the second, ironically, after going through the motion of motion defeats the impulse to free textuality. The central antithesis in "On Innovations" consists in the opposition of the beautifully worded semi-tautology—"those things which have long gone together are as it were confederate within themselves"—against the "new," innovation as such—"whereas new things piece not so well." But the discourse Bacon has just opened up is immediately closed down with an aphoristic analogy containing an antithesis: "[New things] are like strangers, more admired and less favoured." Consequently, Bacon's discourse shifts to a string of aphorisms and covert images such as turbulence and clock time, a string ranging from "All this is true" to the explicit moralization of time, "It were good therefore that men in their innovations would follow the example of time itself." By this second step Bacon's essay is meant to free up the Good from the threat of anti-innovative determinism offered by time at the outset of the essay, where the aphoristic syntax and diction stopped it from realizing even its "forced motion."

Bacon's discursive gambit represents an astonishing conflation of man and God ("the author" of time, itself an "author"), of fortune and fate ("he that is holpen" and "he that is hurt"), of progress and stasis, of discourse and time. The aim of this second step, that is, is to make the essay itself, as aphoristic language, "follow the example of time," force it to move on to a conclusion that will open up the minimal room necessary for good innovations (for free will) to maneuver out of the apparent stasis of determinist time. This stoppage of time, it turns out, is only apparent because time itself "innovateth greatly, but quietly and by degrees scarce to be perceived."

Such an aphoristic series, itself like Bacon's time in moving as a clock moves, by scarcely perceptible degrees, achieves its own demise, and does so in the very effort to extricate itself from itself *as* discourse imitative of time. Sir Thomas Browne's "Urne-Buriall" accepts the implications of a monumentalizing style, which can create a discourse-machine emulating death as the retrograde motion of oblivion; Browne's language memorializes what has been lost, successfully resists time by becoming the act of interment with its sepulchral litanies closing over themselves. The Baconian aphoristic essay, however, opens itself up only by continuing to close itself off from the kind of perpetually open prospects of Machiavellian and Montaignesque essayism.

There is a dramatic difference between Bacon's self-canceling moves to liberate his beliefs in the Good through the magic of aphorism and Machiavelli's cautious yet hopeful reliance on fortune to realize what his discourse in the meantime will sustain by bridging past and future. This contrast originates in their overall intellectual methods: Bacon was the early scientific builder of generalizations from induction, Machiavelli the speculative yet commonsensical reader and antiphilosophical technician of power. Machiavellian "knowledge," as Bernard Crick has described it, "is admittedly not as precise as in the natural sciences and is always conditional. It does not yield any universal methodology for the study of politics, nor any single formula for its conduct: rather, it points to relevant considerations and offers, not iron laws but probable tendencies . . . and [is] always conditional on someone wishing to take up the Greek gift of power" (45). Crick finally acknowledges that this "method" is really nothing other than writing: "Essentially it is the way in which Machiavelli sets about writing, it is not the procedure by which he sets out to validate his conclusions. There is no such procedure" (52).

The different "essayisms" of Bacon and Machiavelli represent two divergent dispositions toward *Fortuna.* As a writer of *discorsi,* Machiavelli is already as free as Montaigne because he loves fortune, however bad his own personal fate in the world of deeds. Her fickleness *is* freedom. For a lover of *Fortuna,* time is undetermined and undetermining. Consequently, his discourse starts out liberated and liberating, an extension of *civiltà,* not its replacement. His writing is the same as his sense of open possibility in history: "So Machiavelli's Fortune is not simply accident, nor is it a kind of deterministic sociology, nor yet the preordained "Doom" of the northern myths or even the fatalism of the inactive cynic: it is the sudden, aweful and challenging piling up of social factors and contingent political events in an unexpected way" (Crick 56). Bacon's practice as an essayist, however, represents an essentially apolitical will to control the thing constantly analyzed as uncontrollable, time. Unlike Machiavelli, whose discourses continue to exult in the imperfectibility of a political reality both "hurt" and "holpen" by *Fortuna,* Bacon keeps aspiring to the rather self-contradictory ideal of perfect worldliness. His weapon is wit, discourse as verbal monument, as a privileged alternative replacing the active pursuit of power. This replacement occurs in both the early essays, such as "Of Studies," and the last, such as "Of Vicissitude of Things." The Baconian essay struggles to liberate itself from itself, whether through the initiative style, which is particularly evident in the earliest essays of 1597, or through the smoothed out yet still aphoristic magistral style that began to dominate in the 1612 and 1625 essays, including revisions of the earlier ones. But the commitment to encapsulation of experience through the aphorism brakes every maneuver for textual openness.

Machiavelli's open-ended discursivity, even with a generalizing introduction and a neatly concluding summation, always extends rather than collapses—while being just as self-reflective as Bacon. This effect is exemplified by Machiavelli's often-cited comparison of Hannibal and Scipio:

> Men are moved in the main by two things; either by love or by fear. Hence it comes about that a person in authority may be either one who makes himself loved or one who makes himself feared. Indeed, a man who makes himself feared is usually better followed and better obeyed than is one who makes himself loved.

It matters then little to a general along which road he travels, provided he has virtuosity, and his virtue gives him standing with men. For when there is great efficiency as there was in Hannibal and Scipio, it counterbalances all the mistakes due to their having made themselves too much loved or too much feared. . . . I conclude, therefore, that it does not matter much in what way a general behaves, provided his efficiency be so great that it flavours [*condisca*] the way in which he behaves [*vivere*, "lives"], whether it be in this way or that. [*Discourses* 462-65; *Discorsi* 288-90]

This is purely self-reflexive, nonreferential discourse. Machiavelli assumes that neither his source, Livy, nor for that matter any empirically discoverable truth about the past could furnish him with the kind of truth he is after. His truth is textuality. The words do their own job, without what is ordinarily called "rhetorical" intentionality and design. Once cited, the two legends unravel as a natural "either/or": both Scipio and Hannibal find themselves deviating from the "true way," whether love or fear, and they pay the consequences.

Neither the "either" nor the "or," it turns out, proves to be so terribly efficient as Hannibal's and Scipio's different kinds of *virtù* would seem to require. Thus instead of proving a prefabricated point in the aphoristic manner of the Baconian essay, the Machiavellian discourse conceives and delivers a new, unforeseeable point: that made by one verb in the conclusion, *condisca* ("flavours"). So *virtù* will be transformed discursively from the controlling political principle of generalship into a condiment. This is the opposite of Bacon's reductionism and self-closure. It may seem that we have descended precipitously from grandeur to triviality. But the discourse proves it is such things as flavoring that make all the difference in politics. And politics for Machiavelli is *Fortuna*—the loved and hated lady herself, not the Baconian threat to the worldly perfectionism of the aphorism. Machiavelli's *condisca*, ironically, is more replete with political delicacy—it is a lover's word of appreciation—than any monument of Baconian inwardness. Discursivity, like Machiavelli's "power," is a way, a political life to be written.

"*Retraite absolue*": Rousseau

In the *Rêveries*, his last and unfinished work, Rousseau describes his situation, advanced old age afflicted by isolation, illness, and straitened circumstances, in such a way that essayistic discursivity becomes completely identified with self. A *rêverie* is a compound of memoir, apology, exploration of psyche, account of health, moral analysis, social criticism, nature observation, meditation—and words uttered for the sake of sustaining voice, the self still alive. The effect sought is that of time itself, its course realized in the rhetorically constitutive action of discursivity as such. Accordingly, the form fashioned by Rousseau consists of ten essays called "promenades," or physical-intellectual "walks," more directed than wanderings yet hardly goal-oriented tracks. This design extends the grasp of prose absolutely, prose retrieved from rhetorical distantiation or deferral and delivered as presence. The voice of the *rêverie*, marked by number but lacking title, no longer needs subjects, not even for pretexts. It becomes its own text, its own pretext and context. The initial phrase of the "Première promenade" announces self-sufficiency, indeed "*fiats*" the self ex nihilo, with an easy slide of pronoun, adverb, and transitional *donc*: "Me voici donc [Me here so: So here I am]."27

Rousseau's essay, then, is more than the rejuvenating digression of Cato the Elder, more than the equally interior-exterior voice of Montaigne growing more communicative as it interiorizes more deeply, more than the arena where Machiavellian discourse dallies with fortune and Baconian aphorisms coerce time. *Les Rêveries du promeneur solitaire* easily accomplishes what Baconian control falls short of attaining: the merger of voice and time, of past reverized into present, by means of the simple substitution of discursivity for a world both lost and rejected, the hating society hated by Europe's first great Romantic-revolutionary pariah.

So complete is this substitution that the voice of the *Rêveries* registers all its operations from within the flow of discourse: "Je me contenterai de tenir le registre des opérations sans chercher à les réduire en système [I shall be satisfied to keep a record of operations (barometric readings) without seeking to reduce them to a system]" ("Première promenade," Roddier 11). Words trace the self tracing itself in words, without any other form-generating principle (*système*) except solitude. Following "Me voici donc" comes Rousseau's declaration of alienation, the phrases prolonging the "Me voici donc" in a void and extending this void, which then assumes the substantiality of time, the palpability of phrasing offering itself as the only world, society attenuating in a rhythmic expiration to "moi-même": "seul sur la terre, n'ayant plus de frère, de prochain, d'ami, de société que moi-même [alone on the earth, no longer having any brother, neighbor, friend, or any other society except myself]" (4).

Once the *vox in deserto* establishes solitude as the self-sufficing occasion of the *Rêveries*, the work of discourse in progress ("l'ouvrage," not "l'oeuvre") delimits itself a space not only withdrawn from the world, as in Cicero and Montaigne, Machiavelli and Bacon, but so extremely alienated that it becomes an altogether other world. This is the world of a secular anchorite dead to *société* and alive only to himself uttering words, *une retraite absolue:* "L'ouvrage que j'entreprenais ne pouvait s'exécuter que dans une retraite absolue [The writing of these *Rêveries* that I would undertake could be performed only in absolute retreat]" (30). The pulse of such a life is the time spent speaking it, a smooth conflation clear from Rousseau's analogy between saying/thinking and day before/day after: "Je dirai ce que j'ai pensé tout comme il m'est venu et avec aussi peu de liaison que les idées de la veille en ont d'ordinaire avec celles du lendemain [I shall say what I have thought exactly as it has come to me, with as little connection as the thoughts of the day before ordinarily have with those of the next day]" (9-10). This is the pulse of an exclusively spiritual life already liberated from the body, the disintegration of which parallels the reintegration of Rousseau's injured soul: "Mais dans ce désoeuvrement du corps mon âme est encore active [But in this coming-apart of the body, my soul is still active]" (10).

Indeed, the whole discursive enterprise of the *Rêveries* is rebirth through the soul's speaking itself. Rousseau writes so that he might in his isolation and old age *read* himself, and thus "double" his existence. Describing his goal, Rousseau attains a degree of frank reflexiveness that Montaigne only approaches in "On some verses of Virgil" (but does aspire to, contrary to Rousseau's judgment):

Je fais la même entreprise que Montaigne, mais avec un but tout contraire au sien: car il n'écrivat ses *Essais* que pour les autres, et je n'écris mes rêveries que pour moi. Si dans mes plus vieux jours aux approches du départ, je reste, comme je l'espère, dans la même disposition où je suis, leur lecture me rappellera la douceur que je goûte à les écrire, et faisant renaître ainsi pour moi le temps passé, doublera pour ainsi dire mon existence. [I undertake the same thing as Montaigne, but with a goal opposite his: for he wrote his *Essays* only for others, and I write my reveries for myself alone. If in my oldest age, on the threshold of death, I remain, as I hope, in the same situation I now occupy, reading them will recall the sweet calm I enjoy in writing them, and so, reviving the past for myself, will as it were double my existence.] [11]

Having set for aims the act of writing and the doubling of his existence through reading his own writing, Rousseau achieves freedom, that peculiar liberty *within* essayistic discourse.

In doing so, that is, in identifying himself as an essayist following but not, in his own mind, imitating Montaigne, Rousseau realizes his lifelong philosophy. In absolute retreat his soul will achieve its "habituel," or characteristic, disposition to solitude. Free of society, Rousseau still differs from his programmatic ideal, as rendered by Émile, for instance, or even the Jean-Jacques of the *Confessions*. In the *Rêveries* the self is old, pariah, with nothing to do but botanize, copy music, take walks—and write. Above all else, it is writing that mediates between his cherished solitude, which except for writing would be crazed estrangement, and his soul. In the opening periods of the "Seconde promenade," the state of nature becomes equated with essayistic discourse, the free-running *idées* seeking their own level ("mes idées suivre leur pente"). The results of this deliberate fusion of essay, solitude, soul, and nature are freedom ("je laisse ma tête entièrement libre") and fulfillment through eternal return upon the self ("je sois pleinement moi"). Constant reflexivity becomes the premier principle of composition in the *Rêveries*. Thus the first paragraph of the "Seconde promenade" further extends the "Me voici donc" initiating the "Première promenade"—extends, prolongs, fills, refines, soothes. More than mere recapitulation, the rhetoric converted into act of discursive self-return defines "essay" in Rousseau as rhythm itself. One essay-reverie-promenade creates out of itself the next, in a kind of musical composition or "absolute music" antedating Rimbaud and Mallarmé by a century. But Rousseau's distinctive essayism also represents a self-sustaining whistling in the dark shadows of imminent death:

> Ayant donc formé le projet de décrire l'état habituel de mon âme dans la plus étrange position où se puisse jamais trouver un mortel, je n'ai vu nulle manière plus simple et plus sûre d'exécuter cette entreprise que de tenir un registre fidèle de mes promenades solitaires et des rêveries qui les remplissent quand je laisse ma tête entièrement libre, et mes idées suivre leur pente sans résistance et sans gêne. Ces heures de solitude et de méditation sont les seules de la journée où je sois pleinement moi et à moi sans diversion, sans obstacle, et où je puisse véritablement dire être ce que la nature a voulu. [Having then adopted my project of describing the characteristic state of my soul in the strangest position a mortal could ever find himself occupying, I saw no way simpler or more certain of bringing off this enterprise than to keep an accurate account of my solitary promenades and of the reveries filling them when I let my brain wander completely free, and allow my thoughts to follow their natural inclination, offering no resistance and suffering no shame. These hours of solitude and meditation are the only ones during my days when I am fully myself, and *to* myself, experiencing no distraction, meeting no impediment, and

when I can truly claim to be what nature has intended all along.]
[13]

Rousseau prolongs his life by writing so that he might read and reread, and "chaque fois que je les relirai m'en rendra la jouissance [each time I reread will provide a return of pleasure]" (9). Essayistic discourse for Rousseau, then, is a matter of prolongation, of sustaining reverie. Each reverie unfurls from its predecessor, ultimately out of "Me voici donc," in successive waves of sheer textuality, each of which serves to "rendre compte des modifications de mon âme et de leurs successions [register the phases of change in my soul]" (10). This technique of prolongation is to Rousseau what mental metonymy is to Montaigne. Examples pervade the ten promenades. The immediate evocation of waves themselves on the lac de Bienne is a central culmination of the "Cinquième promenade": "là le bruit des vagues et l'agitation de l'eau fixant mes sens et chassant de mon âme toute autre agitation. . . . Le flux et reflux de cette eau [there the sound of the waves and the appearance of the ripples on the water's surface capturing my senses and dispelling all my anxieties . . . flux and reflux" (68-69). But this famous prose lyric at the heart of the *Rêveries* merely brings to the foreground what is implicit in Rousseau's style throughout, from the opening sentence of the "Première promenade" to the unobtrusive description of his ramblings after dinner while on l'île de Saint-Pierre in the "Cinquième promenade" (67), to the botanical passages of the "Septième promenade": "Brillantes fleurs, émail des prés [bright flowers, ornaments of the meadows]" (97-98).

A more overt technique than prolongation in the Rousseauistic essay is narrative. For the most part meticulously shaped incidents from his past, Rousseau's narrations sustain more of the discursive burden in the *Rêveries* than anecdotes in Montaigne, formulative historical examples in Machiavelli, aphorisms (which are tacit narratives) in Bacon, or allegories in Cicero and Emerson. Indeed, the entire *Rêveries* tells a story. It emerges throughout the perpetual essayistic discourse in the form of separate, seemingly haphazardly recalled incidents, yet all these narratives point up a moral. Rather, two distinct and often contradictory morals: the isolated voice can either accommodate itself to complete alienation by adopting the rhythmic accents of solitude, or oppose it through self-vindicating tales that show Rousseau to be good-hearted and through recollections that show him reinserting himself into society, which has rejected him.

Narratives of accommodation occur first in the *Rêveries*, as if to demonstrate Rousseau's sincerity in declaring isolation and self-sufficiency as his old man's way and life. Most notable is the set piece in the "Seconde promenade" about his accident, when a Great Dane bowled him over in the road as he walked around Ménilmontant, a hilly suburb of Paris. He fell and was knocked unconscious when he tried to vault over the large carriage dog as it ran toward him, a maneuver he takes great pains to reconstruct in detail. Rousseau allows his reverie to take him back to this violent break in an otherwise continuous existence. For it signifies what reverie itself has come to mean: the self-awareness possible on the very verge of loss of awareness. To one not far from death, this brief interlude of unconsciousness from the past prefigures life felt as it will be in the hour of death: the nullified self oddly in possession of its own relinquishment. The event of this accident for Rousseau is really this unconsciousness, evocations of which he inserts as blanks bracketed by a violent dog, acrobatic man, and serious injuries unnoticed at first because of the shock: "Je ne sentis ni le coup ni la chute, ni rien de ce qui s'ensuivit jusqu'au moment où je revins à moi. . . . On me demanda où je demeurais; il me fut impossible de le dire. Je demandai où j'étais; on me dit [I felt neither the blow nor the fall, nor anything of what followed up to the moment when I came to. . . . They asked me where I lived; it was impossible for me to say. I asked where I was; they told me]" (16-17).

Surrounding this bracketed unconsciousness, a narrative unwinds with an effect matching the pure rhythm of self-reflexive discursivity in the nonnarrative portions of the *Rêveries*:

Il était presque nuit quand je repris connaissance. Je me trouvai entre les bras de trois ou quatre jeunes gens qui me racontèrent ce qui venait de m'arriver. . . . La nuit s'avançait. J'aperçus le ciel, quelques étoiles, et un peu de verdure. Cette première sensation fut un moment délicieux. Je ne me sentais encore que par-là. Je naissais dans cet instant à la vie, et il me semblait que je remplissais de ma légère existence tous les objets que j'apercevais. Tout entier au moment présent je ne me souvenais de rien; je n'avais nulle notion distincte de mon individu, pas la moindre idée de ce qui venait de m'arriver; je ne savais ni qui j'étais ni où j'étais; je ne sentais ni mal, ni crainte, ni inquiétude. Je voyais couler mon sang comme j'aurais vu couler un ruisseau, sans songer seulement que ce sang m'appartînt en aucune sorte. [It was almost dark when I regained consciousness. I found myself in the arms of three or four young men who recounted for me what had happened. . . . The night was deepening. I made out the sky, a few stars, and part of a tree's leafage. This return of sensation was a delectable moment. I was aware of myself only through that feeling. I was born at that instant, and it seemed to me I flowed into the objects I perceived, filling them with my subtle substance. Completely within the present, I remembered nothing; I had no distinct notion of my identity, not the least idea of what had just happened to me; I recognized neither who nor where I was; I felt no pain, no fear, no anxiety. I regarded my blood streaming forth as I would have watched a rivulet, without even imagining this blood was coursing from me.] [16-17]

Such an experience of ecstatic nullity, like Kirilov's before his long-planned suicide in *The Possessed*, differs from *nada*, from nirvana, from simple erasure. What the narrative renders instead is the coursing of the self's deliverance from an outcast's deadened existence, a sense of release from all bonds—including those of the self—retrieved, ironically, by accident in the course of the solitary walker's evasive amblings through the margins of Paris. The rhythmic sequentiality of the words not only describes but simulates the processes of new consciousness emerging from oblivion—but retaining a sense of that oblivion as obliviousness to all the pain of a ruined social existence. Rousseau is really reborn by virtue of the freedom of his narrative discourse to accommodate an alienated self with the translucent presence of his nothingness, his substance subtilized to such a degree that it leaks out, filling the objective world wih pure subjectivity.

In their studied detachment the words avoid ejaculative ecstasy because a particular kind of accommodation is desired: the world of chance passersby can accept a pariah annihilated by a bolting dog; they can preside officially, as conscientious citizens in a society made innocent by the victim's need, over the rebirth of Rousseau. For through discursivity shaped narratively, or time re-created by the essayist-god, he is so entirely at one with his own isolation that he can treat it, as it were, scientifically. This kind of narrative is possible only in an essay-reverie: a semimystical rebirth recounted seamlessly within a discursive fabric unfolding beneath an almost journalistic imperturbability toward a mock death. The point of this kind of narrative is not the psychological sensation, as it would be in the *Confessions*, where the discourse serves the writer's need to justify himself in the eyes of the world. In the *Rêveries* the discourse recovers the accident, a given pretext, so completely that the easy flow of the words merges into easy acceptance of the discourser's nullity as it assumes the narration's form. This form, in turn, accepts the impress of the advancing night of death, the import of the stream of Rousseau's blood. Essayistic discursivity empowering and empowered by narrative thus sacramentalizes pain and death. The final function of *rêverie*, then, is to rewrite history, which, however, has never been anything other than accident *until* written as the curious blend of contingent fact and reflexive textuality afforded by the essay-reverie genre.

In this narrative from the "Seconde promenade," the solitary walker's aim, potentially self-contradictory, of reinserting himself into society as a reborn anonym is an extra, undeveloped side effect. The primary experience remains accommodation of the alienated self to its own estrangement. However, in the "Cinquième promenade" the resocialization of the exile assumes prominence among the functions of narrative discursivity. In 1765, Rousseau happened onto a materialization of his dream of *retraite absolue*. Having been expelled from one temporary haven after another in Switzerland, finally, during a five-week sojourn on l'île de Saint-Pierre in the middle of the lac de Bienne, he had not only enjoyed perfect respite but discovered a way of life that later became transformed by essay-reverie into discursive perfection itself: absolute withdrawal to an enchanted island. On that isle, in fact and reverie, as well as on the wild *petite île* just offshore, Rousseau elaborates a pastorale assembling memories with patriarchal yearnings that match those of his idol, Robinson Crusoe. Words enjoy divine sovereignty on this island displaced from geography to Rousseau's essayistic frame. And the discursive realm, a cloud castle yet sustained by firm narrative supports that lend the credibility of a story-account to what might seem to degenerate into impression and opinion, satisfies the cravings of the old *rêveur* for reunion with society. Such a reunion is unconditional, of course. Just as he has affirmed the independence of personal *âme* at the outset of the *Rêveries* with his constitutive "Me voici," in the narrative sketches of the "Cinquième promenade" Rousseau can luxuriate in an entirely imperial self.

The most aspiring and charming example is his colonializing expedition on which he transported by boat a "settlement" of rabbits from the main island to the *petite île*. Although he commences his narrative as a detached, self-content amateur botanist exploring the varieties of shrubs and flowers on the *petite île*, Rousseau proceeds to join presumptions of Noah-like self-sufficiency with an eighteenth-century flair for charade in casting himself in the multiple roles of subject, narrator, "pilot," and colonizer. Discursivity here supplants remembered experience, which can never achieve such synthesis, with narration:

> Mais une de mes navigations les plus fréquentes était d'aller de la grande à la petite île, d'y débarquer et d'y passer l'après-dînée, tantôt à des promenades très cirsonscrites au milieu des marceaux, des bourdaines, des persicaires, des arbrisseaux de toute espèce, et tantôt m'établissant au sommet d'un tertre sablonneux couvert de gazon, de serpolet, de fleurs, même d'esparcette et de trèfles qu'on y avait vraisemblablement semés autrefois, et très propre à loger des lapins qui pouvaient là multiplier en paix sans rien craindre et sans nuire à rien. Je donnai cette idée au receveur qui fit venir de Neufchâtel des

lapins mâles et femelles, et nous allâmes en grande pompe, sa femme, une de ses soeurs, Thérèse et moi, les établir dans la petite île, où ils commençaient à peupler avant mon départ et où ils auront prospéré sans doute s'ils ont pu soutenir la rigueur des hivers. La fondation de cette petite colonie fut une fête. Le pilote des Argonautes n'était pas plus fier que moi menant en triomphe la compagnie et les lapins de la grande île à la petite, et je notais avec orgueil que la receveuse, qui redoutait l'eau à l'excès et s'y trouvait toujours mal, s'embarqua sous ma conduite avec confiance et ne montra nulle peur durant la traversée. [But one of my most frequent navigations was from the large to the small island, to disembark there and while away the afternoon, either passing through the narrow corridors among the willows, alders, water plants, and all kinds of shrubs or establishing myself on the summit of a shady knoll covered with turf, with wild thyme, flowers, even esparcette and clover, which apparently had been sown there another time, perfect for maintaining rabbits, which could multiply there in peace, without fear and without the power to ruin anything. I let the steward in on my idea, and he sent off to Neuchâtel for some rabbits, both males and females; then we proceeded with pomp and ceremony, the steward's wife and one of her sisters, plus Thérèse and myself, to colonize them in the little island, where they began to spread before my departure and where they will have prospered, no doubt, if they have been able to endure the rigors of winter. The installation of this little colony was a special holiday. The pilot of the Argonauts couldn't have been prouder than I was, leading in triumph both my comrades and my rabbits from the big island to the islet, and I noticed with swelling breast that the steward's wife, who greatly feared traveling on the water and never failed to become seasick, embarked under my leadership with confidence and betrayed no alarm whatsoever during the crossing.] [67-68]

With its ironies contributing a touch of pathos, this gently mock-heroic narrative relies for its effects on the power of nonfictional discourse to fictionalize itself. The adventure becomes a fantasy recapitulation of post-Flood renewal, civilization started over from scratch, only this time according to nature à la Rousseau: a pristine population of rabbits, docile vegetarians, transported to their own brave new world on the islet by a small band of stewards led by a persona non grata on the run from authorities throughout France and Switzerland. Innocence and mythic nobility together make for a mini-*Aeneid*, wrought by discursivity's power blandly to accumulate little, benign details until the point is reached where textuality takes over from reality. The consequence of these inconsequentialities, such as the steward's wife's trust in Rousseau-Aeneas, is automatic reintegration of the solitary into society. The sole context on this *petite île* is the narrative text, wherein Rousseau scouts the terrain, draws up the plan, arranges the company, and escorts all to the new territory, where the only rigor to be suffered is nature's winter. Society, rejecting Rousseau and rejected by him, has been purged of all evil by this narrative. The writing applies a quiet violence that revolutionizes, renewing life at its source, extending it equally to animal and man, and restoring confidence in those who, like the steward's wife, fear nature instead of working with it in the detached wisdom exemplified by the botanizer-guide.

In the "Cinquième promenade" even more markedly than in the "Seconde," Rousseau steers his discourse to its natural harbor. There he experiences not just solitude and freedom from artificial *société,* but also restoration to the arms of that very same society: in the "Seconde promenade," the physical embrace of the "three or four young men" picking up an injured old man from the street; in the "Cinquième promenade," the innocent deference of the company, their trust in the brave patriarch. This redemption is delicately accomplished. How fragile this reestablished social tie can be, how necessary it is for Rousseau to turn repeatedly to discursive narrativity as his only reliable means of retying it, is demonstrated by the "Neuvième promenade," in the anecdote about a walk through Clignancourt (124-25). A child of five or six clasps him about the knees; Rousseau picks him up and kisses him several times, passes on his way, then returns only to find a stranger whispering to the child's father, who looks threateningly at Rousseau. The *promeneur* then turns and leaves, frustrated by his abortive connection with the child, saddened at the ruination of natural innocence by social mistrust. The simple incident conveys no precise message, it neither defends nor attacks, yet the bleakness of the solitary's alienation is contained, restrained, kept at bay by the unembellished sequentiality of the narration. Through its return upon itself for its content, which otherwise equals the nonsequence brutally imposed on spontaneous love by society, this narrative reestablishes synchronically the very sociality shown diachronically to be void.

What Rousseau's discursive narration accomplishes seems so direct, so readily accessible to language, that it might have occurred in Montaigne: rhetoric made constative extends itself to become communication. Despite Rousseau himself, it is not a matter of sincerity or unimpeded impulse; Rousseau in the *Rêveries,* as in the *Confessions* and *Émile,* is as premeditative and distortive as possible. But his essayistic prose does not lie. Montaigne is infinitely communicative, yet Rousseau's discursivity communicates, absolutely. Nor is it just good writing, the kind that functions as it should; Emerson and Nietzsche can be equally efficient.

Nor is it that Rousseau has hit upon a kind of poetic prose like Rilke's prose and poetry. As Europe's first man in "absolute retreat," Rousseau is not self-consciously striving for the hollow effect of some modernist and much postmodernist language, which is language forced from the start to fall on deaf or absent ears.

In fact, he does not even know how to deal with his loneliness and estrangement through writing. Often Rousseau resorts to effusion and preciosities standard during his own time and earlier. Yet even when he is not trying obliquely to resocialize himself in the more or less objective kind of narrative represented by the Saint-Pierre expedition and the Clignancourt encounter, but instead appealing blatantly to the reader's sentimentality, Rousseau somehow allows his discursivity the freedom to communicate, refusing to make it merely serve his communicative urge. For example, neither psychology nor stylistics can explain the independent force of communication in the apparently self-serving pair of proofs positive of the outcast's good-heartedness when a boy: the stories about his refusal to tattle on another child who was responsible for injuring him at his uncle's calico works and about his forgiveness of a boy who struck him on the head with a croquet mallet ("Quatrième promenade," Roddier 56-58).

But the power of essayistic textuality comes from essaying to get something right that has been experienced, whether for good or ill, yet never quite reaching this right, never attaining poetry's hermetic perfection of metaphor and always falling back on the irregular impetus of continuous prosing. This self-reflexive yet never complete discursivity in rendering its own absence becomes a kind of presence. Rousseau can get it wrong, as in the "Cinquième promenade" when he resorts to religious terminology to catch the completeness of synthesized solitude-text in the reverie-essay: "De quoi jouit-on dans une pareille situation? De rien d'extérieur à soi, de rien sinon de soi-même et de sa propre existence, tant que cet état dure on se suffit à soi-même comme Dieu [What does one enjoy in such a state? Nothing from outside the self, nothing except from within and from our own existence; while this state lasts one is self-sufficient, like God]" (71). This is fine for the Académie; it is even apt within the entire spiritual-journal context of the *Rêveries*. Yet when we turn to the Rousseau we know to be annoying, the paranoiac whose desperately won inner balance through identification with estrangement can fashion an essayistic voice with such intensity that it can be offensive, then the self-sufficiency he claims as a *soi-disant* mystic transfers to the process of textuality itself, and the essayist triumphs where the talented complainer and explainer falters.

The technique of narration often saves Rousseau's discursivity from being subordinate to soul and psyche, morality and philosophy; and the essayistic present absence assumes its rightful primacy. As we have noted, the transition from merely good writing, which is efficiently expressive, to self-sufficient discourse often requires the narrative mode. (But not always, as the rhythmic opening paragraphs of the "Première" and "Seconde" promenades show.) Successful transition is particularly evident in the "Neuvième promenade," between the conclusion of a paragraph of psychology and an account of yet another incident of frustrated camaraderie in the wanderer's declining years:

Je ne vois qu'animosité sur les visages des hommes, et la nature me rit toujours.

Je sens pourtant encore, il faut l'avouer, du plaisir à vivre au milieu des hommes tant que mon visage leur est inconnu. Mais c'est un plaisir qu'on ne me laisse guère. . . .

Une de mes promenades favorites était autour de l'École militaire et je rencontrais avec plaisir çà et là quelques invalides qui, ayant conservé l'ancienne honnêteté militaire, me saluaient en passant. Ce salut que mon coeur leur rendait au centuple me flattait et augmentait le plaisir que j'avais à les voir. Comme je ne sais rien cacher de ce qui me touche, je parlais souvent des invalides et de la façon dont leur aspect m'affectait. Il n'en fallut pas davantage. Au bout de quelque temps je m'aperçus que je n'étais plus un inconnu pour eux, ou plutôt que je le leur étais bien davantage puisqu'ils me voyaient du même oeil que fait le public. Plus d'honnêteté, plus de salutations.

[I see nothing but animosity on men's faces, and nature smiles upon me always.

However, I still feel, I have to confess, some pleasure in living amidst people, so long as my face remains unknown to them. But it's a happiness they hardly ever grant me. . . .

One of my favorite walks was around l'École Militaire and to my delight I met here and there several pensioners who, having retained the traditional military *politesse*, saluted me as I passed by. This sign of courtesy, which my heart returned to them a hundredfold, pleased me and increased the good feeling I experienced in seeing them. Since I do not know how to conceal what touches me, I often spoke about these veterans and of the way their demeanor affected me. Nothing more was needed. Some time afterwards I noticed I was no longer unrecognized by them, rather that I was singled out since they began to see me with the same eye as the public's. No more courtesy, no more salutes.] (131-32)

The tinge of preciousness in the sensibility of Rousseau the naturally sociable man closed out of the simplest of pleasurable human exchanges, even the impossibility of gauging the accuracy of his sensitivities from this anecdote—all the opacities of such discourse vanish before the self-sustaining presence-absence of the prose. For Rousseau's essayism carefully picks its way around the particulars, moving as narration moves, back around itself yet always onward, promising a completion that is never fully adequate to what transpires. What *is* revealed in its half-evasive, half-detached indefiniteness is what would be forfeited by Bacon's aphoristic technique, or even by Montaigne's thinking-aloud. The prize captured by Rousseau's narrativity is the quiet hum of time's passing from pleasure to pain, from "Il n'en fallut pas davantage" to "plus de salutations." Or from painless nonentity to the pleasure of simple existence: "J'aperçus le ciel, quelques étoiles, et un peu de verdure." This is writing *as* time.

And, as suggested earlier, when discursivity becomes time, the language of alienation revolutionizes, not only by transmuting *retraite absolue* into sociality through absolute communication, but also by rendering the alienation so starkly that it—the alienation and the rendering made one—announces to the historical world the impossibility of continuing to allow such a stateless state to exist. The completely alienated Word remakes society, by requiring acknowledgment that the present state of society *is* a desert for the voice voicing itself. It is no accident that Fanon, in *The Wretched of the Earth* but particularly in *Black Skin, White Masks*, turned to the Rousseauist essay as his most effective delivery of absolute retort to the racist imperialism of Western humanism.

Aggression and Experimentalism: Emerson and Nietzsche

Emerson at twenty entered in his journal, dated 1823, "Not so much matter *what* as *how* men do & speak. . . . Style not matter gives immortality" (*Writings* 38). Allowing for youth's own immortal aspirations in this entry, readers of the mature *Essays*, including the book-length *Nature* of 1836, first encounter the essay as a genre actually converted into style. This is a style *of* immortality that yet avoids the sterility of Baconian monumentalism. Montaigne's and Rousseau's efforts to free language from subjects permitted the essay to become its own subject, as in "On some verses of Virgil," or to identify itself with subjectivity, as in the *Rêveries*. Emerson's outright equation of essay with style makes it absolute genre, thus nongenerically unbounded, in still another sense. Montaigne and Rousseau *have* style, which is to say their discourse is a complex of techniques, such as Montaigne's mental metonymy and Rousseau's rhythmic prolongation and narrative. These techniques produce distinctive styles. The Emersonian essay, however, *is* style. Essayistic absolutism thus comes to mean the elimination of style as decorum, or the adaptation of words to subject, even when the subject is the language of the self, as in Montaigne, or the self of language, as in Rousseau. And it is the opposite of style as expression; for instead of serving to express things or selves, style in the arch-Romantic Emerson presumes to be the realization of things and of the Self. All is for the Word as divinely potent evaluation of the world; "essay" now stands for "assay."

If we turn back from this transcendent style in Emerson and apply a mundane stylistics, we could characterize his essays in general as aggressively expansionist. An Emerson text above all else *moves*. Movement from phase one to phase two and beyond is the signification prior to all others in any particular one of his phrases, sentences, sequences, paragraphs, or essays. In poetry Shelley's transformational aesthetic is analogous: the dead Keats is transubstantiated into *Adonais*, a text of regeneration; fiat immortality through a series of metaphoric modulations; the world is made Western wind. Like Shelley in this respect, Emerson preempts the French *Symbolistes* in stipulating that creative power as such is theme, form, structure, rhythm. As the working-out of itself, this creative power leaves certain traces. For a proper sense of the Emerson work, the oeuvre, the residue may be seen as the essay genre equated as it is with absolute style, which brings out the contours of that power's presence as *dynamis*. (Emerson's poems, many serving as mottos to the essays, are miniatures, abstracts of the prose forms, among which even the sermons and lectures are to be considered essayistic.) The most typical of these contours, or figurations, is what I shall term the "three-stepper," which becomes the signature of Emersonian discourse.

As a relationship between text and reader, Emerson's style is neither cognitive nor expressive, but seductive: step one designs to get you to step two, and so on. The reading process consists in being moved over and over again from part to whole until the self-renewing textual dynamic becomes habitual. The trick for the reader is to learn how to surrender self to text, phase by phase, one holdout collapsing after another. No hermeneutic program may be brought from outside to an Emersonian essay, for everything is in *its* control. Emerson solves the hermeneutic circle, part to whole to part, by making this very movement not only his message (as in such doctrinal essays as "Circles" and "The Over-Soul") but also his medium: circular power rejoining personal soul and the "NOT ME," whether it be self discovering itself ("Self-Reliance"), self discovering identical other ("Friendship"), self realizing itself in history ("History"), the word discovering itself ("The Poet"), or power as such discovering itself (*Nature* 1836, "Experience").

Like Rousseau's *rêverie*, Emersonian discourse is musical, having not the formats of music, but its *melos*. In fact this inner form, like that of Romantic music—originating in the *bearbeitung* of Haydn, then expanded by Beethoven—is nothing but the hyperunified organization of unit variation, or music articulating itself rather than emulating speech or depicting spiritual states, dramatic gestures, or the passions. First comes a proposition, then a redefinition or refinement or contrast, and finally either an intensification or an opening-out: three steps, each returning into or extending the preceding. Instead of proceeding to new material, the Emersonian text, then, elaborates all or part of the initial material, no matter, since they are synecdochically related. Cadencing the passage, typically, is another three-stepper. This paragraph from "Compensation" shows the form neatly developed; often, however, the changes and returns this whole paragraph runs through may be either packed into one, two, or three sentences or extended in a limited way to a sequence of three plus one, three plus two, even three plus four—or, as always in Emerson, distended to the dimension of the single entire essay:

> [First three-stepper:] There is a deeper fact in the soul than compensation, to wit, its own nature. The soul is not a compensation, but a life. The soul *is*. [Second three-stepper:] Under all this running sea of circumstance, whose waters ebb and flow with perfect balance, lies the aboriginal abyss of real Being. [Third three-stepper:] Essence, or God, is not a relation, or a part, but the whole. Being is the vast affirmative, excluding negation, self-balanced, and swallowing up all relations, parts, and times within itself. [Fourth three-stepper; three plus one, which "one" includes three:] Nature, truth, virtue, are the influx from thence. Vice is the absence or departure of the same. Nothing, Falsehood, may indeed stand as the great Night or shade, on which, as a background, the living universe paints itself forth; but no fact is begotten by it; it cannot work; for it is not. [Fifth three-stepper:] It cannot work any good; it cannot work any harm. It is harm inasmuch as it is worse not to be than to be. [*Essays* 299-300]

Lest his exposition grow too Augustinian, Emerson is never not a sermonizer, so the important theme of compensation receives another rhetorical treatment, one less doctrinal that will hit home. But the form remains the same, one-two-three, one-two-three, with a "plus two" added: "The radical tragedy of nature seems to be the distinction of More and Less. How can Less not feel the pain: how not feel indignation or malevolence towards More? Look at those who have less faculty, and one feels sad, and knows not well what to make of it. He almost shuns their eye; he fears they will upbraid God. What should they do? It seems a great injustice. But see the facts nearly, and these mountainous inequalities vanish" (301).

Ultimately what is this compensation? Nothing else but inner form, contour, style. Everything can be "seen," and everything can be seen "nearly," because the style is expansive, capable of moving in for intense close-up or of telescoping outward for the infinite view. Therefore, all particularities as they seem to be in their fixed state are false. And it is not until the essayistic voice, in Emerson's favorite figure transformed into the "eye," dynamizes them that they can signify what they are, namely aspects of creative power. The "radical tragedy of nature" dissolves as illusory appearance when discursivity first narrows ("nearly"), then expands to the whole. The root ("radical") penetrates to "the aboriginal abyss of real Being." Two ranges of metaphor overlap: on one hand, natural phys- icality—"sea," "abyss," "radical," "More and Less"—and on the other hand, the "eye" of both victims ("shuns their eye") and seer-essayist, which gets "the facts nearly." The cause is a thoroughly expansionist impetus; the effect, no "tragedy." Emersonian metaphor is a heavier artillery than the metonymy of Montaigne. Compensation is style.

Thus the Emersonian text is free to be anything it may be, and it may be anything at all, depending solely on the eye's ability to expand part into whole and to condense whole into part. Author's eye becomes reader's, for each is a microversion of the same circle. Creative power plays along a universal grid, organizing itself around nodes of three that allow compen- satory style to register all particulars as *symboles*. If everything said, as well as everything referred to, is symbolic of every other signifier/signified and referent, and if words and things and selves are all, properly seen, only aspects of universal creative power passing back and forth through a porous Over-Soul—then there need be no ground and no finality of reference. All that is required is circular return. Emerson's style points directly to Nietzsche; it may even serve as an aesthetic explanation of quizzical Nietz- schean themes such as Eternal Return. But the Emersonian essay is a stricter music, phrase-to-phrase, than Nietzsche's discursivity, and always more cos- mic than historical in its irrepressible outward-boundedness.

The result of Emerson's transmutation of the essay genre into style is that text becomes pretext, context, and intertext: omnitext. Emersonian essayism is textualism as such: precise semantic content is minimal, constantly diminishing to zero, while compensatory style as creative power subsumes both form and content. The purpose of Emerson's essay genre is to keep us reading it, for the sake of doing so. No writer in English is more readable and less subject to précis. Like Coleridge and Whitman, as well as his friend Carlyle, Emerson requires the Germans for exegetical frame, whether Hegel and Nietzsche or Schelling and Rilke. The object of essayistic textualism, in other words, is to absorb the reader into the process of its own unfolding, into the rhythms of constriction and expansion, tension and release, this note and that note.

Both Montaigne's *essai* with its metonymy and Rousseau's *rêverie* with its periodicity and narrative make the text approach the self-sufficiency wrought by metaphoric Emersonian textualism. Rousseau, as we have seen, moreover transfers the burden of communication from authorial subject to discursivity itself. Yet there is an important difference, one not simply of degree, either. Preserving its independence from the author, more or less, Montaigne's and Rousseau's discursivity is still progressive: there is always something yet to be said, and what has been said is always inadequate. Stylistic momentum toward something beyond style is maintained in the *Essais* and the *Rêveries*. In Emerson, however, we keep reading not in a free effort to extend the power of discursivity, but as the sole option allowed us by the untrammeled discursivity *of* power. Text becomes appetite for text. And the tyrannizing self, like the "kosmos" of Whitman, gorges itself on the world's metamorphic significations, confident they are all reducible to self: "this tyrannizing unity in his [man's] constitution, which evermore separates and classifies things, endeavoring to reduce the most diverse to one form" (*Essays* 43). The reader no longer reads but is read by the text. One's disposition must be surrender, the Romantic (and perhaps protofascist) attitude toward power that is the cultural inheritance of the aborted French Revolution. In contrast, the abyss between yearning subject and communicating text in Rousseau is pre-Romantic alienation, pregnant with revolutionary potential. Robespierre's "divine Jean-Jacques" was no exaggeration; perhaps Emersonian compensatory style, given post-Romantic to postmodern history, indicates no exaggeration either.

If one reads the Emersonian essay of self-sufficient textualism, one *does* what Nature *is*. The words *are* what they mean, the work symbolizes all in symbolizing itself, and the eye willfully moves closer or turns away to gaze at the starry expanse. A famous example would be the three-stepper from the first chapter of *Nature* (1836): "I become a transparent eye-ball; I am nothing; I see all" (*Essays* 10). Such miracles of metaphor empower the text absolutely, yet discursivity cut so completely loose is no longer liberating. It entraps itself within its perfect mirror. Discourse in Emerson opens door upon door, from the misfortune of lockjaw and the "tragedy of More and Less" to the ethical and metaphysical marvels of history and the universe. But the prospect remains the same: the uniformity of power unmediated, of the essay transformed into a perpetual motion engine of absolute, and absolutist, style.

How unmediated this power style of Emerson's can be is detectable not only in the grand pronouncements such as "I see all" but also, and more clearly, in some of the tamer, primarily cognitive and even bookish, portions of an essay, as in this three-stepper from "Self-Reliance": "Time and space are but physiological colors which the eye makes, but the soul is light; where it is, is day; where it was, is night; and history is an impertinence and an injury, if it be any thing more than a cheerful apologue or parable of my being and becoming" (*Essays* 270). History the power style simply overwhelms with a pseudo-Hegelian joke. By expanding from "eye" to "soul" to "light," Emerson can move effortlessly, without the mediation of "fact," to an equation of history with an "impertinence" that may be overlooked, since the "eye" retains supremacy. The self of the power style thus remains "cheerful." For history is incapable of any other status but that of signifier. If all is a metaphor of and through the eye, the self *reads* evil and misfortune and paradox as mere plot complications in a history reduced to a story, and not a realist narrative at that, but, instead, a self-reflexive "apologue or parable."

The power style of the Emersonian essay rests its case, having converted nature and history alike into text. With a version of Hegel's Absolute Spirit as distorted as his version of Kant's transcendentalism, Emerson looks back from the final phase of the dialectic, to which he has not penetrated but jumped with "the eye makes," and sees all experience as the totality of becoming, which as totality crystallizes into "being." The distance is immeasurable between the sense of history as violent over-determination, a sense realized starkly in the tragic mimesis of Euripides, and Emerson's kind of Romantic essayism, which avails itself of the power style to abolish history altogether by making it nothing but text.

This self-reliance of style in Emerson is more original even than Whitman's poetic voice, and just as vigorous. The trouble, however, is that Emersonian essayism's recourse to words as a self-sufficient power goes beyond the possibilities of liberation intrinsic to discursivity such as that of Montaigne and Rousseau—to willfulness. Rousseau, unable to express alienation adequately in the *Rêveries,* turns to the capacity of discursive narration for autonomous communication. Emerson, worried in "Experience" about diminution of the one thing in the universe he regards as an absolute—creative power—falls back on the power style's self-renewing ploy of verbal recombination. In a sense Emerson is doing nothing different from Rousseau: both are saved from difficulty by reliance on discursivity's potential. But for Emerson everything starts from a transcendent sense of style that embodies a transcendental, if not strictly Kantian, ontology: words, like time and space, are "physiological colors." As he entered in the *Journals* (June 2, 1832), style is the man: "A man's style is his mind's voice" (*Writings* 47).

Rousseau the *rêveur* resorts to the autonomy of discursivity to prove, to manifest and to test, his alienation; his words communicate but stop short of solving this alienation. Like Montaigne, he sees the essay as effort and its vistas as open, not circular. Emerson converts essay/effort into essay/divine assay. In doing so he remains completely Judeo-Christian: "In the beginning was the Word." In "On some verses of Virgil," Montaigne as an old man experiencing erotic revival through the words of the pagan Virgil and Lucretius, as well as his own, still concludes his *essai* to maintain life's fire through writing by humbly abandoning sexual pursuit to the young, who hardly need words to live. Rousseau's anecdotes about reinserting himself as pariah into the hated and hating *société* demonstrate discursivity's autonomous power to communicate alienation when the outcast's immediate expressivity threatens to turn into bathos. Discursivity in Rousseau at the same time, however, discloses the gap between words and reality, thus increasing even to a revolutionary pitch the genuine pathos of everyman's isolation. The *Rêveries* deliver disturbing messages to a future that perhaps will be goaded by Rousseau's words into resolving the malady. Yet "essay" in Rousseau always retains the sense of limitation of "essayer." In Emerson the essay of absolute power, empowering itself, issues in automatic success. Power may wane, but simple yet all-assuming phrases such as "practical power" in "Experience" (*Essays* 492) can always regenerate the transcendentalist's spirit from its crises of exhaustion. The cost, however, is that the essay, in cutting loose so that signifier/signified rests omnipotently self-content, has also lost the power to communicate. Emerson's essays are a heady stimulant; they exhilarate, by lending a sense of transformative power, only to leave one exhausted, with the sole recourse of picking them up again, assured that if words cannot change reality they can change themselves into reality. This is not only a question of aesthetics. The same culmination Carl Schorske has shown to represent a politically ominous regressivism in turn-of-the-century Austrian liberal culture, in the collapse of bourgeois optimism into psychologistic aestheticism (*"Fin-de-siècle" Vienna*). And a similar culmination can perhaps be forecast of the heavy psychologism of liberal culture in all prosperous postindustrial societies.

Nietzsche, particularly in *The Gay Science, Zarathustra, Beyond Good and Evil,* and *On the Genealogy of Morals,* shows signs of having returned from America. Not only does he quote Emerson for a motto to *The Gay Science,* but as Walter Kaufmann and Harold Bloom, among others, have noted, Emerson pervades the major decade of Nietzsche's career, the 1880s. The most obvious Emersonianism is Nietzsche's working-out of the idea of will to power. Yet the subtler, longer-term effect of the German thinker's continued reading, from youth, of the American essayist in translation has to be Nietzsche's adoption of "experimentalism" as the exemplary attitude of the philosopher rehabilitated from truth-seeker into perpetual questioner of "the value of truth" (*Genealogy* 153).

Robert Musil's hero in *The Man without Qualities*, Ulrich, attempts to practice what he calls "Essayism" in self-conscious homage to Emerson as seen through Nietzsche's perspective (300). To the Austrian modernist, Emerson is a philosopher manqué, and fortunately so. For though somewhat obscured by his German borrowings, Emerson shines through, a model of a mind tentatively yet ceaselessly thinking his way through a life often bewildered as well as inspired by creative power. As Nietzsche himself described Emerson in a note, "The author who has been richest in ideas in this century so far has been an American (unfortunately made obscure by German philosophy—frosted glass)" (qtd. in Kaufmann 11-12). Musil's Emerson is an "essayer," one who exchanges the typical intellectual's commitment to what Nietzsche characterizes as the "ascetic ideal" of truth—which is unmasked by experience to show nothing but constant self-deception—for a skeptical yet persistent engagement with diversity and change. The profit to be gained from this exchange is a sense of identity based not on an essential presence but on a critical absence, an identity "without qualities":

The translation of the word "essay" as "attempt," which is the generally accepted one, only approximately gives the most important allusion to the literary model. For an essay is not the provisional or incidental expression of a conviction that might on a more favourable occasion be elevated to the status of truth or that might just as easily be recognised as error (of that kind are only the articles and treatises, referred to as "chips from their workshop," with which learned persons favour us); an essay is the unique and unalterable form that a man's inner life assumes in a decisive thought. Nothing is more alien to it than that irresponsibility and semi-finishedness of mental images known as subjectivity; but neither are "true" and "false," "wise" and "unwise," terms that can be applied to such thoughts, which are nevertheless subject to laws that are no less strict than they appear to be delicate and ineffable. . . . Their [essayists'] domain lies between religion and knowledge, between example and doctrine, between *amor intellectualis* and poetry, they are saints with and without religion, and sometimes too they are simply men who have gone out on an adventure and lost their way. [Musil 301]

Nietzsche and Musil, then, each in his own way, claim for their own the Emerson whose devotion to the essay as both form and attitude is equivalent to a heroic, nontranscendental experimentalism. In brief, they identify their own liberationist critique of the ideological nature of all knowledge—a critique exemplified by Nietzsche most explicitly in the "First Essay" and "Second Essay" of *The Genealogy of Morals*—with the Emerson whose way with the essay and practice of the power style pull up short of willful solipsism. This is the Emerson whose celebration of the freedom implied by the principle of creative power is complete, ignoring Kantian limit and unencumbered by the Hegelian Absolute or by Schopenhauerian pessimism. This is the Nietzschean Emerson who, like the European Whitman, projects the American aboriginal voice—a voice characterized by Nietzsche as expressing "the *instinct for freedom* (in my language: the will to power)" (*Genealogy* 87).

To Emerson, all the universe, natural, historical, and personal, is what to Nietzsche amounts to the individual's power to seize control of existence by acknowledging that there is no truth, just truth-making. The triumphant Nietzschean individual, then, is the self-aware artist of reality. His prize is the same as the self-reliant Emersonian individualist's, minus the Christian-Romantic convictions of divinity and brotherhood: "*freedom above things*" (*Gay Science* 164). This art, I would argue, is to both essayists, Nietzsche as well as Emerson, the art of letting discourse play, the art of evasion and release from all varieties of petrification, moral or religious or scientific: "We need all exuberant, floating, dancing, mocking, childish, and blissful art lest we lose the *freedom above things* that our ideal demands of us. . . . We should be *able* also to stand *above* morality—and not only to *stand* with the anxious stiffness of a man who is afraid of slipping and falling any moment, but also to *float* above it and *play*" (*Gay Science* 164).

Convinced that man's, rather the heroic "over-man's," deepest drive is to will his own constantly changing truth through self-renewing play, Nietzsche shares with both Emerson and Rousseau an affinity for the essay, for discursivity as such. Yet he wants nothing to do with the traces of what he calls "ascetic idealism" imbuing Emersonian transcendentalism, and he is as alien to Rousseau's semimystical *retraite absolue* as he is to Schopenhauer's "Buddhism." Nietzsche the antiphilosopher is saved by a clear-eyed acceptance of what is almost instinctual in Rousseau and only half-conscious in Emerson: the essay as a genre really goes beyond the power style of Emerson, to become pure essay*ism*, the "arts" of metaphysics, ethics, and even science as they can be "played" by discursivity.

What such an essayistic science, or *Wissenschaft*, would be like, Nietzsche demonstrates in both the form of his discourse and its argument in section 22 of *Beyond Good and Evil*, which is a consistently essayistic work. The essayistic antiphilosopher ("someone could come along who . . . ") starts by outwitting positivists with his claim that their "nature's conformity to law" is no "text" at all but just "interpretation"; then he parodies science. The essayist as mock philosopher adduces his own universal and unconditional law of lawlessness "by asserting of this world the same as you assert of it, namely that it has a 'necessary' and 'calculable' course, but *not* because laws prevail in it but because laws are absolutely *lacking,* and every power draws its ultimate consequences every moment" (34).

Interpretation is both the object of Nietzsche's critique and his means, for discourse *is* interpretation. And Nietzsche's anti-interpretive interpretation is a trick of discursive play: to make positivism not so simply by saying it is not so. Thus Nietzsche converts Emerson's power style from a circular pursuit of self and universe *as* word into a means to power *by* the word, the word not as magic spell but as ironic declaration of subversive war. Romantic transcendentalism is retired, the will to power asserted.

CHAPTER SEVEN

Toward a Dialectical Theory of Genre

Most genre theory, from Plato and Aristotle to Scaliger, Goethe, and diverse contemporary theorists such as Bakhtin and Genette, has been a refinement of two mutually reinforcing positions: that all art is representational in one way or another, and that its distinct kinds of representation are classes. Corollaries are that the individual genres serve to guide the production of art and that they condition the consumption and interpretation of both individual works and groupings of works. Gérard Genette, for example, believing that "l'étude des transformations implique l'examen . . . des permanences [the study of transformations implies the consideration . . . of certain constants],"[1] has clarified how genre, if it is identifiable as a network of classes, must be analyzed in order for literary study to proceed securely from such *permanences*.

Adena Rosmarin, in *The Power of Genre*, performs a similarly neat clarification of how representation is inherently classificatory by applying E.H. Gombrich's thesis about visual representation, that "all thinking is sorting, classifying" (Gombrich 301), to both the creation and the theoretical and critical apprehension of literature. Accordingly, Rosmarin explains the relationship between art and reality in Kantian terms, the thing as such "out there" and the categories of understanding (or "schemas," as both Rosmarin and Gombrich call them), which are applied by both conceiver and consumer. The activity of representing, then, consists in aspiring to a perfect match, which is of course impossible, of categories with the objects represented. The end of such activity is rhetorical: the originating understanding selects, distorts, and deceives to convey not the thing in itself but a self-declaring aesthetic illusion that communicates the artist's wishes and aims. The consumer of the aesthetic product engages in a similar procedure, by "reading" the selections, distortions, and illusions intertextually. For one moves beyond similarities in the different things—the object represented and aesthetic production representing—to similarities among different works representing similar objects.

This whole process Rosmarin submits as a special theory of genres that makes them relational forces binding reality to art while never matching the two seamlessly. Genres also become the theorist's and critic's schemas, motivated by desire and managed for rhetorical ends; specific genres establish theoretical argument and critical exegesis according to a "rhythm of schema and correction" (38). And they finally imply for Rosmarin a general theory of genre that apparently avoids the inductive-deductive, particular-universal ambiguity inherent in a "purely representational theory of interpretation" (33), which can never quite fit the particular into the general, or object into schema. Wishing to resolve this remaining gap, which is permanent in Kant, between constituting subject and constituted object, Rosmarin turns to notions of pragmatism, those of William James and the neo-Kantian Vaihinger in particular. Their concepts enable her to claim that genres are heuristic fictions that are expedient to the creation and understanding of art. The schema then acquires "full constitutive power yet shows itself to be fully pragmatic: it is defined in order to serve the purposes of thought, not the other way around" (20).

The contention that schemas underlying genres are primarily instrumental sidesteps the basic issue for the genre theorist, which is *how* after all genres *can* function the way they do. If genres are rhetorical, they may have validity, to be sure. But the key question is whether or not genres have any reality that would make them suitable to be rhetorically selected and applied in the first place. Even Aristotle grants his genres more than rhetorical instrumentality. They are the prime focus of his *Poetics*, as distinct from the *Rhetoric*, because such genres as epic and tragedy maintain constant identities beyond their individual versions of instrumentality: a tragedian engages in *poesis*; he makes something, namely a tragedy—as a builder builds a house—which *then* serves rhetorical purposes, to inspire horror and pity, for example.

In short, to resolve the problem of representation that has nagged genre theory from its inception and burdened the genre theorist with guilt for always being deductive while trying to appear inductive, it is necessary to drive beneath the psychology of perception and beyond the pragmatic dimensions of rhetoric. This necessity exists because genre is intrinsically historical. Texts both originate and accumulate in genres over time, and we register what these texts are and may mean by changes in their genres.

Like the deconstructionists' reduction of genre to the absence/presence of generativity, Rosmarin's and others' representational conceptions of genre as deductive yet pragmatically rhetorical classification are attended by a shadowy sense of history as previous similarity and dissimilarity, to be referred to by the artist addressing the reader and by the reader comprehending the work. However, such conceptions deprive history of its substantial reality. A tragedy such as Kleist's *Prince Friedrich of Homburg* would, were Rosmarin correct, stand as an original event and active aesthetic response, both of which pragmatically relate the nineteenth-century work to the *Persians* as one among many intertexts. But Aeschylus's substantial, even genre-originating example of Athenian tragedy—which genre itself composes part of Athenian and Western history—would then no longer exist, or no longer be allowed existence, in its own right. Pragmatism, again like deconstruction, fabricates an everlasting present from the fumes of a fully consumable past. Not even Marxist or Hegelian theories of the text, which do not deny the substantial reality of the past, however "appropriated," are so reductive as the pragmatic and deconstructionist varieties of consumerism.[2]

Genre cannot be elevated to a Platonic Form, nor can it be reduced to a heuristic notion. And if classification is implied by representational genre, the historicity of genres prevents them from being defined as elements of a class network. Genres are given neither as inapplicable transcendental categories nor as formal schemas. Genres are given as historically generated and modified *operations*. They constitute the reality of history in its aspect of textuality: "The representation of the 'real,' in other words, is an intertextual reference to cultural modes of authority" (Frow 154). This "intertextual reference," however, is *not*—as some post-Althusser Marxists, John Frow and Terry Eagleton, for example, as well as contemporary formalists such as Michael Riffaterre suggest—reducible to "the codes of cultural and literary convention" (154). Unfortunately, though, starting with the Romantics' rejection of restrictive-prescriptive genre and culminating in poststructuralists' textual-intertextual indeterminism, genre has either diminished to a figment or faded into the processes described in literary history, semiotics, and the phenomenology of reading. And despite Genette, certainly genre as even a technical construct is no longer simply identifiable with either the modalities of representation or the thematics of what is represented: such definition is merely taxonomic, empty of significance.

The intrinsic historicity of genre makes it a stronger bridge between the historical and the aesthetic than any other theoretical construct. However, to reconstruct a theory of genre that would be genuinely dialectical requires abandoning altogether the notion that genre in any way possesses a nature. Only then will it be possible to avoid the empiricist triviality of classification schemes and the subordination of the aesthetic to an expression of the historical, a liability afflicting even the most sophisticated code-convention-consensus descriptions. Genre in some of its aspects may be *likened* to material cause: according to Riffaterre, language as the condition, or situation, of works taken individually and collectively. Genre may also be apprehended as efficient cause, as when Alastair Fowler emphasizes the importance to literary history of transformations in the kinds (170-90). Yet genre lacks the status of formal cause: contrary to E.D. Hirsch, it cannot be equated with meaning or assumed to be a hermeneutic program without losing its historicity, as understood apart from epistemology. And Aristotle himself would concur that genre falls short of the teleological absolutism of final cause.

Instead of being regarded as an essentializing presence in the literary work or tradition, genre needs to be decentered, as deconstructionists and pragmatists alike propose. But genre also needs to retain its substantial historical reality. Therefore, the proper methodological angle would enable us to see genre as fully dynamic "set of operations" (Serres, *Hermes* 37).

Among those currently interested in revivifying genre theory, Ralph Cohen, too, believes genres are the historical substance of literature. His continuing argument starts from the position that genre must be considered a nonessential entity: "And since each genre is composed of texts that accrue, the grouping is a process, not a determinate category. Genres are open categories" ("History and Genre" 204). Moreover, according to Cohen, the theory of genre provides criticism with a ground for comprehension and interpretation: "Since genres are interrelated, there seems always a basis for some readability" ("Postmodern Genres" 243). Most important, perhaps, is Cohen's claim that genres, especially in their fluctuating combinations, properly constitute the field of study specifically denominated "literary history."

My own sense of how genre, history, and literary history relate to one another is more extreme than Cohen's. And I think the chemistry of the configuration is fundamentally different from what he perceives to be the case. Not only is genre to be *conceived* historically; genres are themselves incursions *by* texts *into* history. This stance necessarily implies that genres—not the individual texts composing them—are ideological forces and not simply processual groupings. Tragedy, for example, is political in its telos as well as its mimesis-subordinated language; satire is rational in its intentionality and rhetorical in its operation; and the essay is self-referential, with its textualism that transforms rhetoric into reflexive mimesis.

Applying his concept of historical genre, Cohen can cite the gradual formation of the postmodernist essay as a new genre plied by discourse theorists who question the very notion of genre ("Postmodern Genres" 254). However, by applying both the concept of historical genre and the theory that genre is itself a historical force, I would pursue another kind of path. I would observe, for example, that contemporary feminism has in the essay (Woolf, Rich, and several academics have often turned to the essay though it is by no means a dominant feminist form) a genre already proved, by a history beginning with Montaigne, to be a distinctive prospect of power. This is the power of voicing a politics of free self-definition and a subversive critique of ideology. Similarly, I see in tragedy the genre most efficient in working out the power politics of win, loss, or stalemate, whether in its traditional form of nationalism or its modern forms of social, ethnic, and racial revolutionism. And satire, however minor it has become as a separate kind today and however reduced to a flavoring—not even a semi-independent mode—of contemporary dominant genres, will continue to be a favorite weapon, albeit two-edged, of rationalist critique and a promising though problematic prospect of clarified values.

The individual text remains anchored in its status as unique event; it cannot attain the collective, truly historical status of ideology except through its participation in genre. Euripides' *Medea* as a unique event is not ideological; as a tragedy of winner-lose-all, it is. Within the evolution of the essay, the ideology of liberationist textuality once and for all surfaces only after a long history starting with Cicero, developing with Montaigne, and finally culminating with Emerson and Nietzsche; nevertheless, revolution is present as the potency of each *rêverie* written by Rousseau. Cohen, however, would demur: "As for genres possessing immanent ideologies, it would appear that such an assumption disregards the differences among the members of a genre. This is not to deny that texts—such as generic members—can be interpreted as possessing ideologies, but rather that these cannot be deduced from generalizations about the genre" ("History and Genre" 209).

On the contrary, genres are already their own generalizations; no deducing is required. Only the generic can produce the ideological; the member text loses all ideological potency if deprived of its participation in the genre. Genres are exactly like political movements: the collective is all, the individual nothing.

How, then, would my theory of genre as the configuration of power explain the chemistry of genre, history, and literary history? Literary history, I would concur with Cohen, requires genre study, but in a stronger sense than his. Literary history is not just another branch of literary study; it is the study of texts as they are constituted, that is, generically. Or, less absolutely, if Cohen's interest is in the *concept* of genre (as "open category") as it is necessary to literary history if not to other divisions of literary study, my interest is in genre itself as it operates—and it operates as the historical intervention of symbolic prospects of power. I am definitely not asserting what would amount merely to the inverse of Hayden White's aesthetics of history, in other words, that literary texts must be analyzed according to their characteristics as historical formations. Instead, I would lay the quite different claim, in line with the work of Michel Serres, that literature as it is generically constituted is itself a substantially real historical action, and that it mandates genre study as an unavoidable method of studying history.

If genre is construed as power, and literature itself as *potentia* figurally deployed through historically differentiated channels, then understanding a particular genre from its origins to what it becomes as it metamorphoses or expires *is* understanding cultural history in many of its crucial developments. I hope to have proved this hypothesis in my literary histories of tragedy, satire, and the essay. History *is* Aeschylus's *Persians*; or, later, with Büchner's *Danton's Death*, tragedy *is* history: not the deeds at Salamis and Paris, but their status as imitative actions, as *activations* of Athenian identity and modern bourgeois liberty. Such actions, developing through a political mimesis of victory, loss, or stalemate, make tragedy a complete genre unto itself. Incomplete, or semigeneric, satire, with its rational dispersals of generic power, supplants tragedy's language of action with its own language of evaluative rhetoric. Thus it demonstrates how history tends toward crises of stagnation when moral ideas, social and aesthetic biases, and specific political ideologies display their *ex post facto* inadequacy (like Hegel's "owl of wisdom") to the task of embodying culture. And the nongeneric essay frees the self from the crimp of external history as well as from its own inner history through textuality. The essay genre becomes a kind of photographic negative revealing the pressures on the alienated, exiled, typically old self that account for its retreat into the Word as thing—whether these pressures come from Cicero's exhausted Republic, Machiavelli's overthrown republic, Montaigne's civil-war-torn France, Rousseau's prerevolutionary Europe, Emerson's expansionist America, or Nietzsche's rotted bourgeoisie.

Now it is possible to be precise about genre as history, and not merely literary history, as Fowler would have it; nor a product of literary and cultural codes or conventions, as Frow (154) and Eagleton (98-99) argue[3]; nor, indeed, a surrogate for literary theory itself, as Hans Robert Jauss contends. History as such, of course, does not need defining: it defines. It defines us, and it determines our realizations of history's reality, both of which, realizations and reality, are matters of substantial texts. As ground of experience and experience, as determining and being determined, history and texts possess power together. This is power in the mode of violence—not momentum and not continuity. For violence abruptly particularizes, demarcates, figurates, individuates.

The individuating activity, or what I have designated the "operation," of textual power is what I mean by genre. The separate genres are discrete figural deployments of power. Their violence can be maximal: such is the case in tragedy's mimesis of action, which renders with the definitiveness of full genre the political prospects of victory, defeat, and stalemate. This violence can also be moderated, held in check, by susceptibility to the force of other genres, with which it may enter into uneasy alliance. Such is the case, for example, with semigeneric satire's gestural evaluations, rendering in all their ambiguity and ambivalence the rational prospects of right and wrong, acceptable and vulgar, beautiful and ugly, sacred and profane. Or this violence can be dispersed almost completely, as in the essay's prospects opened wide by free-roving textuality, the nongeneric play of discursivity in itself, more or less negligent of the boundaries of word and thing, of signifier, signified, referent.

All these genres, the entire range of individual genres described by these three, are in fact genres; that is, even the nongeneric essay and semigeneric satire are still complete kinds of literature. More important, though, since they are intrinsically historical, genres are degrees of violence; they are gradations of winning, losing, and deadlock that give political shapes to history as they incise their marks into the otherwise amorphous body of intertext. These graded incisions sometimes cut deeply into both history and textuality, as in tragedy. They may erase themselves, becoming mere shadow gestures on the surfaces of history and textuality, as in satire. Or they may channel out elaborate configurations of irresolution and escape, as in the essay. That is the range of generic power expressed in terms of the three possible outcomes of tragedy, the "type" of genre. For satire, as evaluative rhetoric lacking in mimetic action, always ends in stalemate. The essay, as rhetoric made into constative action, or discursivity as such, never loses, never stalemates; the essay genre always wins, but only by default, or by a miracle of finesse, since the essayistic voice perpetually escapes history, which allows the self to plead the Word's immunity.

Thus genres cannot be regarded as either classes, family groupings, or abstract sets and subsets. Nor can genres be thought of as at all representational. As figural deployments of power, they are not; rather, they *operate*. Genre itself can be conceived as *being* only that "ceaseless reciprocality" that Eagleton discerns in the relational practice among history, ideology, text, and structure, "a ceaseless reciprocal *operation* of text on ideology and ideology on text, a mutual structuring and destructuring in which the text constantly overdetermines its own determinations" (98-99). Or, genre as characterized above in chapter 1, following Michel Serres, as a set of operations may now be both energized and substantiated as the specific way literature's difference from life works—that is, according to Bakhtin, dialectically: "All that follows from the point that life is one thing and literature another is that life is not literature; it does not at all follow that there can be no interaction between them. The difference between the two phenomena, on the contrary, is one of the necessary conditions of their interaction. Only differences can interact" (147-48). Genre as a set of operations can further explain just exactly *how* Bakhtin's genre "finalizes" reality: "Every genre represents a special way of constructing and finalizing a whole, finalizing it essentially and thematically (we repeat), and not just conditionally or compositionally" (130).

A number of theoretical quandaries dissolve once genre is seen as power. First, one can detour around the impasse of defining a genre's nature. In itself tragedy has none. Instead, it maneuvers this, that, or another national-social entity or religious-ethical embodiment toward victory, loss, or deadlock, and does so not simply beyond good and evil but irrespective of moral categories altogether, however good or evil the players may be in this serious game. In tragedy it is the power move, which is political because it is aimed at outcome rather than evaluation, that determines genre as a set of operations. Deconstructionists' skepticism concerning genre's possessing a nature is thus borne out. But Derrida's displacement of the question of genre to the presence/absence of the framing *coup d'oeil* (213) is equally impossible. For genre does not exactly generate. Instead, it exerts itself toward political, rational, or textual-libertarian ends, with varying degrees of violence. Also variable are the kinds of social purposiveness achieved by genres: celebration and mourning (tragedy), rational evaluation (satire), and self-liberation (the essay). The elocutionary modes of presentation derive from these ends, as well as from the original degrees of violence: direct mimesis of action (tragedy), rhetorical gesture (satire), and discursivity as such (the essay).

Still another theoretical dilemma, and a crucial one, may also be sidestepped by genre as power. This is the unsolvable problem encountered by post-Althusser Marxists, who multiply "levels" of mediation, each endowed with more or less autonomy ("dominance"), between the base and the somehow nonexpressive superstructure. Their problem of theory is twofold: they conceive genre in spatial terms, and they abstract genre to the point of making it always already alien to the texts it contextualizes and intertextualizes. Both Fredric Jameson (105) and John Frow, for example, follow Bakhtin in emphasizing genre as essential to constructing the literary text so that it dialectically meshes with ideology while retaining its autonomy. Yet Jameson seems to abide by a spatial definition of mediation that requires allegiance to Althusser's notion of "levels." What is needed, however, is Marx's own, rather more Hegelian—that is, temporal—conception, sustained from *The German Ideology* through the *Grundrisse,* of mediation as unrelentingly forceful *intervention.* This intervention is the ceaseless activation of consumption (audience and reader) by production (textuality) and production by consumption, and it subsumes all historical vectors, from the economic ones forming the base to the cultural ones forming the superstructure.

Genre can, as Jameson wishes, mediate between history, ideology, and art without reducing the aesthetic to the historical and the political. However, it can do so only if conceived not as a key element vital to the correct theoretical construction of the text, but, instead, as the *dynamis* of textual construction itself. Genre is not a means of construction any more than it is a representational phenomenon. Genre is the construction of the text, period. Genre is the violent transition between history and ideology and literature.

In *Marxism and Literary History,* Frow acknowledges the problem experienced by contemporary Marxists engaging with genre in their various attempts to formulate an aesthetics that would be true to the literariness of texts. But he persists in approaching genre as a mediatory phenomenon, in the sense of continuousness rather than violent interven- tion, so that genre loses its historical identity as an identifying force and becomes almost imperceptibly gradual. Frow's revisionism leaves genre hanging, along with other theoretical concepts, in a peculiarly spatial and abstract position, as if its "content" were yearning for the embrace of its "categories" so that it might claim its putative "unity" but were unable to bridge the gap: "Literary theory is not *ideologiekritik* but a knowledge of conditions and functions. It forms a unity with literary history, and its descriptive categories are not separable from their content but must adapt themselves to the structuredness of the material" (121). Frow's tenta- tiveness about genre is even more apparent when he moves from a general discussion of it as one element of literary theory and history, which wield genre along with other "descriptive categories," toward a specific, and hopeful, formulation of the problem of genre's relation to intertextuality: "A more difficult (but also a more crucial) question is whether one can speak of an intertextual relation to a genre: that is, a relation which, in simple or complex form, is absolutely determinant for every text and yet which is not, strictly speaking, a relation to an intertext" (156).

These overly sensitive descriptions of genre fail to differentiate genre adequately from intertextuality, and they fail to exploit genre's potential to lend intertextuality the referential specificity it so sorely needs. The source of Frow's uneasiness (peculiar for one otherwise so responsive to Althusser) is his retention of sociological Marxism's notion of ideology as the result of "appropriations": "Given that all discourse is informed by power, is constituted *as discourse* in relation to unequal patterns of power, then political judgments can be made in terms of particular historically specific appropriations of discourse by dominant social forces" (61). Although he successfully evades ontologizing the ideological and thereby reducing the cultural to mere expression of the material base, Frow still cannot imagine literary discourse as being *really* autonomous while at the same time retaining its social significations. The Marxist literary historian is thus left only to trace power patterns showing the "dominant" crudely muscling the varieties of discourse into its service.

Genre adequately conceived for dialectical purposes, however, genre that preserves its proper identity as operation, void of essence and replete with political potency, would abandon this narrow definition of "appropriation" and serve to mediate literary texts with their history. Genre, in short, is neither an abstract repository of codes nor a spatial conception for spanning "levels" of culture—or the various discursive practices composing culture—and the economic base.

Tragedy, for example, the most direct of all the genres, operates its real-time mimesis of win, lose, or draw without degenerating to a merely symbolic register of social values. With its language of action, tragic genre practices its political significations, configuring not what power can be interpreted to be directed toward, either overtly or covertly, but, instead, what power as such *does*: Aeschylean tragedy dominates, Euripidean succumbs, Sophoclean suspends itself. With its language of rhetoric, satiric genre gestures its rational significations, including the directly political, proffering evaluations doomed to paradox by rationality itself. With its relatively pure textual play, the essayistic nongenre is as free of the necessity of interpretation as tragedy or satire. The signifiers of the essay genre practice the artful politics of self-liberation within the sphere of the private, the very articulation of which is a violent counterinsurgency, opposed to the betrayal of the self by public institutions from the political to the scientific, as well as to the external history of exclusion and repression.

Just before the end of *Marxism and Literary History*, Frow does introduce a temporal aspect to his construction of the text-intertext. Only this temporalization occurs, again, between mechanistically distantiated levels where time, however hypothetically "dynamic," must remain inert, inoperative, a mere "structural component of the system" (178). Frow draws an analogy between this system and "framing," both judged to be homologous to genre. Yet the temporality ascribed to the frame is an overly abstract temporality. The frame (*parergon*), which invisibly, as it were, defines both the interiority of the work (*ergon*) framed and the exteriority of what is not the work, relates the two as mutual and as simultaneous. Yet this kind of frame deadens into as nonhistorical a category as Derrida's genre construed as "blink of the eye" in "The Law of Genre." Furthermore, disastrously for a materialist, this refined sense of temporality is too purely Hegelian in both its idealist content and its terminology: "And the frame is rightly an absence insofar as it is a purely relational moment, the point of crystallization of metadiscursive instructions" (224). Indeed, genre understood as frame possesses its temporality as absence, but Hegel himself would demur at Frow's implication that such a frame is a barely imaginable spatial point where encoded instructions proceed from beyond the text into that text through a kind of osmosis.

Genre's rightful temporality resides in its full congruence—as a set of operations—with metadiscursive history. The dialectical time of genre is not "in between," mediating external and internal. For both whole genres and particular works, all possessing some generic dimension, are historical configurations of power, each genre operating in more or less its own distinctive way and exerting its special grade of violence. The theory of genre as the differential deployment of power thus preserves literature's historicity while allowing it to suffer no loss whatsoever in its aesthetic autonomy.

Notes

ONE. *Contemporary Genre Theory*

1. My citations of Derrida follow the English translation listed below in Works Cited. The French original is "La Loi du genre," *Glyph* 7 (1980): 177-232. A particularly helpful application of Derrida's theorizing on genre is that of Jacobus.

2. All three of the works by Hirsch listed below in Works Cited are essential, but especially *Validity*.

3. "Understanding can occur only if the interpreter proceeds under the same system of expectations, and this shared generic conception, constitutive of meaning and of understanding, is the intrinsic genre of the utterance" (Hirsch, *Validity* 81). Or, more extremely, "All understanding of verbal meaning is necessarily genre-bound" (*Validity* 76).

4. Besides Derrida, key references for deconstructionists' approaches to genre are Lacoue-Labarthe and Nancy, Beaujour, Frank, and Kambouchner.

5. A fuller and better, though worse titled, translation of Serres's "Algebra of Literature" appears in *Hermes*—"Knowledge in the Classical Age."

6. See, for example, the recent article by James R. Bennett, "The Essay in Recent Anthologies of Literary Criticism," *SubStance* 60, Special Issue: Writing the Real (1990): 55-67.

TWO. *Tragedies*

1. Although he draws a very different inference from my own, Nietzsche himself, sharing this reference with other classical scholars of his time, also turned to Aristophanes' play, which features a contest between Aeschylus and Euripides, to form his initial estimate of when, as well as why, tragedy died. See Silk and Stern 36-37.

2. Aeschylus, *Agamemnon*, lines 1355-59, Fagles. For all three plays of the *Oresteia*, I will cite either Fagles's or Lattimore's translation, whichever is more apt.

3. Serres, qtd. in Harari and Bell xxvii n.

4. One is reminded of Melville's "Dupont's Round Fight" (November 1861), in *Battle-Pieces* (Melville 12). However, Melville's point is ironically directed against the Union's undeterrable mechanism, which is strangling the Confederacy, and such covertly critical patriotism plays no part in Aeschylus' effect, which is lyric not ironic. This is Melville's poem:

> In time and measure perfect moves
> All Art whose aim is sure;

> Evolving rhyme and stars divine
> Have rules, and they endure.
>
> Nor less the Fleet that warred for Right,
> And, warring so, prevailed,
> In geometric beauty curved,
> And in an orbit sailed.
>
> The rebel at Port Royal felt
> The Unity overawe,
> And rued the spell. A type was here,
> And victory of LAW.

5. This sequence of the production of Aeschylus's works is, however, debated, notably by Herington in "Aeschylus."

6. "When Cimon went to Ithome in 462, or on his unhappy return to Athens, his political opponents took advantage of the situation. In their efforts to increase the democratic elements in the Athenian government they had long been attacking the Areopagus, the most conservative body in Athens, and now, under the leadership of Ephialtes and the young Pericles, they succeeded in carrying through the assembly measures that stripped the old council of all authority except its jurisdiction in homicide cases and other matters of a religious nature. . . . This measure . . . can be dated securely to 462/1 (Aristotle, *Ath. Const.* 25.2)" (Fine 348). Later Fine cites Cimon's "fruitless attempt to support the traditions of the Areopagus. The people, however, freed from the rather ill-defined powers of this archaic and conservative council, had little sympathy with its champion, and in the following spring (461) Cimon was ostracized" (349).

7. Draco's laws "were republished in the year of 409/8" (Fine 190). See also Fine 200-203 on the duration of the coexistence of state law and family law against homicide.

8. Lattimore's is a better translation of this phrase than Fagles's—"the proud heart of the past" (line 848)—which, besides its pro-Athena connotation of "wrong obstinacy," possesses the unfortunate quality of lack of seriousness. While mocking the Furies earlier in the Apollo sections, Aeschylus is careful to acknowledge their intelligence as representatives of the principle of justice as reprisal, and equally careful to avoid making them simply passionate forces of instinct. Aeschylus is like Aristotle in this respect, for the philosopher was hardly a proponent of passion or instinct: Aristotle claims in the *Nicomachean Ethics*, "People seek . . . to requite evil with evil—for otherwise their relation is regarded as that of slaves" (124).

9. I collapse Aristotle's distinction between expression and *dianoia*.

10. All English quotations from Sophocles, *Philoctetes*, in the text are from the Grene translation unless otherwise noted.

11. See Wilson 272-95. Wilson's psychoanalytic view, however, produces neither general tragedy nor specific Sophoclean tragedy of stalemate.

12. Godfrey Bond, note to line 1 of Euripides, *Euripides:* Heracles, p. 63.

13. Pietro Pucci claims that the play's remedial discourse unleashes an "uncontrollable spreading of differences" (84). At the levels of diction-thought and character, which are the only levels of discourse proper, Pucci is right. However, it is precisely the nondiscursive function of the deus ex machina that provides the control on otherwise endless deception and self-deception in *Medea*. Only spectacle in *Medea*, god-authorized pronouncement in *Electra*, or irony undercutting the goddesses in *Hippolytus*— and, in *Heracles*, the brutal "transdiscourse" of irrational violence—can show us an end to the infinite textuality of Euripides' ways with the sophisticated *pharmakon*.

THREE. *Tragic Genre*

1. The designation "histories" can be deceptive; one must recall, for example, that *Richard III*, terminating the first tetralogy, and *Richard II*, beginning the second tetralogy, are both designated in most early collections of Shakespeare as tragedies.

2. Dovzhenko 28-38, 54, 102-3, 121-42, 157-58.

3. Preston Epps, in Aristotle, Poetics *of Aristotle*.

4. To avoid intentionality as it is usually understood, I conflate Aristotelian and Romantic aesthetics.

FOUR. *Satires*

1. Guilhamet thinks satire is basically a mimetic art form that may be more or less distinct from nonfictive discourse. Also differing from my sense of the genre is the linkage he sees in satire between mimesis and rhetoric, which I believe are significantly disparate in their application to the genres, for instance, mimetic tragedy and rhetorical satire. Still, he claims, as I do, that satire is largely dependent on rhetoric: "In some respect all satires are imitations of rhetorical structures. They become satires by deforming the rhetorical structure with strategies calculated to disrupt the normal logic of the rhetorical text" (13). This crucial deformation seems ultimately to account for Guilhamet's sense of satire's genericity, which "transforms" rhetoric into mimesis, or a kind of fictive discourse: "As in all satire, the transformation from the host form (in this case, rhetoric) to generic satire is the dynamic that makes these formal verse satires works of art" (39). However, sometimes Guilhamet seems to install satire in the hinterland *between* rhetoric and mimesis: "Satire depends on maintaining a balance between concern with the real world and involvement with the imaginative one of its own making. An imbalance in either direction results in a generic change toward the purely rhetorical or the wholly mimetic fictional" (126). So satire to Guilhamet is mimetic-fictional, but it imitates rhetoric. Properly generic satire for Guilhamet, then, inheres in the movement back and forth between nonfictional rhetoric and fictional mimesis.

The problematic of satire certainly does involve its rhetorical composition. However, I think Guilhamet's equation of mimesis with fiction, plus his dualist sense of rhetoric and mimesis (so that satire depends on only the "appearance" of rhetoric), obscures a real opposition in satire that makes the genre always at odds with itself. This opposition is between independent discursive formations. On the one hand, satire derives its formal effects from gestural rhetoric; on the other, satire aspires to the definitive outcomes possible only in a truly mimetic genre such as tragedy, the composition of which is *action*, not fiction. Where I see genuine, albeit creative, incoherence as the way the "kind" satire works as only a semigenre, Guilhamet sees purely instrumental incoherence as the very generic operation of satire: "Because *A Tale of a Tub* is an incoherent treatise, it becomes a coherent satire" (139).

2. Women, traditionally victimized by satire, have themselves historically preferred to write and read the harmonious comedy of manners, from the female Restoration dramatists to the practitioners of the mode in novel form from Fanny Burney and Jane Austen to Agatha Christie.

3. Sullivan presents a good discussion about the distinct relationship of moral and aesthetic values to satire in general, and *satura* in particular.

4. Arrowsmith's treatment of this passage in "Luxury" is very sensitive to its complexity but different in explanation from my own.

5. See Frank's references to Lukács, Lacan, and Derrida, 71-72, 77-80.

6. What I signify by "satire against the real" is very different from what Booth (240-45) refers to as "unstable irony" or "romantic irony." First, Cervantes' satire against the real is rational-rhetorical in its operation, however much its content may reflect an interpretation of the absurdity of all human experience. Booth's unstable irony, in contrast, is simply irrational. Second, Cervantes' satire against the real makes authorial intention irrelevant. As a character in the ordinary satire of Part 1 of the novel, Don Quixote has no other options besides despondency when the return of Andrés proves the knight's goodness to be bad in this vale of tears: ordinary satire cannot keep its footing in a world that proves false when compared to the only true world of heaven. Satire against the real, in other words, is an *automatic* result of ordinary satire's proving itself irrelevant. To Booth, however, even unstable irony depends on authorial spin: if it is not intended, irony of whatever variety does not qualify as irony for Booth. Third, Cervantes' satire against the real has clear metaphysical and theological implications that are perfectly compatible with both Platonism and Christianity. A world in which good is bad is precisely *this* fallen world of the New Testament, of Augustine, even of Kierkegaard (one of Booth's exponents of romantic irony). It also corresponds to Plato's definition of the phenomenal, as distinct from the noumenal. Don Quixote as fool of God is entirely inaccessible to the concept of unstable irony, which to Booth requires infinite deferrals of stable meaning, deferrals bearing only the value of "absolute *infinite* negativity" (245). However, the don's despondency during the phase of satire against the real is not "absolute *infinite* negativity," but the serious Christian's dark night of the soul. Don Quixote is a good Catholic, not a romantic existentialist. And the irony in this phase of Cervantes' novel is *satiric* irony, not nihilistic black humor. Booth's entire attempt to make intentional irony, like intentional rhetoric, a theoretical first principle points up the necessity of getting the prior concept of genre right. Irony and rhetoric in literature must always remain secondary to nonintentional genre. For genre controls the direction, thus establishes the meaning, of irony, which is a technique. And genre, which is the deployment of figural power, includes rhetoric as one among other discursive formations.

7. I shall treat only Part 1 of *Hudibras*.

8. That the liberal satirist was deliberating a version of his holocaust finale from the earliest stages of planning *A Connecticut Yankee* is clear from Henry Nash Smith's citation of one of Twain's notes: "One entry, made before the end of April 1885, is particularly relevant because it reveals that at this early date Mark Twain had already conceived the sensational Battle of the Sand-Belt, with which the Yankee's narrative would eventually end: 'Have a battle between a modern army, with gatling guns— (automatic) 600 shots a minute, (with one pulling of the trigger,) torpedos, balloons, 100-ton cannon, iron-clad fleet &c& Prince de Joinville's Middle Age Crusaders'" (3).

9. The question may be raised whether Hašek *would* have made his Menippean satire into a novel had he continued writing. The published parts of *Švejk*, however, unlike the sparse fragments of the *Satyricon*, show no hint of generic transformation. Besides, *Švejk* remains what it is, and if "Menippean" in this case means "unfinished," so it must be.

SIX. *On and of the Essay as Nongenre*

1. Citations of Frame's edition of Montaigne's *Essays* include Frame's A-B-C designations of the "three certain strata in which the *Essays* were composed: A . . . material published before 1588 (generally in 1580 . . .); B . . . material published in 1588; C . . . material published after 1588" (Frame xvi). When the French is cited from the edition of Maurice Rat, Frame's strata markers will still apply.

2. Montesquieu, qtd. in Sayce 103; my translation.

3. Petersson 572 textual endnote;Falconer 4; Hunt 1.

4. Cicero, *De senectute*, pp. 10 and 11; all subsequent citations of both Latin and English will be to this edition by Falconer.

5. An interesting instance of a literary genre specifically dedicated to the rejuvenation of the political exile through a sexualized aesthetics is the *tz'u*. This was a variety of ode written in medieval China; it had mandatory levels of signification, at least seven, and was accompanied by an ink brush drawing. It was a form of poetry reserved for mandarins and generals who lost their positions from bureaucratic infighting and were sent or voluntarily withdrew to the country.

6. Although limited to Barthes's late works (from *S/Z* on) and to Montaigne "Barthesized," Bensmaïa's *The Barthes Effect* also proposes an aesthetic of liberationist reflexivity for the essay genre. What is liberated, however, according to Bensmaïa's postmodernism, is the text from itself: deconstructionist indeterminacy, in short, finds a home in the Barthesian *essai*.

7. Montaigne, qtd. in Frame ix-x, and in Rat vi. My bracketed citations of the French and running revision of Frame's translation are based on Rat's text.

8. See chap. 2, "From the 'Sufficient Word' to the 'Mana-Word,'" in Bensmaïa. The ultimate source of essayistic textuality, or "mana-word," is "body" in Bensmaïa's analysis of the Barthesian essay.

9. "Reconstruction" or "rebuilding" would render more precisely and less moralistically, while still as ironically, the physicality of the program of reforming that Montaigne has in mind.

10. Montaigne's "produict" is stronger than Frame's "brings out"; it has more the sense of actually producing than of eliciting.

11. With "les matieres," Montaigne again emphasizes the materiality of language as its own "subject."

12. Montaigne's "opinions" is weaker than Frame's "ideas."

13. Montaigne's "peneuses" is certainly more forlorn than Frame's "pitiful."

14. Montaigne's "de condition" includes the theological sense of *fallen* nature, of Original Sin.

15. The idea Frame renders as "we don't know what we're doing" is stronger and more sweeping in the French.

16. When the metonymous passages are from Montaigne's different editions, or when they are from different times (Frame's "A-B-C" strata), the principle of association still holds. Since the metonymy occurs after lapses of years, it is all the more remarkably metonymy.

17. Frame's "gives relish to the meat" is too forthright.

18. Montaigne's "Suivons" is less brusque than Frame's translation.

19. The liberty-libertinism-liberality chain of significations is much clearer in the French, as is the customary and legal sense of "convention," which is less binding than the legalistic "compact."

20. A literal translation of the French idiom is awkward, but points up the pertinent bawdry and significations of desire: "The forger mocks the tongs he uses to stir up the fire."

21. Machiavelli's "fastidio," which may be translated "fastidiousness," is psychologically subtler than Walker's "weary" and makes a more intellectual point.

22. "Virtù" is more complex than "virtue," and "regnava" is nobler than "prevailed."

23. The Italian has the implication of "spirited minds."

24. "Offizio" carries much more the sense of "function" than does "duty," though it has just as much implication of morality.

25. Machiavelli, *Discourses* 268-69. The passages quoted in Italian are from Machiavelli, *Discorsi* 136-37.

26. Although Croce and several others were Mann's references for his characterization of Settembrini in *The Magic Mountain* (as Lukács served for Naphta), the Machiavelli of the *Discorsi* would also fit in certain aspects.

27. This opening phrase of the *Rêveries* is untranslatable because the specific positioning of the words *is* their meaning. Rousseau takes full advantage of the idiom's word order, "Me voici donc"; he overdetermines his point about the primacy of the self, first by the initial positioning of the phrase, then by the terminal echoing in the sentence provided by "moi-même": "Me voici donc seul sur la terre, n'ayant plus de frère, de prochain, d'ami, de société que moi-même" (Rousseau 3). All quotes will be from the Roddier edition; the translations are my own.

SEVEN. *Toward a Dialectical Theory of Genre*

1. Genette 84; the translation is my own.

2. What happens to genre when rhetorized or deconstructed is what has happened to Plato's Forms since the nineteenth century, when they began to be understood as "logical universals" lacking the substantial reality they indeed possessed for Plato (Bluck 180-81). Similarly, on the contemporary theory scene, what happens to Julia Kristeva's "intertextuality" when the concept is understood as either too diffuse or too specific is what would be the case were genre to be taken less like a constitutive and more like an explanatory concept. That is, the "intertext" either evaporates into empty discursive echoing or degenerates into positivistic source-study: "The concept of intertextuality can be made workable only if it is focused and given precision of reference; but such a narrowing of its range then weakens its power to describe the full network of textual determinations and relations" (Culler 111). In contrast to intertextuality, Foucault's "discursive formations" composing history, the proper subject of his "archaeology," retain their substantial reality.

3. See also Bakhtin/Medvedev 147-48.

Works Cited

Aeschylus. *Aeschylus One:* Oresteia. Ed. David Grene and Richard Lattimore. Chicago: U. of Chicago P, 1953.

———. *Agamemnon.* Trans. Robert Fagles. Aeschylus, *The Oresteia.*

———. *Agamemnon.* Trans. Richard Lattimore. Aeschylus, *Aeschylus One:* Oresteia.

———. *The Eumenides.* Trans. Robert Fagles. Aeschylus, *The Oresteia.*

———. *The Eumenides.* Trans. Richard Lattimore. Aeschylus, *Aeschylus One:* Oresteia.

———. *Libation Bearers.* Trans. Robert Fagles. Aeschylus, *The Oresteia.*

———. *Libation Bearers.* Trans. Richard Lattimore. Aeschylus, *Aeschylus One:* Oresteia.

———. *The Oresteia.* Harmondsworth, Eng.: Penguin, 1966.

———. *The Persians.* Trans. Philip Vellacott. *Aeschylus:* Prometheus Bound, The Suppliants, Seven against Thebes, The Persians. Harmondsworth, Eng.: Penguin, 1961.

———. *Prometheus Bound.* Trans. Philip Vellacott. *Aeschylus:* Prometheus Bound, The Suppliants, Seven against Thebes, The Persians. Harmondsworth, Eng.: Penguin, 1961.

Altieri, Charles. *Act and Quality: A Theory of Literary Meaning and Humanistic Understanding.* Amherst: U of Massachusetts P, 1981.

Andrewes, A. *The Greek Tyrants.* London: Hutchinson, 1956.

Aristotle. *Aristotle's* Physics. Trans. Richard Hope. Lincoln: U of Nebraska P, 1961.

———. *Nicomachean Ethics.* Trans. Martin Ostwald. Indianapolis: Bobbs, 1962.

———. *The Poetics of Aristotle.* Trans. Preston H. Epps. Chapel Hill: U of North Carolina P, 1970.

Arrowsmith, William. Introduction. Petronius v-xviii.

———. "Luxury and Death in the *Satyricon.*" *Arion* 5, no, 3: 304-31. Rpt. in Rudd 122-49.

Bacon, Francis. *Francis Bacon, A Selection of His Works.* Ed. Sidney Warhaft. Indianapolis: Bobbs, 1965.

Bakhtin, M.M./P.N. Medvedev. *The Formal Method in Literary Scholarship: A Critical Introduction to Sociological Poetics.* Trans. Albert J. Wehrle. Cambridge, Mass.: Harvard UP, 1985.

Beaujour, Michel. "Genus Universum." *Glyph* 7 (1980): 14-31.

Benjamin, Walter. *The Origin of German Tragic Drama.* Trans. John Osborne. Frankfurt am Main: Suhrkamp Verlag, 1963. London: NLB, 1977.

Bennett, James R. "The Essay in Recent Anthologies of Literary Criticism." *SubStance* 60, Special Issue: Writing the Real (1990): 55-67.

Bensmaïa, Réda. *The Barthes Effect: The Essay as Reflective Text.* Trans. Pat Fedkiew. Minneapolis: U of Minnesota P, 1987.

Beroul. *The Romance of Tristan and the Tale of Tristan's Madness.* Trans. Alan E. Fedrick. Harmondsworth, Eng.: Penguin, 1970.

Bloom, Harold. "Whitman's Image of Voice." *Walt Whitman.* Ed. Harold Bloom. New York: Chelsea House, 1985. 127-42.

Bluck, R.S. Appendix 7. *Plato's* Phaedo. By Plato. Trans. R.S. Bluck. London: Routledge and Kegan Paul, 1955. Indianapolis: Bobbs, 1976. 180-81.

Booth, Wayne C. *A Rhetoric of Irony.* Chicago: U of Chicago P, 1974.

Büchner, Georg. *Danton's Death.* Trans. Hedwig Rappolt. New York: TSL, 1980.

Butler, Samuel. Hudibras *Parts I and II and Selected Other Writings.* Ed. John Wilders and Hugh de Quehen. Oxford: Clarendon, 1973.

Cervantes, Miguel de. *Don Quixote.* Trans. John Ormsby. Rev. Kenneth Douglas and Joseph R. Jones. New York: Norton, 1981.

Cicero. *De senectute. Cicero:* De senectute, de amicitia, de divinatione. Ed. and trans. William Armistead Falconer. Cambridge, Mass., and London: Loeb Classical Library-Harvard UP, 1923.

―――. "On Old Age." *On Old Age, On Friendship.* Trans. Harry G. Edinger. Indianapolis: Bobbs, 1967.

Cohen, Ralph. "Do Postmodern Genres Exist?" *Genre* 20, nos. 3-4 (Fall-Winter 1987): 241-57.

―――. "History and Genre." *New Literary History* 17, no. 2 (Winter 1986): 203-18.

Colie, Rosalie L. *The Resources of Kind.* Berkeley: U of California P, 1973.

Crick, Bernard. Introduction. Machiavelli, *Discourses* 13-69.

Culler, Jonathan. *The Pursuit of Signs: Semiotics, Literature, Deconstruction.* London: Routledge and Kegan Paul, 1981.

Derrida, Jacques, "The Law of Genre." Trans. Avital Ronell. *Glyph* 7 (1980): 177-232.

Dovzhenko, Alexander. "Notebooks." *The Poet as Filmmaker.* Ed. and trans. Marco Carynnyk. Cambridge, Mass.: MIT P, 1973.

Eagleton, Terry. "Towards a Science of the Text." In Eagleton, *Criticism and Ideology,* 64-101. London: NLB, 1976.

Ehrenberg, Victor. *From Solon to Socrates.* 2nd ed. London: Methuen, 1973.

Elliott, Robert C. *The Power of Satire: Magic, Ritual, Art.* Princeton, N.J.: Princeton UP, 1960.

Emerson, Ralph Waldo. *Emerson, Essays and Lectures.* Ed. Joel Porte. New York: Literary Classics of the United States-Viking, 1983.

―――. *The Journals of Ralph Waldo Emerson.* Ed. William H. Gilman, Alfred Ferguson, and Merrell Davis. Vols. 2-3, 1822-32. Cambridge, Mass.: Belknap-Harvard UP, 1961-63.

―――. *Selected Writings of Ralph Waldo Emerson.* Ed. William H. Gilman. New York: NAL, 1965.

Euripides. *Euripides:* Heracles. Introduction and commentary by Godfrey W. Bond. Oxford: Clarendon, 1981.

―――. *Heracles.* Trans. Philip Vellacott. *Euripides:* Medea, Hecabe, Electra, Heracles. Harmondsworth, Eng.: Penguin, 1963.

―――. *Medea.* Trans. Philip Vellacott. *Euripides:* Medea, Hecabe, Electra, Heracles. Harmondsworth, Eng.: Penguin, 1963.

Falconer, William Armistead. Introduction. Cicero, *Cicero* 2-7.

Fine, John V.A. *The Ancient Greeks: A Critical History.* Cambridge, Mass.: Harvard UP, 1983.

Foucault, Michel. *The Order of Things: An Archaeology of the Human Sciences.* New York: Random-Vintage, 1970.

———. *Power/Knowledge*. Ed. Colin Gordon. Trans. Gordon, Leo Marshall, John Mepham, Kate Soper. New York: Pantheon, 1980.

———. *The Use of Pleasure*. Trans. Robert Hurley. Vol. 2 of *The History of Sexuality*. New York: Pantheon, 1986. 2 vols.

Fowler, Alastair. *Kinds of Literature: An Introduction to the Theory of Genres and Modes*. Cambridge, Mass.: Harvard UP, 1982.

Frame, Donald M. Introduction. Montaigne, *Essays* v-xiv.

Frank, Manfred. "The Infinite Text." *Glyph* 7 (1980): 70-101.

Frow, John. *Marxism and Literary History*. Cambridge, Mass.: Harvard UP, 1986.

Genette, Gérard. *Introduction à l'architexte*. Paris: Éditions du Seuil, 1979.

Girard, René. *Deceit, Desire and the Novel*. Baltimore, Md.: Johns Hopkins UP, 1965.

Gombrich, E.H. *Art and Illusion: A Study in the Psychology of Pictorial Representation*. Princeton, N.J.: Princeton UP, 1960.

Guilhamet, Leon. *Satire and the Transformation of Genre*. Philadelphia: U of Pennsylvania P, 1987.

Habermas, Jürgen. *Knowledge and Human Interests*. Trans. Jeremy J. Shapiro. Frankfurt am Main: Suhrkamp Verlag, 1968. Boston: Beacon, 1971.

Harari, Josué V., and David F. Bell. "Journal à plusieurs voies." Serres, *Hermes* i-xxxv.

Hašek, Jaroslav. *The Good Soldier Švejk and His Fortunes in the World War*. Trans. Cecil Parrott. Harmondsworth, Eng.: Penguin, 1973.

Hegel, Georg. *The Phenomenology of Mind*. Trans. J.B. Baillie. Selections in *Hegel: The Essential Writings*. Ed. Frederick G. Weiss. New York: Harper, 1974.

Herington, C.J. "Aeschylus: The Last Phase," *Arion* 4, no. 3: 387-403. Rpt. in Rudd 1-17.

Hirsch, E.D., Jr. *The Aims of Interpretation*. Chicago: U of Chicago P, 1976.

———. "Meaning and Significance Re-interpreted." *Critical Inquiry* 11, no. 2 (1984): 202-25.

———. *Validity in Interpretation*. New Haven, Conn.: Yale UP, 1967.

Hunt, H.A.K. *The Humanism of Cicero*. Melbourne: Melbourne UP, 1954.

Jacobus, Mary. "The Law of/and Gender: Genre Theory and *The Prelude*." *Diacritics* 14, no. 4 (1984): 47-57.

Jameson, Fredric. *The Political Unconscious: Narrative as a Socially Symbolic Act*. Ithaca, N.Y.: Cornell UP, 1981.

Jauss, Hans Robert. *Toward an Aesthetic of Reception*. Trans. Timothy Bahti. Theory and History of Literature 2. Minneapolis: U of Minnesota P, 1982.

Juvenal. *Juvenal and Persius*. Ed. and trans. G.G. Ramsay. Cambridge, Mass.: Loeb Classical Library-Harvard UP, 1951.

———. *The Satires of Juvenal*. Trans. Rolfe Humphries. Bloomington: Indiana UP, 1958.

Kambouchner, Denis. "The Theory of Accidents." *Glyph* 7 (1980): 149–75.

Kant, Immanuel. *Prolegomena to Any Future Metaphysics*. Trans. Paul Carus. Rev. James W. Ellington. Indianapolis: Hackett, 1977.

Kaufmann, Walter. Introduction. Nietzsche, *Gay Science* 3-26.

Kleist, Heinrich von. *Prince Friedrich of Homburg*. Trans. Diana Stone Peters and Frederick G. Peters. New York: New Directions, 1978.

Kuiper, Koenraad. "The Nature of Satire." *Poetics* 13, no. 6 (1984): 459-73.

Lacan, Jacques. *Écrits: A Selection*. Trans. Alan Sheridan. New York: Norton, 1977.

Lacoue-Labarthe, Phillippe, and Jean-Luc Nancy. "Genre." *Glyph* 7 (1980): 1-14.

Lattimore, Richard. Introduction. Aeschylus, *Aeschylus One* 1-31.

Lesky, Albin. *Greek Tragedy*. Trans. H.A. Frankfort. London: Benn, 1965.

Lukács, Georg. *The Theory of the Novel*. Trans. Anna Bostock. Berlin: P. Cassirer, 1920. Cambridge, Mass.: MIT P, 1971.

Machiavelli, Niccolò. *Discorsi sopra la prima deca di Tito Livio.* Firenze: Successori le Monnier, 1912.

———. *The Discourses.* Ed. Bernard Crick. Trans. Leslie J. Walker, S.J. Rev. Brian Richardson. Harmondsworth, Eng.: Penguin, 1970.

Melville, Herman. *Selected Poems of Herman Melville.* Ed. Hennig Cohen. Garden City: Anchor-Doubleday, 1964.

Montaigne, Michel de. *The Complete Essays of Montaigne.* Trans. Donald M. Frame. Stanford, Calif.: Stanford UP, 1958.

———. *Essais de Montaigne.* Ed. Maurice Rat. 2 vols. Paris: Garnier, 1962.

Musil, Robert. *The Man without Qualities.* Trans. Eithne Wilkins and Ernst Kaiser. Vol. 1. New York: Capricorn, 1965. 3 vols. New York: Coward-McCann, 1953.

Nietzsche, Friedrich. *Beyond Good and Evil.* Trans. R.J. Hollingdale. Harmondsworth, Eng.: Penguin, 1973.

———. *The Birth of Tragedy and the Case of Wagner.* Trans. with comm. Walter Kaufmann. New York: Vintage, 1967.

———. "The Birth of Tragedy." *Nietzsche on Tragedy.* Ed. and trans. M.S. Silk and J.P. Stern. Cambridge, Eng.: Cambridge UP, 1981.

———. *The Gay Science.* Trans. Walter Kaufmann. New York: Vintage, 1974.

———. *On the Genealogy of Morals.* Trans. Walter Kaufmann and R.J. Hollingdale. New York: Vintage, 1969.

Petersson, Torsten. *Cicero: A Biography.* Berkeley: U of California P, 1920.

Petronius. *Satyricon.* Trans. William Arrowsmith. New York: Meridian-NAL, 1959, rev. 1983.

Pickard-Cambridge, Arthur, Sir. *Dithyramb, Tragedy, and Comedy.* 2nd ed. London: Oxford UP, 1962.

Pope, Alexander *et al. Peri Bathous: or, Martinus Scriblerus, His Treatise of the Art of Sinking in Poetry.* Rpt. in *Eighteenth-Century English Literature,* ed. Paul Fussell, Jr., Geoffrey Tillotson, and Marshall Waingrow, 610-34. New York: Harcourt, 1969.

Pucci, Pietro. *The Violence of Pity in Euripides'* Medea. Ithaca, N.Y.: Cornell UP, 1980.

Rappolt, Hedwig. Introduction. Büchner v-vii.

Rat, Maurice. Introduction. Montaigne, *Essais* 1: vi.

Ridolfi, R. *Life of Niccolò Machiavelli.* Trans. Cecil Grayson. London: Routledge and Kegan Paul, 1962.

Riffaterre, Michael. *Text Production.* Trans. Terese Lyons. New York: Columbia UP, 1983.

Rosmarin, Adena. *The Power of Genre.* Minneapolis: U of Minnesota P, 1985.

Rousseau, Jean-Jacques. *Les Rêveries du promeneur solitaire.* Ed. Henri Roddier. Paris: Garnier, 1960.

Rudd, Niall, ed. *Essays on Classical Literature.* Cambridge, Eng.: Heffer; New York: Barnes, 1972.

Sayce, R.A. *The Essays of Montaigne: A Critical Exploration.* Great Britain: Northwestern UP, 1972.

Schorske, Carl E. *"Fin-de-Siècle" Vienna: Politics and Culture.* New York: Random-Vintage, 1981.

Segal, Charles. *Tragedy and Civilization.* Cambridge, Mass.: Harvard UP, 1981.

Seneca. *Phaedra.* Trans. E.F. Watling. *Seneca: Four Tragedies and Octavia.* Harmondsworth, Eng.: Penguin, 1966.

———. *Thyestes.* Trans. E.F. Watling. *Seneca: Four Tragedies and Octavia.* Harmondsworth, Eng.: Penguin, 1966.

Serres, Michel. "The Algebra of Literature: The Wolf's Game." *Textual Strategies: Perspectives in Post-Structuralist Criticism.* Ed. Josué V. Harari. Ithaca, N.Y.: Cornell UP, 1979. 260-79.

_____. *Hermes: Literature, Science, Philosophy.* Trans. Mark Anderson, David Bell, Suzanne Guerlac, Lawrence Schehr, Marilyn Sides, Susan Willey. Ed. Josué V. Harari and David Bell. Baltimore, Md.: Johns Hopkins UP, 1982.

_____. "Knowledge in the Classical Age: La Fontaine and Descartes." Serres, Trans. Harari and Bell. *Hermes* 15-28.

Shakespeare, William. *The Tragedy of Hamlet, Prince of Denmark.* Ed. George Kittredge. Rev. Irving Ribner. Lexington, Mass.: Xerox, 1967.

Silk, M.S., and J.P. Stern. *Nietzsche on Tragedy.* Cambridge, Eng.: Cambridge UP, 1981.

Smith, Henry Nash. Introduction. Twain 1-30.

Sophocles. *Antigone.* Trans. Elizabeth Wyckoff. *Sophocles One.* Ed. David Grene and Richard Lattimore. Chicago: U of Chicago P, 1954.

_____. *Electra.* Trans. David Grene. *Sophocles Two.* Ed. David Grene and Richard Lattimore. Chicago: U of Chicago P, 1957.

_____. *Philoctetes.* Trans. David Grene. *Sophocles Two.* Ed. David Grene and Richard Lattimore. Chicago: U of Chicago P, 1957.

_____. *Sophocles'* Philoctetes. Ed. T.B.L. Webster. Cambridge, Eng.: Cambridge UP, 1970.

_____. *Sophocles:* The Women of Trachis *and* Philoctetes, *A New Translation in Verse.* Trans. Robert Torrance. Boston: Houghton, 1961.

Starobinski, Jean. *Montaigne in Motion.* Trans. Arthur Goldhammer. Chicago: U of Chicago P, 1985.

Sullivan, J.P. "Petronius: Artist or Moralist?" *Arion* 6, no. 1: 71-88. Rpt. in Rudd 151-68.

Swift, Jonathan. *Gulliver's Travels and Other Writings.* Ed. Louis A. Landa. Boston: Houghton, 1960.

Thucydides. *The Peloponnesian War.* Trans. Rex Warner, Harmondsworth, Eng.: Penguin, 1972.

Tolstoy, Leo. *The Death of Ivan Ilyich.* Trans. Lynn Solotaroff. New York: Bantam, 1981.

Twain, Mark. *A Connecticut Yankee in King Arthur's Court.* Ed. Bernard L. Stein. Vol. 9 of *The Works of Mark Twain.* 12 vols. Berkeley: U of California P, 1979.

Warhaft, Sidney. Introduction. Bacon 1-26.

Wilson, Edmund. *The Wound and the Bow.* New York: Oxford UP, 1929.

Würzbach, Natascha. "An Approach to a Context-Oriented Genre Theory in Application to the History of the Ballad: Traditional Ballad–Street Ballad–Literary Ballad." *Poetics* 12, no. 1 (1983): 35-70.

Index

absurdity, 98, 125-26, 135, 140-43
accommodation: narratives of, in
  Rêveries, 184-86
action(s), 17, 32, 89; language of the
  essay, as, 170; in satire, 128, 145; satire
  as not having, 94-95; writing as, for
  Machiavelli, 173-74
action(s) in tragedy, 15-16, 18, 25, 36, 91;
  Aeschylean, 32-35, 44, 56, 59; contest
  as law of, 91; destructiveness of, 28-29;
  Euripidean, 75-77; language as
  mediating between auditors and, 145;
  language of, 15, 145, 211; as mimesis,
  87, 117, 207; as political, 149;
  Sophoclean, 59-63, 68-69; as telos of
  motive and end, 31-32; use of deus ex
  machina, 75-77, 85
Aeschylean tragedy, 11, 24, 26, 79-80,
  87-88, 147, 211; emotions
  characterizing, 149; as extending
  through early modern European
  literature, 85; inability to demonstrate
  values, 98; models for, as no longer in
  existence, 30-31; political power as
  providing structure of, 74; politics of
  prevalence in 59; progress as fantasy of
  hope in, 132; traces of other genres in,
  25-26; use of character contrasted with
  Sophoclean tragedy, 60; use of deus ex
  machina, 75-76, 84; wrestling as
  metaphor, 85. *See also Agamemnon;
  Eumenides; Libation Bearers;
  Oresteia; Persians; Prometheus Bound*
Aeschylus, 13, 25, 27, 213 n 1
aesthetic realism, 110-19, 127; in prose
  fiction, 138-39
aesthetics, 26, 93, 145, 166-67, 210, 217
  n 6

Agamemnon (Aeschylus), 42-43, 45-46,
  51, 82
agon, 28-30, 43, 84, 86-87, 90
"Algebra of Literature, The" (Serres), 14,
  29
alienation, 114-18, 144; for Rousseau,
  181-82, 184, 186, 192, 196, 198
allegory, 121, 159, 166, 170
Also Sprach Zarathustra (Nietzsche),
  198
Althusser, Louis, 5, 7, 14, 209-10
ananke, 71, 73-74
anarchism, 134-35, 140-41, 148-49
anarchist critique: *The Good Soldier
  Švejk* as, 134-36, 139
anarchist satire, 147-48
antigenre: satire not an, 96
Antigone (Sophocles), 60, 62-66, 70, 74,
  87, 90
aphoristic essay, 174, 176-80
Apollonian rite: purification by, 45-46,
  48-49
aporia: in satire, 101
appearance: relationship to reality in
  Don Quixote, 120, 122, 124-25
appropriations: ideology as result of,
  210-11
Areopagus, 45, 47-49, 56, 214 n 6
arete (functional excellence), 32, 60,
  64-69, 72, 176
Aristophanes, 2, 25, 92, 213 n 1
Aristotle, 13-14, 25, 30, 38, 59, 78, 89;
  genre theory, 26, 202-3, 205; on
  reprisal, 59, 214 n 8; theory of tragedy,
  15, 31-32, 64-65, 83, 92, 144-45
Arrowsmith, William, 111, 118
art, 30-31, 134, 202-3; relationship to
  life, 10-11

polis, 33-34, 47, 52, 60
political identity: Juvenalian tragedy
 concerned with, 107-9
political power, 25, 49-50, 55, 91, 128;
 Bacon on, 173-74; in *Eumenides*,
 47-57; in *Philoctetes*, 59-60; as
 structure of Aeschylean tragedy, 74;
 tragedy as configuration of, 8-9, 15-16,
 18-19, 209; tragedy as deployment of,
 14-15, 88, 147
political satire, 19, 97, 127-37, 139, 145,
 147; confined by issues, 99;
 Connecticut Yankee as example of, 129,
 131-33; generic instability of, 100,
 127-28, 130, 133, 141; Menippean satire
 suited for, 140; periods of consensus
 not conducive to, 100; of 20th-century,
 134. *See also* conservative satire;
 liberal satire
politics, 26-28, 76, 128, 134, 137; for
 Bacon, 173-74; as context for *Hudibras*
 and *Connecticut Yankee*, 129; of essay,
 150, 156, 159, 163-64; for Machiavelli,
 174, 180; of prevalence, 44, 58; role in
 Greek tragedies, 74-77; tragedy as, 87,
 147, 205
Pope, Alexander, 98, 100-101, 139, 144,
 150
post-Althusser Marxist genre theory, 4,
 18, 204, 209-12
postcolonial culture, 16, 147
postmodernism, 101, 119, 147-48, 190,
 205-6, 217 n 6
poststructuralism, 4-5, 7-8, 10-11, 204
Potemkin (film), 83
Pound, Ezra, 103, 133, 140
power, 8, 17-19, 29-30, 36, 82; for
 Cicero, 156; definitions of, 17-18;
 differential, 18-20, 24-25, 98, 149; of
 essay, 18-19, 157, 190, 206; of essay for
 Emerson, 193-98, 200-201; as
 evaluated in satire, 18-19; genre as,
 2-4, 14-18, 22-23, 76, 206-10; for
 Machiavelli, 178-79; for Nietzsche,
 200-201; of omnipotent god parodied
 by Euripides, 80-81; Orestes as agent
 of, in *Eumenides*, 44; Prometheus as
 image of, 44; relationship to discourse
 for Marxists, 210-11; replacement by
 discourse for Bacon, 179; Romantic
 attitude toward, 196; of satire, 131;
 sonnet's capacity for, 16; in Sophoclean
 tragedy, 60-65; in tragedy, 29, 85, 211;
 in tragic mode, 88; transformed by
 power play of language, 176; victory

transformed into, in *Persians*, 32-33,
 35, 38-39. *See also* political power;
 rational power; textual power
power, deployment of, 44, 86, 90, 92-93;
 in Aeschylean tragedy, 44-59; in the
 essay, 150-52; genre as, 14-15, 19-21,
 149, 208; in satire, 140, 146-47, 149; by
 the sonnet, 21; through satire, 96-99;
 in tragedy, 63, 146-47, 149
powerlessness, 88, 96, 121, 124
pragmatism, 203-5
preciousness/preciosity: in Rousseau,
 190, 192
precursive operations: of essay, 16
presence, 8, 12, 181, 184, 190-92
present, 181, 204
Prince, The (Machiavelli), 174-75
Prince Friedrich of Homburg (Kleist),
 84-85, 89, 91, 204
progress, 129, 132-33, 178; problem of in
 Eumenides, 44, 48-49, 69-70, 129
prolongation: as technique, 8, 167, 184,
 192-93
Prometheus: as mythic symbol, 43-44
Prometheus Bound (Aeschylus), 30,
 42-45, 51, 60
propaganda, 28, 56-57, 128, 139
Protestantism: and use of satiric irony,
 141
Pucci, Pietro, 78, 214 n 13
purification ritual: undergone by
 Orestes, 45-46, 48-49
Puritans: as target of *Hudibras*, 129-31

Quintilian, 102
quotable quote, 177

Rabelais, 140
Racine, Jean, 31, 88
racist imperialism: Fanon's retort to, 192
radical leftist satire, 128
Rape of the Lock, The (Pope), 101
rationalist critique: satire as weapon of,
 206
rationality, 40-41, 96; logical
 consequences in *Good Soldier Švejk*,
 136; of satire, 19, 95-99, 128, 133-34,
 148, 205; of satire against the real, 216
 n 6; of satiric evaluation, 146, 209; as
 skewed in *Don Quixote*, 122. *See also*
 reason; reasonableness
rational power: in satire, 8-9, 15-16, 19
reactionary rightist satire, 128
reader, 4, 152-53, 162-63, 193-96